The Jewish Holidays

The Jewish Holidays

A Journey through History

LARRY DOMNITCH

Dear Mr. + Mrs. Silverman
With my very best wishes.

JASON ARONSON INC.
Northvale, New Jersey
Jerusalem

This book was set in 11 pt. ITC Galliard by Alabama Book Composition of Deatsville, AL and printed and bound by Book-Mart Press, Inc. of North Bergen, NJ.

10 9 8 7 6 5 4 3 2 1

Library of Congress Cataloging-in-Publication Data

Domnitch, Larry.
The jewish holidays / by Larry Domnitch.
p. cm.
Includes bibliographical references and index.
ISBN 0–7657–6109–2
1. Fasts and feasts—Judaism—History. I. Title.
BM690.D66 2000
296.4′3—dc21 99–24287
CIP

Printed in the United States of America on acid-free paper. For information and catalog write to Jason Aronson Inc., 230 Livingston Street, Northvale, NJ 07647-1726, or visit our website: www.aronson.com

Dedicated to my wife

Tova

who not only gave birth to our daughter,
Hadassa, *this year, but also encouraged*
my undertaking of this project
and found time to review the manuscript and
make numerous invaluable suggestions to enhance it.

This project was indeed a partnership.

Contents

Introduction

The events surrounding the holidays molded the foundation of the Jews as a nation and are related to their continuity and survival as Jews throughout history. These events did not occur in a vacuum, but rather must be seen in their historical settings.

A known passage quoted in the Passover Haggadah states, "In every generation, a person should see himself as if he personally exited Egypt." (Mishna, Pesachim 10:4) Just as an individual can reflect upon the impact of the Exodus and its relevance on one's life, the events of the Exodus from Egypt did not end with the Exodus but have reocurred throughout history. It is likewise with the other holidays. In every generation the Jews receive the Torah as they did on Shavuot. They wander the Earth as they did the Sinai wilderness for forty years under Divine Protection following their Exodus, as commemorated by Succot. On Rosh Hashanah many Jewish communities begin anew and reassess their conduct, while on Yom Kippur, the Day of Atonement, Jews continually examine their deeds.

The events of Purim and the post-biblical holiday of Chanukah reflect the threats posed to Jewish existence throughout history, threats which they have survived albeit far from unscathed.

On Tisha B'Av, Jews have suffered numerous catastrophes. On that day both the First and Second Temples were destroyed. Six days later, Tu B'Av, which signifies revitalization, arrives. From the ashes of destruction, the remains are rebuilt.

In Pharaoh's Egypt, the Israelites initially sought the acceptance of the society at large although they came from very different backgrounds, dating back to Abraham, and had very different traditions. In Egypt, as in modern times, the Israelites also wrestled with the notion of continuity as Israelites. However, Egypt would undergo change, and it would not be long before they would be forced to endure the Pharaoh's persecutions. After their eventual release, the Israelites would be forced to face grueling trials as they would have to wander the Sinai Desert. The Jews throughout history would face such struggles and most of the holidays contain themes closely related to coping with hardship and adversity.

In that context, many of the essays deal with the struggles and difficulties Jews have encountered as a result of anti-Semitism and persecution. It is a historical reality. And yet the portrayal of events also depicts some of the richness of Jewish life. The cause for the struggle to survive.

Since the holidays commemorate landmark events in Jewish history, many of the events portrayed have had profound impacts upon the Jewish people. Many of the events dealt with in this volume have also occurred in this century. They deal with the early days of Zionism and the struggle for Jewish Statehood, as well as the immense tragedy of the Holocaust. The struggles of Russian Jewry are also dealt with at length as well as the history of American Jewry.

This book attempts to give the reader an appreciation of the cyclical nature of Jewish history and a greater appreciation of the holidays and their relevance throughout Jewish history.

1

Passover

THE PASSOVER THAT MARKED THE ISRAELITE ENTRY INTO THE PROMISED LAND

The first Passover observance in the Land of Israel was unique, as was the first Passover celebrated on the eve of the Exodus. The first Passover sacrifice in Egypt forty years earlier marked the liberation of the Israelites; the first Passover in the Promised Land marked the culmination of the Exodus—the Israelites' entry into the Land of Israel.

Just before their entry, the Israelites were told by Joshua to prepare for war. "Prepare provisions for yourselves for in another three days you will cross the Jordan here to enter and take possession of the land which God your Lord is giving you to inherit."[1] When they reached the Jordan River, it miraculously dried up, similar to the parting of the waters of the Red Sea, and the Israelites crossed into the Promised Land.[2]

---

[1]Joshua 1:11.
[2]Joshua 3,4.

The entire episode, in fact, was strikingly similar to the parting of the Red Sea. At the crossing of the Jordan River, the people came to admire Joshua as they had Moses following the parting of the Red Sea. "On that day God exalted Joshua in the eyes of all Israel. They feared him all his life as they feared Moses."[3] The day the Israelites crossed the Jordan and entered the land was the tenth of Nissan, the same day the Israelites were commanded to offer the Passover sacrifice forty years earlier, prior to their departure from Egypt.[4] The kings on the western banks of the Jordan heard of this miracle and were gripped with fear. "When all the Amorite kings on the western side of the Jordan and all the kings of the Canaanites near the sea heard how God dried up the waters of the Jordan because of the Israelites, until they crossed over, their hearts melted. They had no spirit left in them."[5]

Joshua took twelve stones from the Jordan River and placed them in the area they entered, Gilgal, which would be the site of the Tabernacle for the upcoming Passover sacrifice as well as for the next fourteen years. He told the Israelites, "When your children in the future ask their fathers what these stones are, you shall inform your sons saying; the Israelites passed the Jordan River on dry land."[6]

In Egypt, the Israelites were commanded to undergo circumcision before they participated in the Passover sacrifice. Most of the Israelites in Egypt in the years before their enslavement abandoned the rite of circumcision in their eagerness to assimilate.[7] The situation in Gilgal was not unlike that of Egypt. During their sojourn in the Sinai wilderness, the rite of circumcision was not observed because the climatic conditions of the Sinai Peninsula

---

[3]Joshua 4:14.
[4]Joshua 4:19. The Israelites were commanded on the tenth day of the month of Nissan to offer the Passover sacrifice on the fourteenth.
[5]Joshua 5:1.
[6]Joshua 4:21–22.
[7]Midrash Tanchuma Exodus 6.

made it dangerous.[8] Prior to the offering of the Passover sacrifice, God commanded Joshua to have the Israelites circumcised. "At the time God said to Joshua, 'Make flint knives and circumcise the Israelites again, a second time.' "[9]

Passover soon arrived and the Israelites offered their first Passover sacrifice as a nation within the Land of Israel. "The Israelites encamped in Gilgal on the plains of Jericho, and offered the Passover sacrifice on the fourteenth day of the month in the late afternoon."[10] The Passover celebrated upon their entry into the Land of Israel was a landmark, as was the Passover sacrifice celebrated as the Israelites exited Egypt. Rivers split, miracles occurred, and the nation experienced the freedom of dwelling within its own land.[11]

THE RETURN TO EGYPT: THE RISE AND FALL OF EGYPTIAN JEWRY

When the Israelites hastily exited from Pharaoh's Egypt, little did they know their descendants would return to the land of the Pharaohs and again build thriving Jewish communities there. In

---

[8]Joshua 5:7, Yevamoth 75a.
[9]Rashi's commentary on Joshua 5:2. This was the second mass circumcision since the Exodus.
[10]Joshua 5:10.
[11]Rabbi Sholomo Goren, in his book *Moadei Yisrael*, states that the Passover sacrifice was unlike other commandments that were specifically related to the Land of Israel (with the exception of giving *challah* to the *Kohen*), which were not applicable until the Israelites conquered and distributed the land among the tribes over a period of fourteen years. Additionally, the observance of the laws of the Passover sacrifice were given to the Israelites as they departed Egypt and before the receiving of the Torah at Mount Sinai. The observance of the commandment was therefore of a different nature in reference to its observance in the Land of Israel and not dependent upon the conquest and distribution of the land.

Alexandria, Egypt, a Jewish community was established over seven hundred years after the Exodus. Over time it grew into a massive community that marked a new era in Jewish history. But unlike the Israelite sojourn in Egypt that ended with their redemption, the subsequent era of Jewish settlement would end catastrophically. The events that transpired in Alexandria during those times, which preceded the persecutions, are in many ways similar to those that led to the enslavement of the Israelites in ancient Egypt. Both situations have had a profound impact upon Jewish history.

The first Jews to return as a community to Egypt since the Exodus were migrants from Judea in the years during the Assyrian invasion of Judea in 722 B.C.E. and prior to the destruction of the First Temple (586 B.C.E.). This community did not last long. The prophet Jeremiah warned the Judeans fleeing the destruction inflicted by the Babylonians upon Judea not to go to Egypt. "He [Nebuchadnezzer] will come and smite the land of Egypt. . . . Nebuchadnezzer will wrap up the spoils of the land of Egypt (on whose futile help you are relying), as a shepherd wraps his garment around his shoulders."[12] In Egypt, Jeremiah pleaded for the Jews to desist from the practices of idolatry they had adopted.[13] As the prophet predicted, just several years later the Babylonians conquered the land and ruthlessly exterminated the Jewish community. Only Jeremiah, his pupil Baruch Ben Nehira, and a few others survived.

The beginnings of the later immense Jewish community of Egypt began during the brief rule of Alexander the Great, who invited the Jews to settle in the new city of Alexandria. The Jews arrived seeking freedom and economic opportunity. Alexander the Great granted the Jews of Alexandria citizenship on par with the city's Greek citizens in appreciation to them for their loyal support. After Alexander's rule, it is possible that his son Ptolemy increased Alexandria's Jewish population by returning with many thousands

[12]Jeremiah 44:1–8.
[13]Jeremiah 44.

of captives and soldiers from his numerous raids on Judea.[14] That, too, might account for part of the early influx of Jews into Alexandria. The Jews of Alexandria were given some measure of freedom, and were exempt from worshipping pagan gods and observing non-Jewish rites that were imposed upon others.

The Jewish community of Egypt grew rapidly. Egypt's Ptolemaic rulers[15] were friendly towards the Jews, who prospered and also continued to arrive from Judea and other lands. By the time the Romans occupied Alexandria in 43 B.C.E. there were about one million Jews in Egypt. Most of them had fully settled two of Alexandria's five sections.[16] In Alexandria, the Jews built immense communities with colossal synagogues and institutions. In describing the great synagogue of Alexandria, the Talmud states that it was so large that the sexton stood in its middle and waved a scarf when the time arrived to answer "Amen" to a prayer.[17] The Talmud also described the structure itself, stating: "Whoever did not see this building with the double colonnade, did not see the magnificence of Israel."[18]

Although the Jewish community of Alexandria thrived in a tolerant environment, it faced momentary dangers as well.[19]

Just as the Israelites during their exile in Egypt immersed themselves in Egyptian culture, so did the Jews of Alexandria. They adopted the preeminent culture of the era and sought to make

---

[14]Jacob B. Agus, *The Meaning of Jewish History* (London, New York: Abelard-Schuman, 1963), 1:119.

[15]Ptolemy, son of Alexander, inherited the lower portion of the Empire of Egypt after his father's death in 323 B.C.E. Ptolemy's descendants who inherited the throne were also known as Ptolemy.

[16]Accounts regarding the Jewish population count of Alexandria differ.

[17]Babylonian Talmud, Succah 51b.

[18]Ibid.

[19]The Third Book of Maccabees recalls one event when the Jews refused to worship the god of Dionysus and were forced into a stadium. When they again rejected the king's demands, he ordered that elephants be set loose upon them. Instead of trampling the Jews, the elephants attacked their masters and trainers. The king was duly impressed and released the Jews.

Jewish concepts conform to the non-Jewish world.[20] Members of the Jewish intelligentsia—philosophers, poets, and historians—sought to find common ground between Judaism and Hellenism, although they generally did not accept the latter's religious ideals. At the time, numerous Jewish philosophers emerged in Alexandria who sought to reconcile the contrasts between Judaism and Hellenism.

Aristoblus, a Jewish philosopher from the second century B.C.E., composed a philosophical commentary on the Pentateuch in which he maintained that Pythagoras, Plato, and Aristotle were well influenced by the teachings of Moses.[21] His commentary was allegorical. For example, he stated that the reference "voice of God" referred to "harmony in the structure of creation."[22] "The Divine creation of light [Genesis 1:3]," according to Aristoblus, referred to "the creation of wisdom; the attainment of truth is the apex of man's achievement." All of these ideas are found in Plato.[23]

The most famous of Hellenistic Jewish philosophers was Philo. An observant Jew, Philo was known as the chief interpreter of the highly influential Plato. Philo developed his own outlook on Judaism. He merged the views of Hellenism that praised human ideals with those of Judaism. According to Philo, as well as other Jewish Hellenists, the Bible spoke in allegorical terms: meaning that the stories of the lives of biblical figures were not as important as the ethical message they imparted. The events of the Bible, although all considered actual happenings according to Philo, were secondary to the messages that the biblical figures conveyed.

Philo sought to boost the morale of the Jewish intelligentsia by showing that non-Jews appreciated the Bible as well.[24] Like

---

[20]Samuel Belkin, *Essays in Traditional Jewish Thought* (New York: Philosophical Library, 1956), 130.
[21]Agus, *The Meaning of Jewish History*, 1:121.
[22]Ibid.
[23]Ibid.
[24]Louis H. Feldman, "The Orthodoxy of the Jews in Hellenistic Egypt," *Jewish Social Studies* 22 (1960): 1:221.

many among the upper classes of Jewish Alexandria, Philo attended sports events and the theater despite their Hellenistic religious undertones.[25] Yet, at the same time, he was quick to condemn those Jewish Hellenists whose allegorical interpretations led them to abrogate the observance of the commandments. The Jewish Hellenists walked a fine line between maintaining religious barriers and seeking social acceptance. Although Hellenism was making inroads in Hellenistic Egypt, these ideas were rejected in Judea, and the land of Babylon-Persia—where Jewish tradition thrived.[26]

The willingness of the Jews to adopt some of the philosophies of their Egyptian hosts did not win them the fraternity of their Gentile neighbors.

At that time, an uneasiness that existed between the Jews and their Gentile neighbors worsened when the Romans captured Alexandria. Underlying hostilities surfaced. The Jews had achieved success, which aroused the jealousy of others. In addition, they were granted the consideration of religious autonomy while the petitions by Alexandria's non-Jews for privileges were not granted. Animosity gave way to anger that boiled to a smoldering hatred. Adding fuel to the fire were the Egyptian anti-Jewish propagandists who were busy launching propaganda attacks against the Jews. Such attacks had not occurred since the third century B.C.E., but they were now becoming more common. The most common accusation leveled against the Jews was that they were foreigners living among the Greeks. In particular, a rhetorician and Greek scholar of Egyptian origins named Apion, who lived in the first century C.E., enraged the Alexandrian masses with his vicious orations and attacks against the Jews. The historian Josephus Flavius authored a volume devoted to refuting the numerous attacks on Jews and he saw fit to name it after Apion, *Contra Apionen* (Against Apion). Josephus divides Apion's treatment of the Jews into three sections: the Exodus (offering differing versions of the Israelite Exodus demeaning to the Jews), an attack of the rights of the

[25]Ibid., 225.
[26]Babylonian Talmud, Avoda Zara 18B.

Alexandrian Jews, and a disparagement of the sanctity of the Temple and of Jewish religious customs.[27] Apion asked, "Why, then, if they [Jews] are citizens of Alexandria, do they not worship the same gods as the Alexandrians?"[28] Apion degraded the Jews by borrowing a canard of other anti-Semites of that era. "Apion has the effrontery to assert that the Jews kept an ass's head, worshipping that animal and deeming it worthy of the deepest reverence."[29] Apion was the first person in history to level the charge of ritual murder against the Jews. "They would kidnap a Greek foreigner, fatten him up for a year, and then convey him to a wood, where they would slay him, sacrificed his body with their customary ritual, partook of his flesh, and, while immolating the Greeks, swore an oath of hostility to the Greeks."[30] All that was needed was a spark to ignite the fuel. The Jews became scapegoats for Alexandria's woes and a cloud of danger descended upon the city.

Forces in Alexandria sought to foment hostilities. When a play mocking the arrival of Agrippa, the king of Judea, to Alexanderia in August 38 C.E. was staged in a Greek theatre, the mob and its leaders were slightly apprehensive. Agrippa was a friend of the Roman emperor Caligula and their play could have caused the emperor to turn against them. To offset any possible repercussions, they incited the masses against the Jews. They approached the Roman governor L. Valerious Flaccus with a plan to force all the synagogues of Alexandria to erect a statue of Caligula. Flaccus, also seeking to incite hostilities against the Jews, was all too aware that the Jews would never comply when he enacted the edict. He then issued an edict proclaiming all Jews to be foreigners in Alexandria. The enraged mobs began attacking Jews while Flaccus offered them

---

[27]Menachem Stern, ed., *Greek and Latin Authors on Jews and Judaism* (Jerusalem: Academy of Sciences and Humanities, 1974), 1:389.
[28]Josephus Falvius, *The Complete Works of Josephus*, trans., William Whiston (Grand Rapids: Kregel Publications, 1981) book 2, paragraph 6, line 1.
[29]Ibid., book 2, paragraph 7, line 4.
[30]Ibid., book 2, paragraph 8, lines 8–16.

no protection. That was the beginning. The governor had flashed the green light to the masses; the pogrom had begun and Jewish history would never be the same.

Philo described the horrors that ensued:

> Multitudes of others were also laid low and destroyed with manifold forms of maltreatment, put in practice to serve their bitter cruelty by those whom savagery had maddened and transformed into the nature of wild beasts; for any Jews who showed themselves anywhere, they stoned or knocked about with clubs, aiming their blows at first against the less vital parts for fear that a speedier death might give a speedier release from the consciousness of their anguish. Some, made rampant by immunity and license which accompanied these sufferings, discarded the weapons of slower action and took the most effective of all, fire and steel, and slew many with the sword, while not a few they destroyed with fire. Indeed, whole families, husbands and their wives, infant children and their parents, were burnt in the heart of the city by these supremely ruthless men who showed no pity for old age nor youth, nor the innocent years of childhood.[31]

When the emperor Caligula was assassinated in 38 C.E., many of the Jews were prepared to do battle and take revenge by attacking the Greeks, but the new emperor, Claudius, intervened and called for calm. Claudius, who was more tolerant of the Jews than his predecessor, took measures to prevent further violence. However, he was no friend of the Jews as he also warned against further Jewish immigration to Alexandria.

The Jews soon saw that the violence against them in Alexandria was just beginning. In the year 66 C.E., the year of the beginning of the Jewish revolt against Rome in Judea, the Roman

---

[31]F. H. Colson, trans., "Flaccus," in *Philo with an English Translation* (Cambridge: Harvard University Press, 1940), ix:66–67.

army under Tiberius Alexander, an apostate Jew and nephew of Philo, perpetrated a massacre of over fifty thousand Jews in Alexandria. The local population also massacred thousands. Again, after a period of calm, Egypt was shattered by violence. The Roman emperor Trajan deceived the Jewish fighters of Alexandria who left their homes and were attacked from behind by Roman troops. When they were wiped out, the Romans fell upon the undefended remaining Jews of Alexandria. Hundreds of thousands were killed. By the revolt's end, the Jewish community was nearly annihilated.

The anti-Jewish violence in Egypt at the time also affected Jews in neighboring communities in North Africa and Cyprus who suffered the same fate at the hands of anti-Semites. A Jewish revolt against Roman authority broke out in the year 115 C.E. throughout Egypt and North Africa. An attempt to fight back in self defense against the oppressive rule of the emperor Trajan resulted in disaster for all Jewish communities involved. The Jewish communities of Cyprus, Cyrene, and Libya were also wiped out. Hundreds of thousands perished.

Following the revolt against Trajan, Alexandria's surviving Jewish community experienced a steady decline. The Jews continued to suffer from outbreaks of persecution, which prompted many to emigrate while others joined Christianity to avoid the fate of their brethren. Others simply assimilated into Egyptian society. Over the course of time, the pressure upon the Jewish community continued. In 415 C.E., Bishop Cyril headed a mob that drove all the Jews out of Alexandria. Some Jews drifted back and their descendants later suffered the pressures of forced conversions under the reign of Emperor Mourikios (582–602 C.E.).[32] By 641 C.E., upon the Muslim conquest of Alexandria, the Muslim commander noted that there were forty thousand Jews in the city.[33] Over time the Jewish community continued to dwindle. By the modern era there were few, if any, Alexandrian Jews who could trace their ancestry back to Roman times.

---

[32] Agus, *The Meaning of Jewish History*, 1:136.
[33] Ibid., 1:137.

The once massive and thriving Jewish community of Alexandria had fallen to ruins. Those remaining Jews who survived the persecutions would over time emigrate to other lands or assimilate into Egyptian society.

The first exile in Egypt set the precedent for future experiences. Security led to prosperity and growth, which led to suspicion and ultimately persecution. This scenario has been repeated often. Alexandria, Egypt, was another example of that experience. When the violence began, the horrors that ensued were equal in brutality to any era in Jewish history prior to the Holocaust. The bitterness of the Passover experience has been repeated throughout history as it was in the same land in which the Israelites were enslaved.

EGYPT AND GERMANY: ALMOST TWO MILLENNIUM AFTER THE FALL OF ALEXANDRIAN JEWRY

The events that led to Pharaoh's persecutions of the Israelites in ancient Egypt are in many ways similar to those that preceded the rise of Nazism in Germany despite the separation of the two eras by over three thousand years.

In Egypt, Joseph, who was brought there as a slave from Canaan after being sold by his jealous brothers, eventually became governor after he interpreted Pharaoh's prophetic dreams and devised a plan that saved Egypt from a famine. However, it was not long after Pharaoh's death that Joseph's immense contributions were soon forgotten. As the Bible states: "And a new king arose over Egypt, who did not know of Joseph."[34]

In Germany, Jewish industrialists were instrumental to the growth of its economy. Banking houses such as the Rothchilds helped Germany's international commercial relations and banks like Kahn and the Warburgs helped establish and maintain relations

---

[34]Rashi's commentary on Exodus 1:6.

with America. Walter Rathenau, probably Germany's greatest Jewish industrialist, became the first minister of reconstruction following the First World War and later foreign minister of the Wiemar Republic. Rathenau organized supplies of raw materials for Germany in the First World War. However, his immense contributions to Germany did not earn him the respect nor the admiration of Germany's many anti-Semites. He soon became the target of tirades, and was thought to have conspired to destroy Germany and establish Jewish world rule.[35] Rathenau, who was eventually assassinated by anti-Semites on June 22, 1922, resigned himself to the reality that was Germany. He stated prior to his death that the German Jew "has entered the world as a second class citizen and no amount of hard work and nothing he achieves can ever rescue him from this situation."[36]

Jewish contributions to Germany's economy were soon all but forgotten and the Jews were viewed as being too powerful. The names of Germany's leading Jewish families became the target of hate propaganda espousing the views of the *Protocols of the Elders of Zion* that associated the Jews with an organized international conspiracy. As in Egypt when the "new Pharaoh"[37] viewed the Jews as being too powerful,[38] the influence of Jews in Germany was exaggerated and viewed contemptuously as well.

Pharaoh's Egypt had its propagandists. When Pharaoh planned to enslave the Israelites, he knew he would have to explain his motives to the Egyptian people, many of whom were aware that the Pharaoh in Joseph's time had guaranteed the safety of the

---

[35]H. G. Adler, *The Jews in Germany: from the Enlightenment to National Socialism* (Notre Dame, London: University of Notre Dame Press, 1969) 124.

[36]Rachel Salamander, *The Jews of Germany, Yesterday 1860–1938* (New York: Rizzoli, 1991), 256, quoting "Staat Judentum," *Zur Kritik der Zeit* (N Berlin 1912).

[37]Exodus 1:6.

[38]Exodus 1:7.

Israelites.[39] He thus initiated a propaganda campaign against the Israelites. The Bible states: "And the Egyptians did evil unto us."[40] This verse can be construed to imply that the Israelites were made to appear as evil.[41] Pharaoh depicted the growing numbers and affluence of the Israelites as a threat, telling the people, "Behold, the Children of Israel are numerous and powerful."[42]

The years that preceded the rise of Nazism were awash with anti-Jewish provocation. Journals and public speakers all joined in the fray accusing Germany's Jews of being the cause of the nation's misfortunes. The popular anti-Jewish canards of the time, Jewish domination and control, won wide acceptance and popularity among the German masses, although the Jews numbered one percent of the population. Slogans such as "The Jews are our misfortune" and "Germany awake, Jews perish" became popular.

In Pharaoh's Egypt, the Israelites were described as having "filled the land."[43] Prior to their enslavement, they indulged in Egypt's cultural life. They "filled the theatres and circuses."[44] The Torah scholar and commentator Rabbi Naftali Zvi Berliner, known as the Netziv (1817–1893), explained that the sentence pertaining to the Israelites filling the land (Exodus 1:7) refers to their exit from seclusion in Goshen where they had lived as a distinct entity. Once out of Goshen, they moved throughout Egypt in an attempt to change the public perception of them as being outsiders apart from Egyptian society.[45]

---

[39]Genesis 47:5.
[40]Deuteronomy 26:6.
[41]The Text of the Passover Haggadah contains an explanation of the passage of Deuteronomy 26:6, which likens the passage to Exodus 1:10, in which the Pharaoh speaks of outsmarting the Israelites as he describes them as a threatening entity; a pretext to their enslavement.
[42]Exodus 1:8.
[43]Ibid., 1:7.
[44]Midrash Tanchuma on Exodus 1:7.
[45]Commentary of HaEmek Davar (Rabbi Naftali Tzvi Berliner) on Exodus 1:7.

In Germany, Jews in the major cities were thoroughly immersed in German culture. The two hundred-year struggle of German Jewry for emancipation saw its full realization with the establishment of the democratic Wiemar Republic in 1919. In February 1919, the National Constituent Assembly was convened in the town of Wiemar and a constitution that declared freedom and liberty for all was drafted. For decades the Jews had been devotees of German high culture, be it its music, art, or literature. The Wiemar Republic lifted existing restrictions against Jews; all spheres of life were now officially open to them. Now the Jews could fully reap the spoils of emancipation. Indeed, in Wiemar, Germany, the Jews were instrumental in creating the country's cultural life. Jews were the leaders in most fields of culture—theatre, art, architecture, music, literature, poetry, and journalism. As the historian Walter Laqeuer put it, "Without the Jews, there would have been no Wiemar culture."[46] A German writer described German Jewry within the Wiemar Republic as follows: "As if an age old dam had burst, Jews suddenly appeared in virtually all spheres of literature—poetry, novellas, novels, essays, plays—with achievements that at least a certain stratum of intellectually minded people considered epoch making."[47] The German anti-Semites, viewing Jews as an outside non-German element, reacted with hostility and engaged in anti-Jewish propaganda, launching the beginning of a verbal war against the Jew which would increase over time. In time, many Germans believed that the Jew had achieved too much influence in Germany and perceived the German Jewish culture as foreign and counter-German. As the culture of Wiemar soared, so did Nazism.

In Egypt, the emancipated Israelites were assimilating into

---

[46]Walter Laqeuer, *Wiemar: A Cultural History, 1918–1933* (New York: Putnam, 1974), 73.

[47]Salamander, *The Jews of Germany, Yesterday*, 170, quoting Werner E. Mosse and Arnold Paucker, "Der Beitrag der Juden zu Geist and Kulter," in *Deutches Judentum in Krieg und Revolution, 1916–1923* (Tubingen: Hans Tramer, 1971).

Egyptian society. This became evident after Joseph's death, as most Israelites neglected the commandment of circumcision.[48] Eventually, many engaged in idolatry as well.[49]

In Germany, emancipation was soon followed by the wide scale assimilation of German Jewry and, eventually, baptism by Jews on a massive scale. Many German Jews could not run fast enough from their Jewish heritage. The escape seemed easy, but the German Jewish assimilationists could never run too far. An apt description was presented by German Jew Max Brod who described Franz Kafka's feeling of alienation as a Jew in his work "The Castle." The castle was "the special feeling of a Jew who would like to put down roots in alien surroundings, who strives with all the strength of his soul to draw closer to the strangers around him, to become completely like them—and who cannot achieve this union."[50] In a letter written by writer Kurt Tolcholsky to another writer of Wiemar, Germany, Stephan Zweig, from his exile in Sweden in 1935, the sentiments of multitudes of German Jews were expressed: "I resigned from Judaism in the year 1911, and I know that cannot be done."[51]

Initially, Jews who renounced their Jewish past did so by intermarriage or by living a life void of Jewish practices. But over time many German Jews became zealous about their abandonment of Judaism and sought conversion to Christianity. What was a small trend before the First World War became an epidemic by the 1920s. According to Nazi statistics—which are fairly accurate in this respect—by the 1920s over one hundred thousand Jews had

[48]Midrash Tanchuma on Exodus 6. However, members of the Tribe of Levy continued the rite of circumcision as stated in Deuteronomy 33:9, "They (Tribe of Levy) guarded Your word and observed Your covenant."
[49]Ibid.
[50]Salamander, *The Jews of Germany, Yesterday*, 169, quoting Max Brod, *Streitbares Leben* (Munich, 1960).
[51]Ibid., 155; Laqeuer, *Weimar: a Cultural History*, 73.

converted.[52] Of every one hundred marriages in 1927 involving Jews, sixty-four were mixed marriages.[53]

In Egypt, as well, those who neglected to circumcise their newborn in the hope of assimilating into Egyptian society were not spared the rigors and horrors of servitude when Pharaoh decided to impose slavery upon the Israelites. According to the Midrash, Pharaoh planned the enslavement of the Israelites through deception and by exploiting their allegiance. He declared a national program to build the cities of Pithom and Raamses and fortify them in the event of war. Those who would come forth to work on the project would be given daily wages as well. However, over time, the non-Israelite workers would be quietly removed from the job leaving only the Israelites to labor. At that point taskmasters would be appointed and the Israelites would be forced into servitude. The Israelites, as expected, enthusiastically volunteered to show their loyalty. At the end of one month of labor Pharaoh had already appointed taskmasters who forced them to do heavy labor. He reasoned that the excessive hours of labor would force them to spend their time away from their wives and thus cause their numbers to decrease.[54]

In Germany, the loyalty of the Jews was unsurpassed. This loyalty was exemplified by their involvement with the nation's war effort during the First World War. In World War I, almost twenty percent of the total population of German Jewry served in the armed forces; their casualty rate matched—if it did not exceed—that of the entire German population. One hundred thousand German Jews served in the army; eighty thousand served on the front lines; and twelve thousand were killed in combat. In addition, thirty-five thousand Jews were decorated for bravery.

---

[52]Salamander, *The Jews of Germany, Yesterday*, 131, quoting "In Judaica 4," (Frankfurt am Main, 1984).
[53]H. G. Adler, *The Jews in Germany*, 127.
[54]Sefer HaYashar 125, 126, quoted in Louis Ginzberg, *Legends of the Jews*, trans. Henrietta Szold (Philadelphia: Jewish Publication Society of America, 1940), 246–248.

An appeal to German Jewry by the Imperial Association of German Jews echoed the sentiments of German Jewry:

> German Jews,
>
> In this fateful hour it is once again time to show that, proud of our lineage,
>
> We Jews are among the best sons of our fatherland. The noblest of our millennia
>
> Old history obliges. We expect our young to hasten to the colors voluntarily and with high hearts. German Jews! We appeal to you, in the spirit of
>
> The old Jewish rule of duty, to dedicate yourselves to the service of your fatherland with
>
> all your heart, all your soul, and all your abilities.[55]

Not only did Jews fight for Germany, they also contributed vast sums of money and purchased war bonds, which eventually became worthless. In addition, many Jews contributed their vast talents in many ways to aid the war effort. For example, chemist Fritz Haber's extraction of nitrogen from the air prompted one conservative deputy in the government to state that without Haber the war would have been lost in three months.[56]

A Jew, Ludwig Frank—one of the two members of the Reichstag who was killed in action—wrote in his last letter, "I have the fervent wish to survive the war and then to cooperate in building the Reichstag from within."[57] Such hopes that Jews would be rewarded for their patriotism with acceptance were not to be realized. By the middle of 1916—as it became evident that Germany was loosing the war—the war ministry, under pressure from anti-Semites, ordered a statistical inquiry into the religious

[55]Salamander, *The Jews of Germany, Yesterday*, 260.
[56]Ruth Gay, *The Jews of Germany* (New Haven: Yale University Press, 1992), 285.
[57]Salamander, *The Jews of Germany, Yesterday*, 249.

affiliations of those serving in the armed forces.[58] This was designed as a thinly disguised census of the Jews to verify what percentage of them were among the combat troops. The aim was to give the impression that the Jews were not well represented. To add to the blow, many Germans began to spread propaganda accusing the Jews of betraying Germany during the war. A pseudoanonymous author known as Otto Armin released a fictitious wartime account of the Jews in 1919 that imputed their loyalty. His figures slandered the Jews by stating that 62,000 Jews served in the armed forces, 35,000 served behind the front lines, and only 27,000 ever saw action on the field.[59] There were also other accounts that falsified the number of Jews in active duty. These scurrilous accounts contributed to the rise of anti-Semitism. Massive and costly attempts to report the errors and omissions were to no avail.

During the existence of the Wiemar Republic, (1921–1933), millions of Germans would readily accept this propaganda. The loyalty of German Jewry brought the Jews no closer to the equality they dreamed of. Yet despite the rise of anti-Semitism, the Jews of post-World War I Wiemar, Germany, repeatedly pledged that anti-Semitism would not deter them from their love or duty to their fatherland. On October 27, 1919, the Union of Jewish Clubs declared, "Let the anti-Semites try by any and all means to cut us to the quick, they will not be able to tear our love of Fatherland from our hearts."[60] The director of the Central-Verein Ludwig Hollander protested the exclusion of a rabbi from a ceremony commemorating Germany's war dead, stating that the exclusion changed nothing in the "moral conception" of their fatherland.[61] In 1929, Hollander declared, "German Jews–Jewish Germans, constitute parts of the German people and for all future time

---

[58]Ruth Pierson, "German Jewish Identity in the Weimar Republic" (Ph.D. diss., Yale University, 1970).
[59]Gay, *The Jews of Germany*, 243.
[60]Pierson, "German Jewish Identity in the Weimar Republic," 251.
[61]Ibid., 252.

members of the German people."[62] At an R.J.F. convention in Rhineland in 1925, the speaker Ludwig Haas stated, "It was as German soldiers that we defend ourselves against those who drag our honor through the gutter—and our Germanality is our honor."[63] But it was all to no avail.

The Passover Haggadah states: "In every generation there have been those who have risen against us to destroy us." The first exile in Egypt served as a blueprint for many to follow throughout history. Not only do Pharaohs reemerge in different times and places, but the circumstances that faced the Israelites in Egypt have reocurred in pre-Nazi Germany and throughout history as well.

THE COLOR OF WINE

When Passover night arrives, the cups of wine are filled and the prayers and songs of the holiday are joyfully chanted. In today's times Passover has often become synonymous with vacation as newspapers are filled with advertisements for Passover getaways to places ranging from the Canadian Rockies to Miami Beach to the French Riviera. But that's not how Passover was celebrated for the Jews of medieval Europe. For them, wine—traditionally a symbol of gladness and holiday celebration—also signaled a time for contemplation on Passover. When Passover arrived, Jews celebrated with extreme caution and fear, unsure of the violence that could be unleashed against them. That time of the year coincides with the Easter season, a time when Christians commemorate the Crucifixion. Too often, Jews, who were blamed for the Crucifixion and resented for their rejection of Christianity, became targets of hatred and superstitions. Often it was their use of wine on Passover that prompted those attacks.

On Passover, the bizarre blood libel accusations were often

---

[62]Ibid., 275.
[63]Ibid., 273.

leveled against the Jews. These accusations usually led to violent attacks against Jewish communities. There were hundreds of blood libels throughout history, resulting in the deaths of thousands. The blood libel theme rarely deviated. A child—almost always a young boy—was lost. Allegations then arose that the Jews murdered him and used his blood for ritual purposes. Usually those leveling the accusations had murdered the child themselves in order to accuse the Jews. Sometimes the child was a victim of an accident or later found unharmed. The cruelest methods of torture were often used to force confessions and the fabricated charges would serve as a pretext to slander and attack Jewish communities.

By the fourteenth century, ritual murder charges became common at Passover time. The fact that human sacrifice and the use of even animal blood for any purpose are strictly forbidden according to Jewish law did not matter to those perpetrators and believers of lies. Reason is abandoned when hatred and ignorance rule. Repudiations of blood libels by many popes throughout the ages did little or nothing to stop them.

The first ritual murder accusation in history against the Jews goes back to Egypt at about 40 B.C.E. when a propagandist named Apion, intent upon inciting the masses against the Jews of Alexandria, slandered them with a blood libel accusation.[64] Not until over one thousand years later did the accusation resurface. On Passover 1144, in Norwich, England, a young man named William, a tanner's apprentice, disappeared during the week of Easter, which coincided with Passover that year. Charges immediately arose that the Jews killed him as part of a ritual murder. According to the accusation, the Jews "bought a Christian child before Easter and tortured him and on Long Friday hanged him on a rod."[65] Since no body was found, the Sheriff of Norwich ignored the charges and granted the Jews protection. But the story was not forgotten and

---

[64]See "The Return to Egypt: The Rise and Fall of Egyptian Jewry," page 3.
[65]*Encyclopedia Judaica*, vol. 4 (Jerusalem: The Macmillan Co., Keter Publishing House, 1972), 1121.

the missing boy, William, became a martyr amongst the town's people. A short time later, the Jews of Norwich were attacked by mobs seeking vengeance and were forced to flee.

Eleven years later, the blood libel resurfaced bringing horrific consequences to Jews attending a wedding in Lincoln, England. A Christian boy named Hugh was found in a cesspool where he apparently had fallen. After subsequent forced, tortured confessions, nineteen Jews were hanged. Soon, the anti-Semites of England accused all of England's Jews of participating in ritual murder. The many accusations that followed were often accompanied by violent attacks against Jewish communities.

In 1171, the blood libel reached France. In the city of Blois, rumors spread that Jews committed murder in order to extract blood for Passover *matzot.* On May 26, 1171, two months after Passover—without the recovery of a corpse—the thirty-three members of the Blois Jewish community, which included seventeen women, were burned at the stake after they refused the chance to save themselves by accepting Christianity. French Jewry were shocked and horrified by the event. The rabbinical scholar Rabbeinu Jacob Tam proclaimed the day of the massacre, the twentieth day of Sivan, a fast day to commemorate the tragedy. Tragically, many more such horrors would follow. Ten years later, the accusation reached Spain at Saragossa.[66] The merchants of hate and perpetrators of lies found a new frontier for their poison and more countries lay in their path.

In the seventeenth century, catastrophe struck Polish Jewry as Cossack troops attacked and massacred entire Jewish communities during the Chmielnicki Revolt. Rabbi David Halevy Siegel, who lived during that era and authored a commentary on the *Shulchan Aruch* (Code of Jewish Law) entitled the *Turei Zahav*, issued a ruling intended to protect Jews from the blood libel. He ruled that the traditional red wine used at the Seders be substituted with white wine in lands of persecution in order not to arouse suspicion. "In

---

[66]Historically, blood libels were not as pervasive in Spain.

lands where false accusations are made, we refrain from using red wine."[67] On Passover night white wine was consumed thereafter. In his own life, Rabbi Siegel managed to flee from the Chmielnicki massacres, but he was not spared great personal suffering when two of his sons were murdered in a pogrom in Lvov, Poland, in 1654.

Over the next three hundred years, as the modern era approached, there was a slow decline in blood libels but they did continue. In 1840, the Damascus blood libel drew protests from Jews worldwide and signified the entry of blood libels in the Middle East. The infamous Kishinev pogrom of 1903 began on the last day of Passover as the result of a blood libel.

Although blood libels became less frequent over time, their rhetoric and the power of their accusations helped to set the stage for new conspiracy theories. With the approach of the era of modernization and the Industrial Revolution, accusations arose against the Jews of conspiracy for world domination. Canards of Jewish control and aspirations for global domination became the new theme for the hate propagandists.

As Jews celebrated Passover in bygone eras, they were aware of the risks involved. At the Passover Seder, they drank the four cups of wine that symbolized freedom, but not in the traditional color. When they gazed at the white wine that adorned their holiday tables, they were reminded of their own sufferings and of their precarious existence. They lived in hostile environments and they suffered, yet they could celebrate the freedom experienced by their ancestors as they exited Egypt and they could nonetheless sit and recline in the manner of nobility and drink white wine celebrating their legacy as Jews. Today, we who drink red wine at our Seders can think about our ancestors of Europe and their trials and triumphs.

THE PASSOVER SACRIFICE

> "And Moses called the elders of Israel and he said to them, draw forth (your hands) and take for yourselves a lamb for your

---

[67]Orach Chaim, section 472, paragraph 11, Magen David, Taz.

> households and slaughter the Passover sacrifice."[68] Rabbi Yose the Gallilean states that the words "draw forth" imply "draw forth your hands" from idolatry and cling to the [Torah's] commandments.[69]

When the Israelites gathered lambs on the tenth day of the month of Nissan and set them aside for slaughter on the afternoon preceding Passover they declared themselves free of the influences of the idolatrous practices of the Egyptians. Although the Israelites in Egypt had maintained a distinctive national character during the duration of their enslavement, many, if not most, adopted the idolatrous practices of the Egyptians.[70] The slaughtering of the lamb—considered a deity to the Egyptians—before their oppressors was a public and communal repudiation of idolatry by the Israelites. The Israelites were truly worthy of leaving Egypt only after slaughtering the Passover sacrifice. However, when the Israelites left Egypt, their repudiation of idolatry was not final. The worship of idols would continue to plague the Israelites over the next thousand years until the destruction of the First Temple in 586 B.C.E.

During the chaos of the First Temple era, a righteous Judean king prevailed upon the people to desist from their idolatrous practices and mend their ways. This king's emergence and call for change coincided with the approaching Passover holiday. Those changes were characterized by the Passover sacrifices brought by a repentant nation.

Judea had both upright and evil kings. Often the rule of evil kings was followed by the rule of just kings. At the young age of 25, King Hezekiah of Judea inherited a troubled kingdom from his father Achaz, who had lured the Judeans into idolatry and showed contempt for the holiest site in Judaism—the Temple. Achaz

---

[68]Exodus 12:21.
[69]Mechilta (a Midrashic source on the biblical Book of Exodus).
[70]Midrash Tanchuma on Exodus 1:7.

plundered the Temple of its wealth and brought sacrifices to strange gods and placing *bamot* (prohibited altars) throughout the land.[71] He also sought the alliance of the powerful Assyrians in the north as protection from Judea's many surrounding enemies. In his desire to mimic the ways of his northern ally, he removed the Temple's copper altar and constructed a likeness of an Assyrian deity in its place. During his rule, Achaz cancelled the Temple service, prevented the study of the Torah, and permitted immoral practices.[72]

Immediately upon ascending the throne, Hezekiah sought to right the wrongs of his father. He gathered the Levites and priests and instructed them to purify the Temple. He reminded them of their mission: "My sons do not forget, for the Lord chose you to stand before Him to minister to Him and to be His ministers and to burn incense."[73] He also recalled the failures in Judea's history: ". . . for our fathers acted treacherously and did evil in the eyes of the Lord, our God and forsook Him, and they turned their faces away from the Tabernacle of the Lord and turned their backs."[74] Many of the Levites and Temple priests did not hastily heed the king's call. Rather, they delayed their preparations for the Temple service. They did not take the new king seriously, nor did they trust his motives. They did not initially believe that the son of Achaz could be so vastly different from his father, but when they investigated the matter and found Hezekiah to be righteous, they returned to Jerusalem.[75] When the holy work was completed, the Temple was consecrated and offerings were once again brought to the Temple.

As Passover was approaching, Hezekiah called upon the nation to come to Jerusalem to celebrate the holiday. He dared to send letters to the tribes who were Judea's adversaries, in the

---

[71]During Temple times, sacrifices were prohibited from being brought outside the Temple walls.
[72]Babylonian Talmud, Sanhedrin 103b.
[73]2 Chronicals 29:11.
[74]2 Chronicals 29:7.
[75]Rashi's commentary on 2 Chronicles 30:15.

Northern Kingdom,[76] inviting them to Jerusalem. Although his attempts to have Judah's northern secessionists reunite with their brethren had not been a complete success, some from the north did journey to Jerusalem. When Passover came, the nation assembled in Jerusalem. "And the entire congregation of Judah and the priests and the Levites and the entire congregation that come from the Land of Israel, and those who dwelt in Judah rejoiced."[77] Prior to the offering of the Passover sacrifice, all idols were removed from their midst. Jerusalem was once again free of idolatry. "And they arose and removed the altars that were in Jerusalem, and all the altars for incense they removed and cast them into the Kidron Valley."[78] The people arose, cleansed of their impurity, and offered sacrifices.[79]

Following the Passover sacrifice, the nation, in a renewed spirit of dedication, destroyed the idols throughout the land. "All the Israelites who were present went out to the cities of Judah, and they smashed the monuments and cut down the *asherim*,[80] and they demolished the high places and the altars from all Judah and Benjamin and in Ephraim and Menashe until they had completely destroyed them."[81]

Just as at the time of the Exodus from Egypt, preparations for the Passover sacrifice involved the collective elimination of all forms of idolatry that the Judeans had adopted from their neighbors. That Passover, the Jews experienced a spiritual renaissance, just as their

---

[76]The Jewish people were divided into the Israelite Kingdom in the north and the Kingdom of Judah and Benjamin in the south.
[77]2 Chronicles 30:25.
[78]2 Chronicles 30:14.
[79]The commentary of the Radak on 2 Chronicles 30:14 states that there were those who came to Jerusalem remaining ritually impure without properly undergoing purification according to Jewish Law and although unfit to offer the Passover sacrifice and other holiday sacrifices, did so. The king prayed on their behalf and his prayers were answered.
[80]*Asherim* are trees that were used as part of idolatrous rites.
[81]2 Chronicles 31:1.

ancestors had in Egypt before the Exodus took place. The Israelite Passover was followed by their redemption. In Hezekiah's time a few years later, the Assyrians—formerly the ally of Achaz were to advance towards Jerusalem and threaten the kingdom of Judah. On Passover night, as the Assyrians surrounded Jerusalem and prepared its capture, a plague broke out among the troops stationed around Jerusalem. The Assyrian army was decimated. However, the triumph of Hezekiah's Passover did not endure. His son Menashe was as evil as his grandfather Achaz, and under his rule the Judeans once again immersed themselves in idolatry. However, history would repeat itself as Menashe's son Josiah would campaign against idolatry, and again the Passover sacrifice would be offered in the purified Temple.

Just as when they left Egypt the first Passover did not eliminate the Israelites' lust for idolatry in subsequent years, the Passover that was celebrated during Hezekiah's rule did not eliminate idol worship, nor did Josiah's. Even so, the Passover celebrations profoundly impacted the Jews in their time and strengthened their commitment to their heritage, as had been the effect of the first Passover.

MATZAH: AN ETERNAL SYMBOL OF FREEDOM

On Passover—the holiday that celebrates freedom—there were times when Jews of the Soviet Union did not have the freedom to obtain *matzot*. Matzah, the symbol of both slavery and freedom, was consumed by the Israelites during their bitter enslavement in Egypt[82] and upon their hasty departure. In the late 1950s, the Soviets went out of their way to obstruct the attempts of Jews to receive *matzot* for Passover.

Despite difficulties in procuring *matzot* since the Russian Revolution in 1917, Soviet Jews, to some degree, were allowed to

---

[82]Deuteronomy 16:3.

either obtain packages from the West or bake *matzot* in synagogues. But beginning in 1957, the authorities began to prohibit the baking of *matzot* in synagogues, while they did continue to permit the distribution of *matzot* within some major cities. In smaller cities, *matzot* were often baked clandestinely.

By 1962, the Soviet government for the first time prohibited the baking of *matzot* throughout the entire Soviet Union. Following worldwide condemnations, the Soviets appeared to make some concessions the next year. A month before Passover, Soviet diplomats abroad responded to the inquiries of Jewish religious leaders' on the matter and stated that Jews may bake *matzot* privately.[83] However, private homes were inadequate for baking and supplying sufficient quantities for the thousands in need. What made the Soviet "concession" more disturbing was that there were additional arrests and incarcerations of individuals who baked *matzot*.

Within the Soviet Union the prohibition had not in fact been lifted and the outcry from Jewish communities in the West intensified. That Passover, a special prayer added to the Seder by the chief rabbi of England, Rabbi Israel Brodie, articulated the increasing identification of World Jewry with the plight of their brethren. "Behold this Matzo, the symbol of our affliction but also of our liberty. On this festival may our hearts be turned to our brothers and sisters in Russia who were not permitted to bake Matzo and to celebrate this Passover in the traditional, reclining attitude of free men."[84]

One can only speculate the Soviet's motives for the prohibitions of *matzot* at that time and the subsequent arrests of Jews found privately baking *matzot*. Perhaps, just as Pharaoh would not buckle under the pressure of the plagues, the Soviets were not yet ready to concede to world pressure and grant religious freedom to

---

[83]"Matzot Can Be Baked Privately," *The Jewish Chronicle* (March 8, 1963): 1.

[84]"Special Seder Prayer to be Recited," *The Jewish Chronicle* (April 5, 1963): 12.

Soviet Jewry. The prohibition against *matzot* was their way of demonstrating this.

The Soviets slowly did respond to protests. In 1964, while the public baking and sale of *matzot* remained prohibited, the Moscow Jewish community was given a slight concession. Just prior to Passover, they were permitted to rent a small bakery to bake *matzot*.[85] By 1965, the Soviets again allowed some synagogues in some major cities to be used for baking *matzot*.[86] They also allowed Soviet Jews to receive individual packages of over ten thousand pounds of *matzot* sent from abroad.[87] In 1966, the bans were lifted in some capitals of the Soviet republics and in Oriental Jewish communities.[88]

By 1969, the Soviets lifted all the restrictions. Over time more easing would follow. Soon afterwards, the emigration of Soviet Jews would begin. In 1971, over thirty thousand Jews immigrated to Israel. The Soviet's easing on *matzot* restrictions was part of an early trend of concessions and the beginning of many more to follow. Thus, for Jews of the former Soviet Union, after their many experiences, the connection between *matzot* and freedom is inseparable.

THE HEALING OF A COMMUNITY'S WOUNDS

Since the time of the Israelite Exodus from Egypt, Passover has been a time for families to gather together and celebrate the momentous occasion. Passover is also a time when the Jewish community must make substantial efforts to ensure that no Jew is without the provisions needed to observe the holiday.

---

[85]William Korey, *The Soviet Cage: Anti-Semitism in Russia* (New York: Viking Press, 1973), 47.
[86]"British Matzot Parcels for Russia," *The Jewish Chronicle* (April 23, 1965): 1.
[87]Ibid.
[88]Nora Levin, *The Jews in the Soviet Union Since 1917: Paradox of Jewish Survival* (New York: University Press, 1988) 2:626.

As the nation was divided during the Civil War, so too were the Jewish communities of the North and South. Each community felt passionately for their cause and sacrificed on behalf of their side's war efforts. As the war was nearing its end and the war-torn Confederacy was in ruins, the Jews of the South sought to rebuild their broken lives. When Passover approached, they did not have the means to observe the holiday and they looked towards their Northern brethren for support. The Northerners immediately put aside their differences and ensured that their Southern co-religionists would have adequate provisions. They did so with compassion and understanding.

In February 1865, two months before Robert E. Lee's surrender at Appomatox, the Jews of Savannah addressed a request to their Northern brethren for Passover *matzot*.[89] The requests were sent to Isaac Leeser, spiritual leader of Congregation Mikve Yisrael of Philadelphia and publisher of the Jewish newspaper *The Occident*, and to Meyer S. Isaacs, a prominent Northern Jewish businessman.[90] Other appeals soon followed.

On March 3, 1865, a Jewish periodical called *The Jewish Messenger* appealed on behalf of Savannah's Jews in an editorial. "An appeal has been made through Mr. N. J. Brady, now at Savannah, on behalf of the Jewish residents of that city. It is desired to procure for them about five thousand pounds of *matzot*. Many of the inhabitants, formerly wealthy, are in extremely straitened circumstances, and besides, have lost entirely the means of baking for the ensuing Passover."[91] The editorial urged support, noting the generosity of Savannah Jewry in the past: "The Israelites of Savannah as a community here, in former years, have been prompt and generous in response to calls for aid."[92]

The first response came from Congregation Shearit Yisrael of

---

[89]Savannah was then under Union control.
[90]Bertram Korn, *American Jewry and the Civil War* (Marietta, Georgia: Bernis Publishing, 1995), 112.
[91]*The Jewish Messenger* (March 3, 1865).
[92]Ibid.

New York with a donation of $100; others followed. Three weeks later, a notice in the *Jewish Messenger* from the Savannah Relief Fund publicized the responses to their appeal which contained a list of thirty-five synagogues, companies and individuals who contributed a total of $502.90. "We have obtained transportation for and have shipped on steamer Arago three thousand pounds of *matzot* baked here, together with two thousand pounds sent as a contribution for the Israelites."[93] Contributions continued to come in from various northern cities.

That Passover, in a nation divided by civil war, the unity of the Jewish community was affirmed. Soon after, appeals would be sent from the beleaguered Southern Jewish communities of Charleston, North Carolina and Columbia, South Carolina. Those appeals would also be answered. The Jewish periodical *The Occident* printed in its July 1866 issue an appeal on behalf of Charleston's Jewish community. "We were pleased to see that the appeals were not looking with mute despair on the past, but working with hope to repair the losses with new success in the future."[94]

That Passover of 1865 the wounds of the Jewish community caused by the division of the nation began to heal.

NAPOLEON AND THE ESTABLISHMENT OF ISRAEL

On April 20, 1799, General Napoleon Bonaparte of France made a most intriguing proclamation. Deeming the conquest of the Land of Israel as imminent, he proposed to grant the Land of Israel to the Jews. The day of the announcement was also the fifteenth day of the Hebrew month of Nissan, the first day of Passover.

The first step toward Napoleon's proclamation began with

---

[93]Savannah Relief Fund, "Letter to the Editor," *The Jewish Messenger* 27, no. 12 (March 24, 1865).
[94]*The Occident* 24 (July 1866): 185.

France's conquest of Egypt. Napoleon sought the defeat of France's enemy, England, via Egypt—the gateway to British-controlled India. On July 1, 1798, Napoleon arrived in Egypt with a fleet of 180 ships carrying 17,000 soldiers, 1,000 cannons, and 800 horses and set about his conquest.[95] The Turkish and Mamelukian forces were swiftly defeated and Egypt came under French control. While in the Sinai Peninsula, Napoleon received word that the Turks were planning to drive him out of Egypt. On February 10, 1799, Napoleon and his troops left Cairo and journeyed northward toward Turkish-controlled Palestine to confront Turkish forces. After two grueling months of travel through the Sinai Desert, the French army reached Gaza. After its conquest, they proceeded to move up the coast and captured Ramle and then Jaffa on March 7. Napoleon's forces continued their advance northward, capturing the Carmel Mountains and then Haifa, until they reached the Turkish-controlled fortress of Acre. Aside from being surrounded by five towering, formidable walls, a British fleet of four ships had arrived before Napoleon's army and was anchored in its port, making the conquest of well-fortified Acre even more difficult. French troops settled in and dug trenches, marking the beginning of a siege.

But before the assault on Acre could begin, Napoleon had to defend the siege itself from outside attacks. An army of thirty thousand troops—comprised mostly of Turks—was sent from Syria to relieve the besieged city. As they made their way through the northern hills of the Galilee, they were met by the French and routed. Napoleon's most outstanding victory occurred at the foot of Mount Tabor in the Galilee on April 10. On that day, his troops, outnumbered eight to one, defeated Turkish forces.[96] With the Turks driven back, all that remained for the French was the capture of Acre. As Napoleon turned his attention back to the siege, word reached him that heavy artillery was on its way. Victory now seemed

---

[95]Yadin Roman, "Napoleon's Folly," *Eretz Magazine* 4, no. 1 (Winter 1988–1989): 39.
[96]Ibid., 75.

certain and Napoleon would soon become history's next ruler over the Holy Land. From Acre, Napoleon would then plan the conquest of Jerusalem.

The next day, April 20, 1799, Bonaparte issued a proclamation to the Jewish people declaring his alleged intentions to restore Jewish sovereignty over the Land of Israel. A portion of the proclamation reads:

> Rightful heirs of Palestine!
>
> The great nation which does not trade in men and countries as did those who sold your ancestors unto all peoples [Joel 4:6] hereby calls on you not indeed to conquer your patrimony, nay, only take over that which has been conquered and, with that nation's warranty and support, to maintain it against all comers.[97]

In its conclusion, the Jews were encouraged to rise up after two thousand years of oppression:

> Arise! Show that the once overwhelming might of your oppressors has not repressed the courage of the descendants of those heroes whose brotherly alliance did honor to Sparta and Rome [Maccabe 12:15], but that all the two thousand years of slavish treatment have not succeeded in stifling it.
>
> Hasten! Now is the moment which may not arise for thousands of years, to claim the restoration of your rights among the population of the universe which had been shamefully withheld from you for thousands of years, your shameful existence as a nation among nations, and the unlimited right to worship Ye-hova in accordance with your faith, publicly and in likelihood forever [Joel 4:20].[98]

---

[97]Franz Kobler, *Napoleon and the Jews* (New York: Schocken Books, 1975), 56–57.
[98]Ibid.

The proclamation was addressed not just to the Jews who lived in Palestine, but to Jews worldwide.

The statement was made, but the conquest of the land was not yet complete. Soon after, the fortunes of France's victories on the battlefield were reversed. The heavy cannons never arrived, they were intercepted by the British. Nevertheless, on April 24 Napoleon ordered an attack on Acre. Assault after assault met with failure as the city and its defenders, aided by the British, managed to hold off the French. By May 20, after sustaining heavy losses, Napoleon raised the siege. The French soon withdrew to Egypt. Napoleon's triumph was short-lived.[99]

With French defeat in the region imminent, Napoleon left Egypt, and was eventually followed by all the French forces. The Turks resumed control. Before the ink on the proclamation had dried, the French were gone and it was of little value.

The proclamation, however, did bear fruit. It was a precursor to Zionism, heightening awareness of the cause of Jewish Statehood. Others around the world began to seriously contemplate the notion of Jewish Statehood in Palestine. Many saw Napoleon's gestures as fulfillment of biblical prophecy that foretells of the restoration of the Jews to their land. The idea drew many adherents, especially in England. English writers echoed the theme of Jewish Statehood. James Bicheno, in his book *The Restoration of the Jews: The Crisis of all Nations* (1800), presented the return of the Jews to the Holy Land as one of the world's pressing problems. Bicheno reflected on the fact that it was the French who endorsed Jewish Statehood: "I can not help feeling that we (i.e., the English) are not the favored nation."[100] Edward King, author of *Remarks on Signs of the Times*, also interpreted the events as a fulfillment of biblical prophecy that foretells of the return of the Jews to the land. He concluded that the restoration of the Jews to the Holy Land was

[99]Roman, "Napoleon's Folly," 79.
[100]Kobler, *Napoleon and the Jews*, 86.

inevitable.[101] Another English writer, Henry Kett, also believed Napoleon's proclamation to be prophetic, but suggested that the English, rather than the French, would ultimately return the Jews to Zion.[102]

Napoleon's dealings with the Jews remain an enigma. Why did he give them so much attention? Napoleon granted the Jews emancipation and declared a Jewish State. Perhaps he wanted to play a special role in history, to enshrine his name as the liberator of the Jews, securing his name next to those of the most revered biblical figures. Or maybe he had less lofty motives. It could have been mere propaganda, an attempt to enlist Jewish support for the French war effort against the Turks. Or perhaps there were other motives. There were rumors that Napoleon wanted to establish his own kingdom in the east from India to Ethiopia. That too might account for his actions.

The day of the proclamation was the first day of Passover—the day of the Israelite Exodus from Egypt. On the same day over thirty-five hundred years earlier, in a covenant with Abraham, the Almighty promised the Land of Israel in its full boundaries. On the first night of Passover throughout history, many wonders have been performed for the Jewish people. However, the fulfillment of Napoleon's plans was not destined for that Passover. Yet the ideas he expressed found the admiration of many and were, therefore, a step closer to the eventual creation of Israel. One hundred and eighteen (118) years later the British would issue the Balfour Declaration that called for a Jewish Homeland. Thirty-one years later, in 1948, Israel was recognized as a sovereign state by popular vote in the United Nations General Assembly. Perhaps it can be said that Napoleon's premature announcement on the first day of Passover played some small role in the creation of the State of Israel.

---

[101] Ibid., 84.
[102] Ibid., 84.

ENTERING THE PROMISED LAND

When the Israelites left Egypt, they found themselves confronted by new, unexpected challenges. They encountered harsh elements, received manna as provision, and were subjected to attacks from the nation of Amalek. There was a strong temptation to turn around and leave the Sinai Desert. The Israelites frequently complained and spoke about returning to Egypt. But there was no turning back. Destiny called and the Israelites would eventually enter the Promised Land.

Destiny also called out to the first wave of Zionist settlers. These Jews came to the Land of Israel from Russia to develop agricultural settlements in early 1882. They had no agricultural training nor were they prepared for the difficulties that they would encounter. The first group of Zionist pioneers, the original members of B.I.L.U.,[103] reached the shores of Jaffa and brought with them the idealism that had propelled them toward the Land of Israel. They set about the task of building one of the first Jewish agricultural settlements, Rishon L'Tzion (First to Zion). But the conditions were difficult and they faced many hardships. Some of the original members of B.I.L.U. lost heart and returned to Russia after the failure of their first harvest season. When eight members of B.I.L.U. attempted to build the settlement of Chadera in December 1884, their efforts again met with failure and more members opted out and emigrated. The prospect of living out in the open wilderness and facing the possibility of starvation was too much for them to bear. A member of B.I.L.U., Chaim Chassin, wrote in his diary of his despair, "I am leaving this country and shall return only when I am able to build my life here with my own hands."[104] However, the setbacks did not prevent the continued development

---

[103]The Hebrew acronym for Beit Yisroel L'chu V'nilcha (House of Israel Arise and Go), a passage from Isaiah 2:5.
[104]Howard Sachar, *A History of Zionism: From the Rise of Zionism in Our Time* (New York: Alfred A. Knopf, 1979), 32.

of the land. Other settlers from the Zionist movement Chovevei Tzion arrived. They increased the Zionist foothold in the land by building the settlements of Zamarin and Rosh Pinah. They too encountered opposition—the heat was oppressive, the workload was unbearable, they were menaced by flies, and Bedouins periodically robbed them of their livestock. The settlers and their families suffered exhaustion and many contracted diseases. Not accustomed to such circumstances, the members of the Chovevei Tzion, like the Biluim, began to wilt under the conditions.[105] Just like the Biluim, some members of Chovevei Tzion went to live in the cities and others returned to their native lands. The development of the Land of Israel initially seemed hopeless.

Between 1905 and 1914, thirty thousand immigrants arrived in what became known as the Second *Aliyah*. As with the prior wave, life was difficult and full of hardships. Poverty, disease, and despair abounded. One immigrant—a 19-year old student and the future first prime minister of Israel, David Ben Gurion–contracted malaria. A doctor advised him to return to Europe. This advice was not unusual in those times; possibly eighty percent of the members of the Second *Aliyah* returned to Europe or moved to America within weeks or months of their arrival.[106] However, the few who stayed kept the dream alive, elusive as it may have appeared. Over time new immigrants arrived, adding to the dwindling ranks of the first pioneers.

Those Israelites who exited Egypt left with a purpose. In modern times, the early pioneers of the Jewish State arrived with a mission. As in the Sinai wilderness, the difficulties and the harsh conditions that confronted the pioneers in Israel would not prevent their mission. Most of the generation of Israelites would not reach the Promised Land; so too, most of the early pioneers would not see the establishment of the State of Israel. The task of each generation was to face the challenges and forge the path to the

---

[105]Ibid., 29.
[106]Ibid., 73.

Land of Israel so that the next generation could fulfill their destiny to reach the Promised Land.

THE DREAM OF REDEMPTION

The origin of Ethiopian Jewry, also known as Beta Israel (House of Israel), remains somewhat a mystery despite the many theories. They were located in an area where they had no contact with other Jewish communities and yet they never gave up the dream of redemption and their return to the Jewish Homeland. They lived as a community in isolation from the rest of the Jewish world, and they desperately sought to maintain some measure of independence within a dangerous and ruthless environment. Just as in other lands where the sufferings of Jews prompted the growth of messianic movements, the Jews of Ethiopia had their own movement started by a man named Abu Mahari who claimed to have a messianic vision. He promised to lead the Beta Israel through the waters of the Red Sea as Moses had done.

It is no wonder that the Beta Israel were beguiled by his promise. As Jews in other lands, they had endured incredible sufferings. Successive wars and persecution greatly diminished the numbers of Ethiopian Jews. It is a wonder that they even survived.

Their worst suffering was during what is known as Ethiopia's Period of the Wars. From 1270–1632, there were massive executions of Falashas and tens of thousands were sold into slavery. In 1270 Emperor Yekuno Amlek vowed to end the independence of Beta Israel. His declaration was made at the beginning of a series of religious wars in Ethiopia, which would last for hundreds of years.[107] In the beginning of the fourteenth century, the Beta Israel were caught in the middle of inter-tribal conflicts. Amda Seyon, commander of the Amhara, sent his forces with the command to

[107]Louis Rapoport, *The Lost Jews* (New York: Stein and Day, 1980), 142.

"devastate the Falashas and subject them to the rule of Christ."[108] During the rule of the next Amhara, Emperor Dawit I (1382–1411), warfare against the Falashas continued.[109] His successor, Yeshaq (1413–1430), sent an army against Falasha tribes. Those Falashas who cooperated with him were rewarded while the others faced severe hardships.[110] Zar'a Yaqob, Yeshaq's successor, ordered all Jews to accept Christianity or be put to death.[111] His order was in response to the many Ethiopian Christians who sought to convert to Judaism at the time.[112] Upon the death of Zar'a Yaqob, Baeda Miriam (1468–1478) led forces against the Beta Israel that resulted in wide scale massacres until he reached a truce with the Muslim states.[113]

Soon, the Portuguese arrived and the Falashas aided them in a successful war against their Muslim foes. However, the arrival of the Portuguese would prove disastrous for the Falashas as well since they brought firearms into Ethiopia, some of which soon fell into the wrong hands. The Falashas managed to repulse Amhara forces in 1559. However, those forces were armed with the guns and cannons brought over by the Portuguese and they eventually managed to crush a twenty-two-year Falasha revolt. Thousands of Falashas were killed. For the next thirty-five years, sporadic fighting continued as Falashas still attempted to hold on to what remained of their independence while continuing to suffer at the hands of Amharic leaders who called for their extermination. Emperor Negus Suseynos (1607–1632) put to death all Falashas who refused to accept Christianity, including their king Gidion. He also confiscated all lands belonging to Beta Israel. By the late 1700s, the Falashas were a beaten, downcast nation numbering two hundred thousand. Yet most surviving Falashas remained steadfast in their

---

[108]Ibid., 144.
[109]Ibid.
[110]Ibid., 145.
[111]Ibid.
[112]Ibid., 146.
[113]Ibid.

faith and never lost hold of their dream of returning to the Promised Land.

In 1862, the Falashas faced a new crisis—an invasion by Protestant missionaries who had the backing of the emperor. The Falashas were prepared to resist all pressures of baptism. It was at that time that several Falasha monks and Abu Mahari claimed that they had a vision that the time for the redemption had arrived. Abu Mahari claimed that he would lead his people to Jerusalem. He also predicted that as they approached the Red Sea, it would split for them as it had when their forefathers left Egypt. The Falashas heeded the call, assembled, and headed toward the north.

From its start, the trip was a dismal failure. Stranded in a harsh climate without proper provisions, the Exodus met tragic failure as thousands died from starvation and malaria. Some settled in the southern part of the Tigre Province in northern Ethiopia. Others turned around and headed toward their former homes, with many dying en route. Over the next twenty years, Beta Israel would often flee the missionary menace, running from region to region, but that was their last collective attempt toward returning to the Promised Land in that century.

Still caught in the middle of wars and invasions, the Beta Israel continued to endure hardships, which further reduced their numbers. In the 1930s, the Beta Israel fought tenaciously against Italian fascist invaders. The Italians, who waged a merciless campaign, wiped out entire Falasha villages. The Ethiopian Jews were singled out for harsh treatment throughout the six-year occupation of the Italians.[114] By the latter part of the twentieth century, the Beta Israel numbered only about thirty thousand.

Still, the Beta Israel continued to hope for their redemption to the Promised Land. Although Abu Mahari led their fathers astray, ultimately the majority of the survivors of Beta Israel were brought to Israel through Operation Moses in 1985 and Operation So-

[114]Rapoport, *The Lost Jews*, 153.

lomon in 1991.[115] The generation of Beta Israel who are now living in Israel are the actualization of their fathers' dreams. They were the ones to cross the Red Sea.

THE LAST EXODUS

There have been Jewish communities in almost every Arab land since the Second Temple era. These communities lived under Muslim rule since the Islamic conquests of the seventh century. They were forced to live as "Dhimmis," a term literally translated as "writ of protection" or protected ones, which refers to those who constituted an underclass who were obliged to follow the rulings set for them by their Muslim overlords. Being an underclass is a most humiliating existence, but it is not necessarily intolerable. Some rulers were tolerant, while others were not; however, all too often Jews in Arab countries suffered persecution.

When Israel was declared a state in 1948, there were 850,000 Jews living in the Arab world. From the early twentieth century, their existence had become increasingly difficult with the rise of Zionism. Riots broke out against Jewish communities as Arabs vented their anger upon them. Jews feared for their very lives and fled to Israel. Unlike the Israelites' Exodus from Egypt where they left with great wealth,[116] the vast majority of Jews from the Arab lands who were fortunate enough to make a swift exit left empty handed, prohibited from taking their assets.

Over the next few years, there was a massive Exodus from the Arab world. The following population figures shed light on the Jewish Exodus from Arab countries. In 1948, there were 110,000 Jews in Morocco, by 1974, 2,000 remained. In Tunisia there were 55,000 in 1948; in 1974, 2,000. In Yemen there were 55,000 in

---

[115] As of September 1998 several thousand Ethiopian Jews still awaited their rescue.

[116] See Genesis 15:14 and Exodus 3:22.

1948; in 1974, 500. In Libya there were 38,000 in 1948; in 1974, 20. In Algeria there were 140,000 in 1948; in 1974, 500. In Iraq there were 135,000 in 1948; in 1974, 400. In Egypt there were 75,000 in 1948; in 1974, 350.[117]

The one country that continued to possess a large Jewish community was Syria. While the number of Jews in Syria did decline, there was, nonetheless, a sizable community that remained. In 1943, there were 30,000 Jews in Syria; by 1946, the community declined to 18,000. By 1974, 4,500 Jews remained in the country, held against their will.

Jews left Syria when faced with anti-Jewish violence in the 1940s. When the Syrians gained independence in 1945 anti-Zionist demonstrations increased, as did Jewish emigration. The distribution of pamphlets calling for the boycotting of Jewish businesses became more common.[118] The authorities made emigration increasingly difficult and many Jews were forced to escape to Lebanon. From there they would attempt to go to Palestine. Those caught would be imprisoned or subjected to torture and often murdered; yet the flight continued. In 1947, anti-Jewish attacks continued with greater intensity. Mobs raced into the Jewish quarter of Aleppo,[119] setting the synagogues, shops, and homes ablaze. In early 1948, bombs, which killed and wounded many, were placed in the Jewish quarter of Damascus. The authorities showed little sympathy and demanded that the Jewish community make a declaration to the effect that the incident in Damascus was "ordinary" and that the Jews received full assistance from the authorities in providing for their protection.[120] Upon the declara-

---

[117]Martin Gilbert, *Atlas of Jewish History* (New York: Dorset Press, 1976), 67–68, 78, 91–92, 109, 114–115.
[118]Hayyim Cohen, *The Jews of the Middle East* (New York/Toronto: A Halstead Press Book, John Wiley and Sons, Jerusalem: Israel Universities Press, 1973), 46.
[119]The second largest Jewish community in Syria.
[120]Cohen, *The Jews of the Middle East*, 46.

tion proclaiming the establishment of Israel in 1948, hundreds of Jews were arrested and the persecutions continued.

Over the years, a slow trickle of Jews continuously managed to exit Syria clandestinely despite the risks involved. According to the Joint Distribution Committee's figures, 620 Syrian Jews arrived in Israel in 1962.[121] Due to an early, successful diplomatic effort, the Syrians permitted a few Jews to emigrate after former congressman Stephan Solarz intervened on behalf of fourteen young women who were permitted to emigrate as brides due to a shortage of young marriageable Jewish men in Syria.[122] In the early 1980s, President Hafez El Assad of Syria eased travel restrictions but still denied visas to families. During that time, two young women were permitted to emigrate each month until only 350 young Jewish women remained in Syria. But a few thousand Jews, most of whom lived in Damascus and Aleppo, remained, still waiting for their day of freedom.

That day came at the conclusion of Passover in 1992.

The last day of Passover that year seemed like an ordinary day for the Jews of Damascus and Aleppo. In accordance with their tradition, they stayed awake the entire night reading passages recalling the Exodus from Egypt and the splitting of the Red Sea, which occurred on that day. About that time rumors had circulated that they would soon be permitted to emigrate. The news was initially greeted with skepticism. Was it indeed true? It seemed hard to believe that their long-awaited freedom had arrived. In the early morning hours, as congregations met for prayers, they all learned that the news was indeed fact. In one Damascus congregation known as the *minyan*, morning prayers had begun. At about that time, word spread among the approximately one hundred congregants present that they would be permitted to

---

[121]Larry Yudelsohn, "Syria Free At Last: Secret Syrian Exodus Declared Complete," *Long Island Jewish World* 23, no. 38 (October 21, 1994): 23.

[122]Many of the young men had succeeded in escaping Syria over the years.

emigrate.[123] The news seemed like a "dream." As the psalmist states about the Jews return from Babylonian captivity to Judea, "we were as dreamers."[124]

Over the next five months, half of the Jewish communities of both Aleppo and Damascus and a few smaller Jewish communities were permitted to emigrate; the rest of the Jews would be permitted to emigrate over the next two years. Only a handful decided to remain behind. For the Jews of Syria, a long ordeal had ended.

The news of the final Exodus came as the Syrian Jews were commemorating the parting of the Red Sea. Like those who left Syria and other lands of oppression before them, the Exodus had already occurred but the final splitting of the "Red Sea" had yet to take place. On the last day of Passover, it occurred and the last of the Jews held against their will finally crossed through its parted waters.

[123]The events were related to the author by Joseph Zalta, an emigrant from Syria.
[124]Psalm 126:1.

2

Lag B'Omer

A CELEBRATION TO REMEMBER

Lag B'Omer is a day of celebration amidst a period of semi-mourning between Passover and Shavuot. It is customary on Lag B'Omer to go on an outing or to attend a party or celebration. One particular Lag B'Omer in the Bronx celebration represented an end of an era. It was one of the last celebrations of its kind.

The story of Bronx Jewry is similar to those of most inner-city Jewish neighborhoods, whether the Brownsville section of Brooklyn, the South Beach section of Miami Beach, or the north section of Boston. These inner-city ghettos were in essence a halfway stop for an entire generation in American Jewry's upward climb.

The Bronx once contained a Jewish population of six hundred thousand. By the Second World War, Jews numbered half the population of that borough. The history of the Jews of the Bronx is a significant, but brief, chapter in American Jewish history.

As transportation became available at the turn of the century, Jews migrated to the Bronx from the Lower East Side and Harlem seeking improved accommodations. By the 1920s Jews were arriving en masse. But by the 1960s, Jewish flight from the Bronx was as rapid as their arrival as Jews again left in search of improved conditions. The flight first began from the South Bronx. The construction of the Cross Bronx Expressway in 1961, which tore through Jewish neighborhoods, contributed to urban migration from the South Bronx, as did the construction of Co-Op City in the North East Bronx, which attracted seventy-five thousand Jews from other areas of the borough. From Co-Op City and other Jewish neighborhoods, the flight soon continued.

By the 1980s, the once thriving Jewish community of the South Bronx numbered in its entirety only a few thousand of mostly elderly, often destitute, Jews who were scattered throughout the area. One who passed through the South Bronx would not think that so many were still there, but the most lonely always seem to be less visible. They are not numbered among crowds where they do not mingle. They can only be counted separately. In fact, "a few thousand" could have been a gross underestimation.

A few small but cohesive Jewish communities remained in their virtual isolation amidst the most heavily populated Jewish community in the world. In 1986, one of the last Lag B'Omer celebrations was held in one of the remaining shuls in the South Bronx.

The synagogue was quite a sight to behold. Its abysmal condition testified to years of neglect. Paint chips fell from the ceiling, decaying walls revealed their wooden interior, floor tiles were missing, as were most of the light fixtures. Regardless of its condition, to its elderly members it was their shul and a day for celebration had arrived.

The synagogue was in a rough, drug-infested, crime-ridden neighborhood known as Soundview, which bordered on the Hunts Point section of the Bronx. Walking through its streets was not safe, but the congregants came, slowly trickling into the synagogue. Some arrived in small groups, while many came alone. Some were dressed in their holiday best; others came wearing shabby, old garments. Many of the women brought small handbags hoping to leave with some leftovers. As they entered the synagogue's narrow lobby, volunteers—mostly college students who organized and ran the event—met them.

Seated on folding chairs and old synagogue benches, they exchanged greetings. Some reacquainted themselves with old friends. Some spoke to each other frequently, while others met only on rare occasions. Then there were those who ventured out from their seclusion only to catch a glimpse of a holiday celebration. The sounds of lively conversations in both Yiddish and English reverberated throughout the room as information on recent neighborhood news and Jewish current events were relayed while a festive meal was being prepared. An amateur musical band of student volunteers arrived and began unloading their instruments from a van. Moments later, a yeshiva student arose and, nervously swaying slowly from side to side, spoke about Lag B'Omer and the reasons for its celebration as all listened attentively. As he concluded the D'var Torah, he received a generous applause and the conversations resumed. And then the meal was served.

Across long paper-coated picnic tables, the congregants sat while volunteers ran back and forth with plates full of chicken, kugels, and salads. Soon, the band started playing and volunteers and congregants danced the hora. The melodies played were a mixture of popular Hebrew songs and old Yiddish tunes. Those too old and frail to dance clapped their hands or sang along, but everyone participated. Some joined in with the band, singing tunes from a microphone. As the meal progressed, the mood in the room became more upbeat; there was no melancholy, only joy.

The event began at noon and came to a close at about three o'clock. In a jovial mood, the participants slowly left the synagogue, carefully making their way down its stairs as they ventured back to the troubled streets of their neighborhood and to their isolated worlds. But the memories of Lag B'Omer would linger. As they left, some spoke with anticipation of future synagogue events.

That synagogue was an old decaying building hardly resembling the Jewish centers that one is accustomed to seeing presently, but it was a haven for its Jewish community. It might not have had a congregational rabbi, but the synagogue was, nevertheless, full of joy and smiles that Lag B'Omer day. The enthusiasm and spirit appeared like that of an ordinary party or *simchah*, but there was nothing ordinary about this event. The forgotten lives of golden-agers living in an area where there were no hotels or boardwalks or golf courses were uplifted and momentarily transported to another time and place.

Over the years, the Jewish community in that neighborhood dwindled even more. Few members from that congregation remain and the shul's doors have since been closed. But their celebration of that Lag B'Omer reflected the joy they could experience despite all the obstacles.[1]

LAG B'OMER AND YOM HA'ATZMAUT: THE TWILIGHT AND THE DAWN

Lag B'Omer and Yom Ha'atzmaut are thirteen days apart on the calendar. The political events that surround both days are separated by eighteen hundred years, and yet they are connected. Lag B'Omer is a semi-holiday that celebrates a day of relief during tragic times when the Jewish nation fought for its very survival. Yom Ha'atzmaut celebrates the realization of a national dream following a prolonged exile.

The events of Lag B'Omer date back to the second century. The Talmud relates that a plague took the lives of thousands of students of the Mishnaic sage Rabbi Akiva during the Omer—the forty-nine-day period between Passover and Shavuot—during a year (presumably the last) of the Bar Kochba Revolt (132–135 C.E.). On the intermittent day of Lag B'Omer, the thirty-third day of the Omer, that plague ceased.[2] On Yom Ha'atzmaut, the fifth day of Iyar, 1948, the State of Israel was proclaimed.

---

[1]The description of events is based upon a personal experience of the author's.
[2]Babylonian Talmud, Yevamot 62b.

The Bar Kochba Revolt arose in the aftermath of over 150 years of anti-Jewish persecution throughout the Roman Empire. It was a fight for Jewish continuity. The Roman emperor Hadrian, who ascended to power in 118 C.E., followed the reign of Trajan who perpetrated massacres against Jews in North Africa and Cyprus. Under Trajan hundreds of thousands of Jews perished. Entire communities were decimated. By the revolt's end, the Jewish community of Cyprus and virtually all the Jews of Libya were wiped out. Upon his ascent to power, Hadrian could either provoke more hostilities or create an atmosphere that would restore some tranquility. The new emperor was initially friendly toward the Jews, but over time he became their bitter antagonist. Hadrian had reneged on a promise to rebuild the Temple, and the hopes of the Judeans were dashed.[3] Hadrian also further provoked the Jews. According to the Roman historian Dio Cassius, he rebuilt Jerusalem as a pagan colony and renamed it Aelia Capitalina—named after pagan Greek gods—while he placed a statue of the pagan god Jupiter on the Temple Mount, Judaism's holiest spot.[4] An act that would no doubt affront the Judeans. It seems that Hadrian, an ardent Hellenist, sought to transform Jerusalem into a Hellenistic pagan colony. Another possible cause for the revolt was stated in *Historia Augusta* by its anonymous author, "At this time also began the war, because they were forbidden to practice circumcision."[5]

The revolt's leader, Simon Bar Kochba, received widespread support in Judea and the backing of the pre-eminent scholar of the time, Rabbi Akiva, who claimed that Bar Kochba was the redeemer of Israel.[6]

---

[3]Midrash Genesis Raba 64.

[4]Dio Cassius, *Roman History LXTX*, 12:1 quoted in Menachem Stern, ed., *Greek and Latin Authors on Jews and Judaism* (Jerusalem: Academy of Science and Humanities, 1974), 392.

[5]*Historia Augusta*, 14:2, trans. D. Maggie, quoted in Stern, *Greek and Latin Authors on Jews and Judaism*, Vol. II, p. 619.

[6]Jerusalem Talmud, Taanit 4:68a. Midrash Lamentations Raba 2:2. Maimonides, "Laws of Kings" *Mishna Torah*, 11:3. Drawing from a

The initial successes of the Judeans electrified the nation. Victories were achieved by Bar Kochba's soldiers, and it is very possible that Jerusalem was also captured from the Romans.[7] At the time, the prospect of reestablishing a Jewish State seemed imminent. But the revolt eventually took a tragic turn for the worst. The Romans, determined not to be defeated, soon sent their finest legions to counter the rebels and summoned one of their finest generals, Julius Severes, from Britain. The Romans eventually gained the upper hand as they laid siege to town after town throughout the Judean countryside, cutting off supplies and causing massive starvation and death.[8] Dio Cassius wrote that, "fifty of their most important outposts and 985 of their most famous villages were razed to the ground."[9]

It was at that time—during the counting of the Omer[10]—that thousands of Rabbi Akiva's students suddenly died. The Talmud states, "Rabbi Akiva had 12,000 pairs of students . . . and all of them died at the same time."[11] The Talmud considers the plague punishment for the lack of respect they showed one other. An eighth century rabbinic sage known as Rav Shriria Gaon, wrote "Rabbi Akiva raised up many disciples, but there was a destruction

---

Talmudic source (Sanhedrin 93b) states that all the leading rabbinic scholars of that generation considered Bar Kochba to be the Messiah.
[7]Various Talmudic and Roman sources allude to this but it is not stated definitively.
[8]Cassius, 13:3, trans. E. Cary, quoted in Stern, *Greek and Latin Authors on Jews and Judaism*, 393.
[9]Ibid., 14:1, trans. E. Cary, quoted in Stern, *Greek and Latin Authors on Jews and Judaism*, 392.
[10]A forty-nine-day period between Passover and Shavuot when each individual day is counted in accordance with the biblical commandment to "count seven full weeks after the day following the (Passover) holiday." (Leviticus 23:15–16) At that time an *omer* (measure) of barley was brought to the Temple as a token of gratitude for the ripening fruit and as a prayer for a bountiful harvest in the coming year.
[11]Babylonian Talmud, Yevamoth 62b.

(*shemada*) upon the disciples of Rabbi Akiva."[12] Most probably, the destruction was the result of battles fought during the war. That destruction ceased on Lag B'Omer.

The revolt came to its end following the Roman siege of the Judean city of Betar. In total, Dio Cassius claims that 580,000 men were killed in various battles and a number beyond estimation died from famine and pestilence.[13] During the destruction that followed the war, Hadrian oppressed the Judeans and sought to crush their spirit of defiance by outlawing all Jewish rites and practices as he scorched the land hoping to eliminate any Jewish connection to it. The people again resisted, disobeying Hadrian's edicts as they struggled to maintain their identity in the most adverse climate. They resisted and suffered, but their spirit and their dreams could not be crushed.

Circumstances forced the Jews of modern Judea to take a stand against another empire eighteen hundred years later. Under the British mandate over Palestine, the Jews were permitted to build a cultural and economic infrastructure. But the freedoms of the Zionists were severely restricted. The Yishuv (Jewish community of Palestine) vigorously opposed the imposition of the disastrous Passfield White Paper of 1939—the product of British appeasement to Arab pressure—which severely restricted Jewish immigration into Palestine. But active opposition was limited. The Yishuv hoped that the British would soon reverse the White Paper. More importantly, as World War II was underway the Yishuv was compelled to cooperate with its British allies whose forces protected Palestine from German invasion. By 1944, as the war was turning in the allies' favor, the Irgun Tzvai HaLeumi, under the leadership of Menachem Begin, broke ranks with the Yishuv and along with the Stern Group (who never called a truce with the British) initiated a

---

[12] *Iggeres of Rav Sherira Gaon*, trans. Rabbi Nosson Dovid Rabinowich (Jerusalem: Moznaim, 1988), 10.

[13] Cassius, History of Rome, 14:1, quoted in Stern, *Greek and Latin Authors on Jews and Judaism,* 393.

campaign of violence against the British. However, most of the Yishuv continued to cooperate in the hope that British policy could be changed by other means.

As the war ended and Jewry were coming to terms with the enormity of the Holocaust, Jews in Palestine and around the world looked with anger toward intransigent Great Britain. Their refusal to reverse the White Paper subjected hundreds of thousands of Holocaust survivors to languish in DP camps throughout Europe and in Cyprus. Jewish anger was exacerbated when newly elected prime minister Clement Atlee, of the new Labor Government, pledged to maintain Britain's long standing White Paper in July 1945. By September little had changed. Under intense international pressure, the British raised its Palestine immigration quota to a meager fifteen hundred Jews per month. The Yishuv's patience ran out.

On October 1, 1946, David Ben Gurion sent a coded message to the Hagganah to begin an armed uprising against Britain known as the "Resistance Movement." The revolt no longer involved just segments of the Yishuv but was now conducted with the support of almost the entire community.[14] On November 1, 1945, the Resistance Movement blew up the Palestine railway in over 160 places and destroyed British ships in the port of Haifa. The British responded with mass arrests of Zionist activists and leaders of the Jewish agency, but that did little to stop the revolt. The violence, along with British reprisals, escalated. The Zionists also aggressively attempted to break the British blockade by trying to smuggle immigrants illegally by both land and sea, as the world watched scenes of British gunboats and troops preventing the entry of ships with refugees on to Palestine's shores.

The Yishuv's opposition to the British mandate had reached a

---

[14]The joint Hagganah–Irgun campaign lasted for nine months. When the Hagganah suspended its military campaign against the British, it did not cooperate with the British in their efforts to stop the underground as it had in the past.

crescendo. The British, no longer willing or able to control the people, now saw the mandate as an increasing burden. By October 17, 1947, the British announced their decision to leave the mandate to the UN, which soon endorsed partition and the creation of the Jewish State.

The soldiers of the Hagganah, Irgun, and Lehi, as their ancestors, fought their foreign occupier to achieve independence from a hostile ruler. On Israel's Independence Day 1948, the first law enacted by Israel's new provisional government was to open the gates of immigration to all Jews. No longer could White Papers be imposed.

The events of Lag B'Omer and Yom Ha'atzmaut both involved insurrections. In both generations, the people were forced into rebellion. Lag B'Omer came amidst a time of tragedy and misfortune for the Jews. Yom Ha'atzmaut followed Jewry's greatest tragedy, the Holocaust, yet it concluded with the triumphant declaration of Israel's independence. In the course of the events surrounding one holiday a dream was defeated, but it lived on. The latter holiday celebrates the realization of that dream.

3

Yom Yerushalayim

THE ROAD OF HEROISM

On the twenty-eighth day of the month of Iyar 1967, the Old City of Jerusalem was liberated by Israeli troops. Nineteen years earlier, during the War of Liberation, the Israel Defense Forces fought tenaciously to hold on to the Old City, which was under a prolonged siege by trans-Jordanian forces. Eventually, the survivors of the fierce battles were no longer able to hold out and they surrendered along with the Old City's remaining Jewish population.

During the war, West Jerusalem—"the new city," with a population of one hundred thousand—faced the possibility of loosing vital supplies as Arab armies besieged the Jewish capital. Without ample food supplies, the people would starve. Without ammunition, the city would become more vulnerable to an Arab attack. But the threat was averted and the city was saved by an ingenious and courageous plan to construct a road that would serve as a lifeline to Jerusalem.

The operation was named "Operation Nachshon" after the biblical hero Nachshon Ben Aminadav who entered the Red Sea just before it parted. Operation Nachshon was described in the classic novel *O Jerusalem*, by Larry Collins and Dominique Lapierre, "They (the Israelis) were going to try to achieve with sweat, ingenuity and mechanical skill what they had failed to accomplish with arms—opening a road to Jerusalem."[1]

The Road of Heroism was a sixteen mile long road that linked Jerusalem to a road leading from Tel Aviv. For four weeks, soldiers and civilian volunteers labored in its construction. They worked under the cover of night while within range of Arab mortar. The work was difficult as the workers maneuvered through the steep Judean hills. Diversionary tactics were used to draw the enemy's attention. Rocks on the hills were blasted so the road could be cleared and supplies could be rushed to Jerusalem. At one point, there was a hill that no jeep could pass, so food and supplies were loaded upon shoulders and carried to trucks waiting on the other side to be brought to Jerusalem.

Upon its completion, which took eight weeks, on June 11, the Road of Heroism[2]—a thin, hazardous dirt road—was the lifeline to the residents of Jerusalem. But it could only be temporary. When winter's rains arrived it would no longer be usable. Thus the next task began of clearing Arab forces from the area and then rebuilding the road, which would be paved and five meters wide. Then the next major hurdle would be averted.

The completion of the Road of Heroism was an astonishing feat. It took the Turks eight years to construct a highway that linked Jerusalem and Jaffa. During the British mandate a similar highway was built in two years. But it took only eight weeks for poorly equipped soldiers and volunteers comprised of elderly and young students, professionals, ear-locked Orthodox, and members of the friendly Arab village Abu Gosh to build this road.

---

[1]Larry Collins and Dominique Lapierre, *O Jerusalem* (New York: Pocket Books, A division of Simon and Schuster, 1972), 598.
[2]The Road of Heroism was also known as the Burma Road, named after a 750 mile long road constructed by the Chinese in Burma.

In the official ceremony marking the opening of the road, also known as the Kvish HaGevurah (Road of Heroism), many of those responsible for its construction were present. A strange parade of those who participated in the road's construction marched past David Ben Gurion as he stood upon the reviewing stand. It consisted of soldiers of the Hagganah who had captured Arab towns and hills near the roadside, making construction possible; the young and elderly who had slaved long hours in its building; the bullet-pierced jeeps, along with egged buses, which carried supplies, and donkeys used to carry supplies when the jeeps could not.[3]

Today, many of the armored cars remain alongside the road as a memorial to the actions of those who saved Jerusalem. A plaque upon the location reads, "To our comrades who blasted the rock, routed the enemy, and made this road. . . . If I forget thee O Jerusalem, let my right hand forget its cunning."[4]

The day of the completion of the Kvish HaGevurah was the twenty-eighth day of the month of Iyar—the same day that Israeli troops would liberate the Old City of Jerusalem nineteen years later.

In 1948, on Yom Yerushalayim, a road was completed that saved West Jerusalem. On the same day in 1967, the Old City was liberated. Thus, it can truly be said that on Yom Yerushalayim all parts of Jerusalem were united.

---

[3]Marie Syrkin, "Siege of Jerusalem," *Jewish Frontier* 16, no. 10 (175) (November 1949): 25.
[4]Ibid.

4

Shavuot

THE ULTIMATE SACRIFICE

Right before Shavuot, many horrors did befall me, when savagery broke loose upon Israel.[1]

On the third day of the month of Sivan, three days prior to Shavuot, Moses told the Israelites to prepare themselves over the next three days for the moment of receiving the Torah. In the city of Mainz on the same day—the third of Sivan—in 1096, when the Jews should have been preparing to celebrate Shavuot, they were instead preparing themselves for their own slaughter, to die *al Kiddush HaShem*—in the sanctification of God's name. On that day a community of eleven hundred Jews was virtually wiped out.

On November 27, 1095, Pope Urban II called upon his followers to liberate Jerusalem from Muslim control. Those who heeded the Pope's call became known as the Crusaders, meaning those who wear the crucifix. Figuring that the Crusaders' destina-

[1]The Prayer Zulat, which is read in synagogues on the Sabbath prior to Shavuot.

tion was the Holy Land, the Jewish communities of Europe initially did not pay them much heed. However, in a frenzy of religious zeal, the Crusaders did not wait until their arrival in the Holy Land before they erupted in violence against Jewish communities en route along the Rhine River to "avenge the crucifixion." On the month prior to Shavuot (Iyar) of that year violence already broke out; Jewish communities along the Rhine River of Germany were attacked. On the fifth of Iyar (May 3), the community of Speyer was attacked and eleven Jews were murdered. On the twenty-third day of the same Hebrew month (May 21), the community of Worms was destroyed.[2] Most chose to die martyrs' deaths, often at their own hands, rather than submit to forced conversion. The few who did convert returned to Judaism when the storm subsided.[3] The carnage intensified against the Jewish communities of the region. About twelve thousand Jews were slaughtered during the first Crusade.

As Shavuot approached, a massacre of one of the great communities of early Ashkenazic Jewry occurred. On May 25, the first day of the Hebrew month of Sivan, the Crusaders encircled the city of Mainz. Two days later, with the help of burgher sympathizers within the city, the Crusaders were able to enter its city walls. The Jews of Mainz, weakened from fasting as a petition to the Almighty, attempted to put up a fight and set up defenses. The Crusaders were seasoned warriors and the Jews' efforts failed. Like the community of Worms, destroyed days earlier, the Jews of Mainz were given an option for survival by their tormentors—that of conversion. They rejected the notion and prepared themselves for martyrdom. Many of those who were slaughtered went to their deaths without a fight and did not even attempt to flee from their tormentors.

An account from *Mainz Anonymous* describes the horrors:

> The enemy, immediately upon entering the courtyard, found there some of the perfectly pious with Rabbi Isaac ben R.

---

[2]Rabbi Yosef HaCohen, *Emek HaBacha* (Crackow: Typis, Joseph Fisher, 1895), 10.
[3]Ibid., 10.

> Moses the subtle thinker. He stretched out his neck and they cut off his head immediately. They [Rabbi Isaac and his followers] had clothed themselves in their fringed garments and had seated themselves in the midst of the courtyard in order to speedily do the work of their Creator. They did not wish to flee to the chambers in order to go on living briefly. Rather, with love they accepted upon themselves the judgement of heaven. The enemy rained stones and arrows upon them, but they did not deign to flee. They [the Christian attackers] struck down all those whom they found there, with blows of sword, death, and destruction.[4]

Rather than offer their lives for slaughter, many took their own lives and thus denied the Crusaders the use of their swords and spared themselves the torture that might be inflicted upon them before their executions. The last moments of such martyrs are described in the following account. "Ultimately we must not tarry, for the enemy has come upon us suddenly. Let us offer ourselves up before our father in heaven. Anyone who has a knife should come and slaughter us for the sanctification of the unique name [of God] who lives forever. . . . They all stood—men and women—and slaughtered one another."[5]

Each case of martyrdom reflects the heroism of the Jews of Mainz. The book *The First Crusades and the Jews* discusses a woman who "slew her four children, and then was cut down by the Crusaders with her martyred children by her side."[6]

The same book also tells of a young man who professed his desire to convert after the Crusaders massacred his entire family. "He was led to the Bishop's courtyard where he pulled out a knife hidden under his clothes and managed to kill the nephew of the

---

[4]Robert Chazan, *In the Year 1096: The First Crusades and the Jews* (Philadelphia: Jewish Publication Society of America, 1996), 109.
[5]Chazan, *In the Year 1096: The First Crusades and the Jews*, 110.
[6]Ibid., 111.

bishop along with two others before his knife had broken and he was then torn to pieces."[7]

On that day, eleven hundred Jews were massacred, and the jewel of early Ashkenazic Jewry was wiped out. "On that day the crown of Israel fell. Then the students of Torah fell and the scholars of Torah disappeared. The honor of Torah fell."[8]

Such horrific carnage became a new facet of the war waged against Jewry by anti-Semites and a precedent for future attacks. The descriptions of the horrors tell of unprecedented massacres in central Europe. Another bleak reality that emerged from the aftermath of the attacks was that no friend or fortress could offer them lasting protection from their enemies. The promises of protection were made, but those who offered protection either betrayed the Jews or were unable to protect them. From that dark era, Jews no longer stood as they did before in Europe. They were alone—open targets for those who sought their destruction.

Rabbi Shlomo bar Shimon, a chronicler of the first Crusades writes, "On the third day of Sivan, a day of sanctification and abstinence for Israel in preparation for the giving of the Torah, the very day in which our Master Moses, may he rest in peace, said: 'Be ready for the third day'—on that day the very community of Mainz, saints of the Most High, withdrew from each other in sanctity and purity, and sanctified themselves to ascend to God all together."[9]

As the Israelites who had prepared themselves at Mount Sinai to receive the Torah, the victims of Mainz affirmed their perfect faith in that Torah. Their sacrifices, in effect, helped to strengthen the resolve of Jews in their many coming struggles to preserve their heritage at all costs.

---

[7]Ibid., 104.
[8]Ibid., 34.
[9]Rabbi Shlomo bar Shimon, "Gezeirot 1096" (1140), quoted in Rabbi Yom Tov Levinsky, comp., *Sefer HaMoadim* 4, 169.

THE LESSONS OF FREEDOM

Shavuot, which celebrates the giving of the Torah, also celebrates freedom but not in the political sense of the term. The freedom granted the Israelites on Shavuot was an inner freedom that no despot could ever take away.

Over three thousand years later, the Jews of Europe reveled in a different kind of freedom. After centuries of persecution and forced seclusion, an era of enlightenment arose in France and other corners of Western Europe that offered the Jews a way out of the ghetto. Beyond the ghetto there was freedom. That era, known as "The Emancipation," signified an end to the division that separated Jews from society at large. The Emancipation also shook many Jews from the traditionalist foundations that they had tenaciously clung to for millennium.

German Jewish philosopher and Emancipation leader Moses Mendelssohn (1729–1786) advocated civic emancipation and fidelity to Judaism. He urged Jews to absorb themselves into the "culture of nations" while privately remaining observant Jews.

After the storming of the Bastille in 1789 and the onset of the French Revolution, the French followed the American example by declaring freedom and equality with the Declaration of the Rights of Man. Two years later, emancipation was granted to the Jews of France. Exuberant Jews celebrated, comparing the new laws to those given at Mount Sinai. Many laws called for the cessation of their observance.

Soon emancipation was declared in Holland and then in other lands. In a new environment, Jews sought to immerse themselves in science, medicine, commerce, and many other fields once denied to them. The Western European Jew entered the New World leaving behind the old. Yeshiva education was replaced with institutions that taught secular studies. The type of clothing Jews wore changed, as did their spoken language. All facets of their lives represented the dominant culture of society. Despite the frequent revocation of emancipation rights in many regions due to wars and border changes, its memory remained with the Jews and they would continue to strive for its return. By the late 1860s, all Jews of Western Europe were granted emancipation.

The walls of the ghetto fell and drastic changes followed. Like momentum down an endless hill, there were no limits to emancipation. No lines of demarcation could be drawn in a world where acceptance of the Jew seemed to be based on the condition that they modernize. Traditional Judaism was viewed as a barrier separating the Jew from society. While many of the emancipated maintained some measure of Jewish observance, their children—who sought complete acceptance as equals—abandoned their Jewish identity, many choosing to undergo baptism. The writer Heinrich Heine (1797–1856), who himself was baptized (but later did return to Judaism), referred to baptism as the "entrance ticket to European society." During Heine's era, well over a quarter million Jews followed that path. Only a generation later some of Mendelssohn's own children underwent baptism. A century later Mendelssohn had no surviving Jewish descendants. In a world of individual freedoms, remaining Jewish was voluntary, and Western European Jewry was eroding. Mendelssohn had his own vision of emancipation while others had theirs.

The rabbinical leadership among the Chasidim and the Mitnagdim (yeshivas of Lithuania) bitterly opposed the Maskilim or Emancipationists. As the eastern annex of the Emancipationists slowly made inroads into Russia, the traditionalists built more yeshivas and fortified them with students to counter their influence. The ideological differences that they feuded over for centuries seemed far less significant next to the emerging threat of emancipation. For them, it was better to live as a Jew confined to a ghetto and rejected by the outside world than with the freedoms that came with emancipation. The worlds of the traditional and the modern became locked in a bitter struggle that continued in Eastern Europe until the Second World War.

America in essence is not unlike Western Europe, although achieving equality came easier to American Jews. The majority of

American Jews today—descendants of those who stepped off boats onto Ellis Island a century ago—have been a part of mainstream American life for years. They are living their great-grandparents' dreams of success, but as assimilated Jews. The majority were denied meaningful Jewish education and have foregone the traditions and observances passed down from generation to generation from Sinai, unaware of what they have forfeited. Can American Jews reconcile tradition with modernity? Can American Jewry withstand the pressures of freedom?

There are different connotations to freedom other than the free exercise of one's rights. The Mishnah delves into the meaning of freedom. "Rabbi Yehoshua ben Levi stated . . . It says: 'The Tablets [containing the Ten Commandments] are God's handiwork and the script was God's script [Charut] engraved upon the Tablets.'[10] Do not read Charut [engraved], but rather Cherut [freedom]. For there is no freer man than one who engages in the study of the Torah."[11] Freedom is the ability to resist outside influences in a world of diverse paths and maintain one's Jewish convictions. When one is truly free, one is not captive to one's impulses. Despotic regimes might have controlled the lives of the ghetto dweller, but not their spirits.

When the Israelites left Egypt, they also left its culture replete with idolatry and immorality. There were many Israelites who became too enamored with Egyptian civilization and never left, preferring Egypt's culture to joining the mission destined for the Israelites. Soon after the Exodus, the Israelites at Mount Sinai declared their readiness to accept the Torah and, on Shavuot, they heard the Ten Commandments proclaimed and received the Torah. There is no greater freedom than that.

---

[10]Exodus 31:16.
[11]Mishnah, Pirkei Avot 6:2.

RENEWING THE COMMITMENT TO JEWISH SCHOLARSHIP

During the Second Temple era, Torah education was generally passed from father to son.[12] However those children who were fatherless or whose fathers was unable to teach them often missed the opportunity for such studies. A sage and High Priest who lived in the first century B.C.E., Joshua ben Gamla, established an innovation—local yeshivot (centers for Torah education) in every community throughout the land of Israel. This innovation revolutionized the study of Torah. Rabbi Joshua's accomplishment was considered so great that the Talmud states that "if it were not for Rabbi Joshua ben Gamla, Torah study might have been forgotten in Israel."[13]

In early nineteenth-century Lithuania, another great luminary achieved a similar accomplishment. This great Torah luminary, who left an indelible mark on the spiritual and intellectual life of the Jewish people, was Rabbi Chaim Volozhiner. He was born in 1749, on the second day of Shavuot. A prized disciple of the Vilna Gaon, Rav Chaim was one of the foremost scholars in his generation and possessed many gifts. One of these gifts was his ability to disseminate Torah knowledge to the Jewish community through his unique educational methods. His influence strongly impacted the Jewish people and earned him distinction as the "father of the Lithuanian yeshivot."

At the turn of the nineteenth century, Rav Chaim of Volozhin saw a Jewish community in Lithuania where Torah study was lacking. Poverty abounded and the masses were preoccupied with survival and eking out a living. They found only limited time for Torah study and their commitment to learning was withering. The devotion of the affluent to Torah study had also declined and few continued to finance yeshivas.

---

[12]There were some yeshivot in the big cities.
[13]Babylonian Talmud, Baba Batra 21A.

It was due to this situation that Rav Chaim sought to establish a yeshiva in Volozhin that would stress the study of texts of Talmud and Jewish law. This methodology was based on that of his mentor Rabbi Elijah, son of Solomon Zalmon, otherwise known as the Vilna Gaon. The Gaon emphasized inner criticism, the establishment of the intent of the Talmud itself and its plain meaning by way of rational analysis.[14] In his yeshiva, Rav Chaim stressed the understanding of the *pshat*—a basic understanding of Talmudic texts through logical reasoning. This differed from the method of other yeshivas called *pilpul*—a technical method of analysis which was deeply analytical and focused on subtleties. Such a method, although of great value, lost the interest of many among the masses.

There were a few smaller yeshivas in existence in Lithuania at the time that were attended by members of their local communities. The Yeshiva of Volozhin, however, was intended to be a large institution; a central body bringing together the finest students in the entire region and, eventually, throughout the entire continent. Rabbi Yosef Krynki, one of the Yeshiva's first students, recalls its founding in a fundraising letter:

> During the first year the House of the Lord was founded in Volozhin, I saw many merchants who went out of their way in order to pass by Volozhin to see what a Yeshiva is all about and what one does there. . . . And when they saw that several tens of great Torah scholars were sitting and studying all night with remarkable assiduousness, they wondered and marveled at this very much.[15]

Rav Chaim's yeshiva, which he established in 1803 with a few dozen students,[16] soon developed the reputation as a landmark

---

[14]Norman Lamm, *Torah for Torah's Sake: In the Words of Rabbi Hayyim of Volozhin and His Contemporaries* (Hoboken, New Jersey: Yeshiva University Press-Ktav Publishing House, 1989), 29.
[15]Ibid., 24.
[16]Ibid., 26.

institution. The purpose of the yeshiva was to raise the general level of learning by producing a generation that would include leading Torah scholars. Rav Chaim instilled in his students that their motivation for studying Torah must be *lishma*—learning solely out of the love of learning and of Torah, and out of the thirst for increased Torah knowledge. Torah *lishma* became the hallmark of Rav Chaim's philosophy of study.

Over the next several years under Rav Chaim, the school grew to between fifty and one hundred students.[17] Soon, the Yeshiva of Volozhin produced noted scholars and rabbinical leaders. Each rabbi led his community and oversaw its spiritual growth while at the same time producing future students for Volozhin and other yeshivas that sprang up to cater to the increased flow of students.

Rav Chaim changed the landscape of Lithuania. He built a yeshiva and nurtured it with a methodology of study that caused it to flourish. But what he built was more than a yeshiva. He established an entire network of Torah scholarship in a land where just years earlier Torah study was in decline. He created a renaissance in Torah study. This renaissance was not confined to Lithuania alone. Eventually, yeshivas reflecting Rav Chaim's methodology emerged throughout Europe and wherever Jews found themselves. The traditions of the Vilna Gaon and the Yeshiva of Volozhin continue to flourish in yeshivas around the world. These yeshivas are the beneficiaries of the wisdom of the Vilna Gaon and Rav Chaim of Volozhin—a wisdom that has survived the passage of time.

Rav Chaim's accomplishments are truly immense. He instilled within the masses of Lithuanian Jewry a renewed interest in Torah study, thus perpetuating the values received at Sinai over three millennium earlier.

---

[17]Ibid., 28.

THE LEGACY OF A CONVERT

On Shavuot, when the Israelites accepted the Torah on Mount Sinai, they actually became a nation of converts. That is one of the reasons why the Book of Ruth, which tells of the Moabite woman's ordeal and conversion to Judaism, is read on Shavuot. Another famous convert in Jewish history was Valentine Potocki.

Count Valentine Potocki came from a long line of Polish counts. He lived a privileged life of royalty, but his intrigue with Judaism ultimately led him to study its principles and undergo conversion. Not only did he give up an easy existence, he also gave his life willingly for his convictions. Being of Polish royalty, conversion to Judaism no doubt put him in extreme danger. If discovered, he would face the severest of punishments. Potocki, who disappeared from a papal academy in Rome after his decision to convert, resettled in the small Lithuanian city of Ilya, near Vilna. He lived there protected by his fellow Jews under his new Jewish title—Avraham ben Avraham. Meanwhile, the authorities continued to conduct a thorough search for the missing count.

Eventually, an evil informant tipped off the authorities and told them that Avraham was the former Count Potocki. As Avraham was about to be married he was apprehended by the authorities, placed in chains, and taken away. Polish officers who recognized that he was the son of a duke could not understand what prompted him to become a Jew. They asked, "What did you see in this stupidity to become a scorned Jew?"[18] Avraham ignored the question. When they persisted he denied that he was Count Potocki, since according to Jewish law a convert assumes an entirely new identity upon his conversion. Interrogations and torture brought no information; he remained insistent that he was not Count Potocki but Avraham ben Avraham—the Jew. His

---

[18] M. Dayak, "Story of the Ger Tzedek," quoted in Rabbi Yom Tov Levinsky, comp., *Sefer HaMoadim* 4, 716.

mother came and pleaded with the convert to confess and spare his life.[19]

The count's conversion was an embarrassment that the church would not tolerate. After repeated attempts to induce a confession, he finally broke his silence. He told officials, "My name is no longer Potocki and you are addressing me by a foreign name, therefore I am not responding. My true name is Avraham and I am within the exile as all Jews, but Potocki is the prince of all Gentiles and I am not him."[20]

A man managed to bribe his way into prison. He told Avraham that he could be saved: "Rabeinu Eliyahu Vilna Gaon could use Kabbala to save you." Avraham refused the opportunity and explained to the perplexed visitor what induced him to such lofty ideals: "When the Almighty went around to all the nations of the world and offered them the Torah, not all the people in each nation rejected it. Only the refusals of their peers prevented them from fulfilling their aspirations. The souls of those who did not reject it are those who become converts, who come in every generation to claim the share once offered them."[21]

In the year 1748 on the second day of Shavuot, Avraham was taken to the main square of Vilna. Many of the townsfolk came out to mock him and witness the obscene spectacle of his execution. The bishops and the hierarchy of the church were also in attendance along with Avraham's mother, who, dressed in black, pleaded for his life. Once again the bishops offered Avraham the opportunity to confess and save his life. He again refused. And then the fires were lit and Avraham was martyred. As the flames consumed him his lips uttered the words of the blessing over the sanctification of the name of the Almighty, "Blessed art Thou O Lord . . . who sanctifies Thy name before multitudes."

---

[19]Selig Schachnowitz, *Avraham ben Avraham* (Jerusalem/New York: Feldheim, 1977), 216.
[20]M. M. Yashar, "Generations of the Chafetz Chaim," quoted in Levinsky, comp., *Sefer HaMoadim*, 171.
[21]Ibid.

Out of fear of the Gentiles' anger over the matter, the Jews did not venture outdoors on that day. One Jew with no beard dressed himself incognito and managed to offer the executioner a bribe that would allow some of the martyr's remains to be collected after the holiday so they could be interned in a Jewish cemetery.[22]

Every year on the second day of Shavuot the Jewish community of Vilna recited a special *Yizkor* (memorial) prayer in Avraham's memory.[23]

As the Israelites were accepted into the covenant with the Almighty at Mount Sinai on Shavuot, Avraham exemplified his devotion to that covenant and died as a martyr on Shavuot.

Rabbi M. M. Yashar relates the following in the book *The Generations of the Chafetz Chaim*:

> On the day of Erev Shavuot, all tables and benches in the large study hall of the Yeshiva were removed. This was done to make room for the young men to dance and enjoy the holiday. In the middle of the dancing, the Dean, Rabbi Hirsch Levinson, would silence the cheerful crowd. With deep fervor and emotion, he would begin to tell the story of the righteous convert, how he was able to reach a lofty stage that he would give his life for the sanctification of God's name on the day of the giving of the Torah. And how in the end he was betrayed.[24]

THE ACCEPTANCE OF THE TORAH IN LIBERATED BUCHENWALD

The family of S. B. Unsdorfer and three thousand other Jews who lived in Slovakia under Nazi occupation attempted through nego-

---

[22]Ibid., 177.
[23]Amud Beit Yehudah, "Amsterdam, 1776," quoted in Levinsky, comp., *Sefer HaMoadim*, 171.
[24]Ibid.

tiations to save themselves the horrors of Nazi persecution. Their efforts to find shelter did not last the duration of the war. In 1944, they were arrested by the Gestapo and transported to Auschwitz. On the day of the roundup, the world of nineteen-year-old S. B. Unsdorfer was destroyed. His family soon perished in Auschwitz, but he would live to survive and tell the tale of his survival in Auschwitz and Buchenwald.

When American forces entered the camp in April 4, 1945, they found several thousand survivors. Emaciated and wearing the scars of their horrific ordeal, the survivors began to come to terms with their harrowing experiences and reconcile themselves with the reality that they indeed were the surviving remnants of their friends and families. Their world was in the past, and it was hard for the survivors during those times to envision their futures and what kind of lives they would live. Unsdorfer, who chronicled his ordeals in *The Yellow Star*, describes with surprise the events that transpired with the arrival of Shavuot just before they left Buchenwald. As Unsdorfer prepared to depart Buchenwald in just a few days, announcements on loudspeakers proclaimed that a U.S. Army chaplain would lead services for the coming holiday. The services held that Shavuot were no doubt unforgettable for those thousands in attendance. Unsdorfer describes the event as follows:

> Since my childhood I had always looked forward to our wonderful and inspiring festivals, and particularly so in the tragic war years. But I wondered whether we weren't being put to a test too soon. Who among those thousands of physical and mental cripples would want to attend services and prayers so soon after their tragic experiences? The Festival of the Receiving of the Torah! Within a few weeks after liberation, religion, which seemed to do so little for us, was now challenging our loyalties and us.
>
> But just as you cannot measure the physical strength of an oppressed people, so you can not gauge its spiritual wealth and power.
>
> On that evening, Buchenwald staged a fantastic demon-

> stration of faith and loyalty to God. Thousands upon thousands of liberated Jews crowded into the specially vacated block for the first postwar Jewish religious service to be held on the soil of defeated Germany. The Muselmaenner, the cripples, the injured, and the weak came to demonstrate to the world that the last ounce of their strength, the last drop of their blood, and the last breath of their lives belonged to God, to Torah, and to the Jewish religion.
>
> As Chaplain Schecter intoned the Evening Prayers, all the inmates in and outside the block stood in silence re-accepting the Torah whose people, message, and purpose Hitler's Germany had attempted to destroy. Jewish history repeated itself. Just as our forefathers were liberated from Egypt accepted the Law in the desert, so did we, the liberated Jews of Buchenwald, reaccept the same Law in the concentration camps in Germany.[25]

The Torah was given at one moment to the Jews at Mount Sinai, but it is accepted each year every Shavuot, and every day when the Torah's laws are studied and obeyed. Acceptance, however, is often amidst the most difficult of circumstances, especially at times when one searches for meaning after emerging from the madness of genocide. Such acceptance is the truest sign of one's convictions. That was the situation for the thousands of survivors of Buchenwald who reaccepted the Torah received by their forefathers.

STANDING AT MOUNT SINAI, 1997

Rabbi Meir Shapiro was an illustrious scholar and communal leader who conceived of a novel idea that would enhance the universal

---

[25] S. B. Unsdorfer, *The Yellow Star* (New York/Jerusalem: Feldheim, 1983) 199–200.

knowledge of the entire Talmud within world Jewry. He proposed the study of *Daf Yomi*—the studying of a page of Talmud each day. For seven years, 2,711 pages would be studied. Congregations and individuals around the world would study the same pages of Talmud every day. Not only would the *Daf Yomi* enhance the universal understanding of Talmud, but the tractates that were less often studied would be learned as well.

As leader of the Polish faction of the organization Agudath Yisroel, Rabbi Shapiro proposed the idea at the organization's 1923 congress. The idea was accepted and it also drew support from Jewry's most revered scholars. The great rabbinical scholar, Rabbi Yisrael Meir Kagan HaCohen, the Chafetz Chaim, said the *Daf Yomi* brought joy to heaven. The Gerrer Rebbe announced to his Chassidim that he would be teaching the first folio of the first tractate, *Berachot*, and would study *Daf Yomi* thereafter. Agudath Yisroel archives report that by 1929, 250,000 Jews were studying in the program.[26]

Seven years later, on Tu BiShvat 1930, the first *Siyum*[27] was held in Lublin, Poland. Rabbi Shapiro presided over the celebration. At the event, the *Hadran* was recited. A *Siyum HaShas* was also held in the Jerusalem neighborhood of Mea Shaarim where Rabbi Yosef Chaim Sonenfeld recited the *Hadran*.[28] Afterwards, memorial prayers were recited for those sages who had passed on since the inception of *Daf Yomi*.

Seven years later, the next *Siyum* was held in the absence of Rabbi Shapiro who did not live to see the next completion of the Talmud. Twenty thousand Jews converged upon Lublin. Masses also gathered in Jerusalem and New York. By the late 1930s the

---

[26]Jonathan Mark, "Garden Party for the Ages" "The Edge of Town," *The New York Jewish Week* (October 30, 1997), 22.
[27]Ceremony marking the completion of the study of a tractate of the Talmud.
[28]Traditional prayer following the completion of a portion of the Talmud.

program became so popular that more than a million Jews were studying *Daf Yomi*.[29]

The destruction caused by the Holocaust did not end the *Daf Yomi* program. Even in the concentration camps, small groups assembled to study pages of the Talmud which they knew by memory.

Following the war, Rabbi Shapiro's novel idea would again gain momentum. Each *Siyum* would receive increased attendance. By 1997 over one hundred thousand Jews attended *Siyum* celebrations around the world. The largest celebrations that year were held in New York, where forty-eight thousand *Daf Yomi* enthusiasts filled Madison Square Garden and the Nassau Coliseum on Long Island. Satellite hook-ups in over thirty other American cities allowed an additional thirty thousand people to participate in the tenth *Siyum HaShas*.

The people came to celebrate the completion of the Talmud and to experience the *Siyum* itself. The *New York Times* quoted one long-time participant in the *Daf Yomi* program who stated, "exciting is not the word for this. This is the thrill of a life: to see everyone united in the service of our Creator."[30]

The program began with the recitation of the afternoon prayers and was followed by a succession of inspirational speeches.

Rabbi Avroham Chaim Feuer, chairman of the event, told the audiences, "In America alone we have over 70,000 Jews gathered to celebrate this *Talmud Torah* [study of Torah]. This is a powerful demonstration of the *nitzchius* [eternity] of Torah."[31]

Following a *Kaddish* (memorial prayer) recited in memory of the six million Holocaust victims and the recitation of the *Hadran*, joyful songs of celebration were sung as dancing filled all the packed theatres and auditoriums. More speeches followed.

---

[29]Mark, "The Edge of Town," 22.
[30]Frank Bruni, "Thousands Celebrate Completion of Talmud Study," *New York Times* (September 29, 1997): City section, 1.
[31]Tova Domnitch, *Florida Jewish Journal* (October 3, 1997): 3.

Rabbi Yaakov Weinberg, dean of the Yeshivat Ner Yisrael in Baltimore, described the significance of the event by stating, "All of Clal Yisrael [Jewish people] and all of humanity are uplifted with the finishing of Shas [The Talmud]. . . . In life itself, the only path to achievement is through closeness to the source of all existence."[32]

Rabbi Matityahu Solomon, the spiritual advisor at the Lakewood Yeshiva, delivered the final address of the evening. He described the nature of the celebration by comparing the significance of the *Siyum* to another event—the receiving of the Torah at Mount Sinai. Rabbi Solomon recalled the Torah portion of *Nitzavim*, which was read the week before the *Siyum*. The portion begins, "Today you are assembled before *HaShem*." He continued, "There is no greater description than the assembly here this evening, the Baal HaTurim [a commentator on Bible and Jewish law] explained that the only place you find the word *Nitzavim*—standing—is by Matan Torah. It describes a resolute assembly, not an assembly of celebration. The Jewish people were assembled to reaffirm their commitment to the acceptance of the Torah."[33]

On September 28, 1997, thousands of Jews around the world gathered to celebrate the completion of the Talmud and also the increased intensity of Torah study throughout the world. The multitudes simultaneously heard their leaders' encouragement as they proclaimed their love for the Torah to which they devote so much of their lives. As their ancestors stood at Mount Sinai over thirty-three hundred years earlier and affirmed their readiness to accept the law, the Jews assembled at the *Daf Yomi* celebrations around the world made the same affirmation.

THE MAGIC OF THE MOMENT

Over the centuries Jews have made pilgrimages to Jerusalem for the holiday of Shavuot as they had on all three pilgrimage holidays. On

[32]Ibid.
[33]Ibid.

Shavuot, there was also the custom to visit the grave of King David, since tradition holds that he was born and died on this holiday.

When Shavuot arrived in 1948, a month after the establishment of the State of Israel, Jews could no longer continue to make the pilgrimage to the Western Wall because they were denied access under the Jordanian occupation (1948–1967). However, the pilgrimages to King David's grave on nearby Mount Zion, located on the Israeli side of divided Jerusalem, continued. Over the next nineteen years crowds of pilgrims made their way to Mount Zion. From there they could see the Old City and view the Temple Mount.

On the morning of Shavuot, June 15, 1967, just six days after the liberation of the Old City of Jerusalem following the Six Day War, the Old City was officially opened to the public. For the first time in almost two thousand years, masses of Jews could visit the Western Wall and walk through the cherished streets of Judaism's capital city as members of the sovereign Jewish nation. Each Jew who ventured to the Western Wall on that unforgettable day represented the living realization of their ancestors' dreams over the millennium. It was one of those rare euphoric moments in history. In the late hours of the night, thousands of Jerusalem residents streamed toward the Zion gate eagerly awaiting entry into the Old City. At 4 A.M., the accumulating crowds assembled at Mount Zion were finally allowed to enter the area of the Western Wall. The first minyan (traditional quorum of ten) soon began. Fifteen hundred people shared in that unprecedented moment. As the sun rose, there was a steady flow of thousands of Jews who had made their way toward the Old City. In total, two hundred thousand Jews visited the Western Wall that day. It was the first pilgrimage en masse of Jews to Jewish-controlled Jerusalem for a Jewish festival in two thousand years, since the pilgrimages for the festivals in Temple times.

The *Jerusalem Post* described the epic scene:

> Every section of the population was represented. *Kibbutz* members and soldiers rubbing shoulders with the Neturei

Karta. Mothers came with children in prams, and old men trudged steeply up Mount Zion supported by youngsters on either side, to see the wall of the Temple before the end of their days.

Some wept, but most faces were wreathed in smiles. For thirteen continuous hours a colorful variety of all peoples trudged along in perfect order, stepping patiently when told to do so at each of six successive barriers set up by the police to regulate the flow.[34]

An eyewitness described the moment as follows:

I've never known so electric an atmosphere before or since. Wherever we were stopped, we began to dance. Holding aloft Torah scrolls we swayed and danced and sang at the tops of our voices. So many of the Psalms and songs are about Jerusalem and Zion and the words reached into us a new life. As the sky lightened, we reached the Zion gate. Still singing and dancing, we poured into the narrow alleyways beyond.[35]

On the day of Shavuot 3,320 years earlier, the Israelites stood at Mount Sinai and felt the gravity of the moment as a unique relationship was formed between themselves and their Creator. On the day of Shavuot following Israel's amazing victory in the Six Day War, multitudes ascended to the Western Wall as their ancestors had done in the past and they also celebrated the holiday just a short distance from the Temple Mount. They, too, felt the magic of the moment.

---

[34] *Jerusalem Post* (June 15, 1967), 1.
[35] "Voices of Jerusalem—Crowd of Tears," *Hadassah Magazine* 77, no. 9 (May 1996): 23.

BIKKURIM

Shavuot, among other things, is known in the Bible as the Day of *Bikkurim*—First Fruits. When Shavuot arrives, the first fruits begin to ripen in the land of Israel. Shavuot inaugurates the season when the Torah commands a landowner to bring the first fruits to the Temple.[36]

The Talmud tells of a time in the history of the Temple when an unnamed ruler—most likely a Greek or Roman—prohibited the bringing of *Bikkurim* to Jerusalem. His intent was apparently to sever the ties of the people from their beloved capital and Temple.[37] This ruler posted guards on the roads leading to Jerusalem to prevent the bringing of *Bikkurim*.[38] However, many Judeans were determined to maintain the practice of bringing the *Bikkurim* and would not be deterred. They devised a means to bypass the guards.

They took the baskets of *Bikkurim*, covered them with dried figs, and carried them to Jerusalem with a pestle on their shoulders. When they reached the guards, they were asked where they were going. They would respond "to make cakes of pressed figs with the mortar in a nearby place that is before us with the pestle on our shoulders." When the guards allowed them to pass, they decorated their baskets of *Bikkurim* and brought them to Jerusalem.[39]

Bikkurim consists of the first ripened harvest of seven specific species mentioned in the Bible in reference to the Land of Israel—wheat, barley, grapes, figs, pomegranates, olives, and dates.[40] The

---

[36]The actual moment of the inauguration of the *Bikkurim* season began with the offering of the "two loaves" sacrifice brought in the Temple on Shavuot day, which consisted of the new crop of barley.

[37]This was done in a similar manner by Yeravam ben Nevat. See "Tu B'Av: A Day of Restoration."

[38]*Megilat Taanit*, ch. 5, "The Month of Av."

[39]Mishna, Tractate Bikkurim, ch. 3. The reference to the event cited in chapter 5 of *Megilat Taanit* indicates that the event took place during Hellenistic times.

[40]Deuteronomy 8:8.

obligation to bring *Bikkurim* fell upon one who owned land that produced any of these species. They were to be brought to the Temple priests in Jerusalem. Those who went on pilgrimage to Jerusalem for Shavuot brought *Bikkurim* with them. If they came from afar, the fruits brought were dried; if they lived close by, they were fresh.[41] From Shavuot until Succot, the *Bikkurim* were brought and a special accompanying prayer was recited. The *Bikkurim* were decorated as those bringing them approached the Holy City. Upon entering Jerusalem, their arrival was formerly announced by the city elders.[42] Right after the *Bikkurim* were brought to the Temple priests, the following proclamation of gratitude was recited:

> An Aramite[43] sought to destroy my father,[44] and he went down to Egypt and lived there in small numbers, and it was there that he became a great and numerous nation. And the Egyptians did evil unto us and they made us suffer and they imposed slavery upon us. And we cried to God, Lord of our ancestors, and God heard our voice and saw our affliction, our harsh labor and our suffering. And God took us out of Egypt with a strong hand and an outstretched arm, with great visions, and with signs and miracles. He brought us to this place and gave us this land flowing with milk and honey. I am now bringing this first fruit of the land that God had given to me.[45]

The offering of *Bikkurim* showed appreciation to the Almighty for his kindness and bounty and the acknowledgement that nothing could be produced without the Almighty.[46]

---

[41]Mishna, Bikkurim, 3:3.
[42]Ibid.
[43]Laban—the uncle of Jacob who sought to kill him after his departure from the land of Aram Naharaim.
[44]Jacob.
[45]Deuteronomy 26:6–10.
[46]*Sefer HaChinuch*, Commandment no. 606. *Sefer HaChinuch* (Book

When Shavuot arrived, masses of Judeans continued bringing *Bikkurim* to Jerusalem despite the difficulties involved. As the *Bikkurim* proclamation speaks of the Exodus and the Israelite entry into the land that occurred against all odds, those who managed to bring the *Bikkurim* under duress and recite the verses of the proclamation did so despite the difficulties.

---

of Education) is a thirteenth century classic composed by an anonymous author, known only as Rabbi Aaron HaLevi, that explains and details the Torah's precepts.

5

Tisha B'Av

TRAGEDIES OF TISHA B'AV

Bad things on an unlucky day. (Taanit 29B)

Tisha B'Av, the day of mourning, has been historically a day of tragedy. On Tisha B'Av, the destruction of the First and Second Temples of Jerusalem and many other calamities befell the Jewish people. The following events are some of those tragedies that occurred on Tisha B'Av. Each calamity deeply impacted the history of the Jews.

The Mishna states that the following five tragic events occurred on Tisha B'Av.[1]

1) On Tisha B'Av, the Israelites took the reports of the spies who had maligned the Land of Israel to heart. They cried out in anguish and bemoaned their fate although their inheritance of the land was assured by the Almighty.

[1]Taanit 4:6.

Consequently, it was decreed by the Almighty that the Israelite men above the age of 20, excluding those from the tribe of Levy, would not enter the land of Israel.

2) The First Temple was destroyed in 586 B.C.E.

3) The Second Temple was destroyed in 70 C.E.

4) The city of Betar—the last stronghold of the Bar Kochba Revolt was captured.

5) The Roman commander Tarnus Rufus plowed the Temple Mount and the surrounding area.

In addition, according to the commentator Isaac Don Abarbanel, the destruction of the Jewish community of Alexandria, presumably perpetrated by the Roman emperor Trajan, also took place on Tisha B'Av.[2]

Since the codification of the Mishna in 210 C.E., many other tragedies have befallen the Jewish people on Tisha B'Av throughout history.

In 613, in Visigoth Spain, a royal decree was issued imposing either forced conversion on all the Jews of the land or exile. (The decree was later annulled.)

King Edward of England ordered the expulsion of the Jews on July 19, 1290.

On August 2, 1492, the last of approximately 250,000 Jews expelled from Spain left Spanish soil.

On July 26, 1555, the Jews of Rome were forced into the newly established ghetto.

On July 28, 1648, Bogdan Chmielnicki's Cossacks massacred three thousand Jews in Konstantynow.

On July 26, 1670, the last Jews left Vienna following their expulsion.

On July 25, 1882, the Turkish Government reacting to the

---

[2] *Abarbanel Commentary on the Latter Prophets* (Elisha Publishing House, Tel Aviv: Elisha, 1946), 311.

first wave of Zionist pioneers in the Land of Israel prohibited land sales to Jews. This was one of the first official acts of Arab opposition to the Zionist cause.

On August 1, 1914, World War I broke out. It was a most disastrous day. The First World War, which caused untold horrors to Jewish communities, also led to the Second World War.

On August 2, 1941, a decree expelling all Jews from Hungarian Ruthenia was issued.

On July 23, 1942, orders for the deportation for most of Warsaw's five hundred thousand Jews began.

On Tisha B'Av, 1955, El Al airlines lost its only passenger plane when it was shot down after it accidentally wandered into Bulgarian airspace.

As no other day, Tisha B'Av signifies the sufferings of the Jews throughout history.

COMMEMORATING THE CRUSADER ATTACK UPON JERUSALEM

Tisha B'Av recalls the destruction of the First and Second Temples of Jerusalem and other disasters which befell the Jewish people. Long after Roman forces turned Jerusalem into a Roman colony, empires and armies continued to attack Jerusalem and claim its hollowed ground as their own. During Jerusalem's long history of conquests, the attack of the Crusaders stands out as one of the most brutal. Jerusalem's Jews were tragically caught in the middle of a conflict between Christians and Muslims over Jerusalem. On Tisha B'Av, the Crusader attack should also be remembered.

Under Roman and then Byzantine rule, which extended for most of the next five hundred years following the Bar Kochba Revolt, Jews were only permitted to enter Jerusalem on Tisha B'Av.[3] When the Muslims conquered the city in 638 C.E., a small

---

[3]See "Tisha B'Av: The History of the Western Wall," page 103.

number of Jews were readmitted and allowed to reestablish a Jewish community. The Crusaders, upon their conquest of Jerusalem in 1099, would wreak devastation, destroy its rebuilt Jewish community, and again prevent Jews from residing in their holiest city.

On November 27, 1095, Pope Urban II urged a Crusade to liberate the Holy Land and Jerusalem from Muslim rule. The first group of Crusaders gathered in France under the leadership of Godfrey of Boullion, who urged violence against the Jews as "revenge" for the Crucifixion. By January 1096, Crusaders began attacking Jewish communities, wreaking devastation, and threatening death to those who would not submit to baptism. As the Crusaders made their way into Germany, the Jews there faced the same horrors. Unleashing their hatred and fury against the Jews, the Crusaders committed atrocities whose horrors are etched upon the annuls of martyrdom in Jewish history. Of the thousands of Jews offered the choice of baptism or death, the vast majority—over 10,000—chose to die as martyrs. It was the Crusader mission toward Jerusalem to fight the Muslims that brought about these horrors.[4]

Prior to the Crusader invasion, the Jews of Jerusalem lived under the rule of Muslim empires for most of the past 500 years, since their conquest of the city in 638 C.E. Under Muslim rule, Jews and Christians were permitted to live in Jerusalem as *Dhimmis* (Protected Ones), who are considered subordinates to the dominant Muslim rulers as in all Muslim controlled societies. Some Muslim rulers were tolerant; others were not. Just prior to the Crusader invasion, the Fatamids—who were generally more tolerant—ruled Jerusalem.

The Crusaders advanced southward and occupied Syria. Following a grueling two-year siege of the Syrian capital Antioch, they eventually overcame its defenders and continued their campaign southward. They reached the Land of Israel in the spring of 1099 and headed toward Jerusalem. Their advance sent fear into those

---

[4]See "Shavuot: The Ultimate Sacrifice," page 59.

who lay in their path. When the Crusaders reached the cities of Jaffa and Ramle, they found them empty because the entire population had fled in terror. On June 7, they arrived at a mountain overlooking Jerusalem, the burial place of the prophet Samuel. There, they prayed and prepared for the upcoming siege of Jerusalem.

The city's defenders—Jews and Muslims—prepared the best possible defenses, well aware of what awaited them should the Crusaders overcome those defenses. Jerusalem, surrounded by high walls and deep valleys was already prepared for a long siege. Under the leadership of Godfrey of Boullion, the Crusaders set siege to the city's northern walls at the Damascus Gate and from the south, Mount Zion. They continuously hammered away at the city's walls while its defenders feverishly worked to repair them. However, the Crusaders' repeated attempts to breach Jerusalem's walls failed as its defenders waged a fierce campaign in its defense. As at the siege of Jerusalem by the Roman general Titus one thousand years earlier, a special siege machine was constructed to enable the Crusaders to scale Jerusalem's well-fortified walls. On Friday morning, July 15, 1099, an assault machine was lowered upon the city's walls and battlements, making Jerusalem accessible.

At noon of that same day, with the sound of trumpets and shouts of encouragement, the crusaders forced their way into Jerusalem from the north, entering the city's Jewish Quarter. As they streamed into the city, its panic-stricken defenders and residents fled through the narrow streets. A massacre of the city's residents ensued. Tens of thousands of Muslims and Jews were slaughtered. Many of Jerusalem's Jews were burnt alive as they were forced into synagogues that were then set aflame. Others desperately attempted to hide, but were hunted down and slaughtered. The few who survived were sold into slavery.

Following the carnage, the knights of the Crusades changed their blood-stained clothes and went to pray at their holy places, where they offered prayers of thanksgiving. Over the following days, the Crusaders sacked the city, plundering its wealth. Each marauder claimed the house he entered as well as its possessions.

Soon, Jerusalem's population would be replaced with Latins,

Syrian Christians, and other Christian minorities. Under Crusader rule, the city's infrastructure was developed with the expectation that Crusader Jerusalem would be permanent. Remnants of their construction are clearly visible today.

Under Crusader rule, with one rare reported exception, Jews were again forbidden to live in Jerusalem. The Jewish connection to its eternal capital was no longer marked by the presence of a Jewish community—a presence that helped instill hope within Jews over the centuries.

Soon Tisha B'Av arrived and the Jews living in a world of fear and increasing persecution had even more reason to mourn. The loss of the Temple and exile of the Jews was compounded by the loss of Jerusalem's Jewish community.

But in its desolation, one could envision Jerusalem free of Crusaders and a Jerusalem whose ancient splendor would someday be restored. During the dark days of the opression that hope never faded.

THE EXPULSION FROM SPAIN

On March 31, 1492, King Ferdinand and Queen Isabella of Spain signed an edict of expulsion against Spain's Jews. The decree, disseminated throughout Spain between April 29 and May 1, left Spain's Jewish community in shock. Nowhere else in the history of the Diaspora did a Jewish community reach the level of affluence as in Spain. With the expulsion, fifteen hundred years of history came to an end. The final day of the expulsion from Spain was August 2—Tisha B'Av, 1492.

There were many tragic events that were a prelude to the disastrous end of Spanish Jewry. A century prior to the expulsion, in 1391, anti-Jewish violence broke out as Dominican priests led frenzied mobs into Jewish communities demanding conversion or death. When the violence eventually ceased, fifty thousand Jews had perished in the city of Seville alone. Thousands were also sold into slavery. During the attacks there were many who outwardly converted and yet privately maintained Jewish practices.

The *Anusim* (forced ones) underwent baptism in order to save their lives when faced with the choice of baptism or death. They were often the wealthy who could be saved with the help of funds. The number of *Anusim* exceeded two hundred thousand. Over the course of time, as anti-Jewish policies increased in Spain and endangered the livelihoods of Jews, there were also some who, not threatened with conversion or death, voluntarily accepted baptism in order to protect their occupations and assets, but who also lived secretly as Jews.

The vast majority of Morranos—those who lived secretly as Jews—continued their clandestine lifestyle for generations. They maintained Jewish communities and observed Jewish traditions. Throughout that time, their children only married other Morranos and an underground Jewish community flourished in Spain. Aware of the wide scale adherence of conversos to Judaism, the church became increasingly hostile toward them. Over time the situation for all of Spanish Jewry worsened. In 1469, the call for purges of "heresy" became louder. At the same time, the wedding of King Ferdinand of Aragon to Isabella of Castile merged the two largest provinces of Spain. Both the King and Queen sought to implement a campaign to "root out heresy" as an effective means to unify their empire.

Eleven years later, Ferdinand and Isabella convened with Pope Sixtus VI and established the Inquisition, which would continue until the nineteenth century. Its purpose was to find and root out the Morranos. Under Thomas Torquemada, the barbaric enforcer whose slogan was "one kingdom, one people, one faith," the Inquisition was enforced. Spies were sent throughout Spain in search for Morranos. The thousands who were found or suspected of maintaining Jewish observances became victims of the Inquisition's torture chambers. At the *Auto-Da-Fe* (act of faith), thousands were sentenced by the inquisitors as "heretics" and handed over to the authorities for sentencing. Many faced public executions and many were burnt alive after already suffering unspeakable horrors. Despite the protests of the Pope against the monarchy's barbaric practices, the determined king and queen maintained their policies. But despite the terror, the Morranos continued to live their secret lives. Fredinand and Isabella were aware that the Inquisition did not stamp out "heresy" as Morrano communities continued to exist. At the behest of Torquemada, the monarchy eventually ordered the expulsion of all Jews from Spain.

On April, 29, 1492, in the central square of Toledo—a city where Jews had lived for over a millennium—an officer of arms flanked by three trumpeters, two local magistrates, and two bailiffs read out the proclamation of expulsion. Ferdinand and Isabella issued the expulsion edict that blamed all Jews for corrupting Morranos by secretly encouraging their adherence to Judaism.

The revered rabbinic scholar, financier, and leader of Spanish Jewry, Isaac Don Abarbanel attempted repeatedly to persuade the monarchy to reverse the decree. He reported on his efforts to persuade the king, "I pleaded with the King many times. . . . But he sealed his ears as if he were deaf, and utterly refused to reconsider."[5]

The expulsion was motivated by religious hatred. However, the prospect of plundering the assets of the exiles who were prohibited from leaving with their capital was also a major factor. The expulsion was also another attempt to proselytize Spain's Jews; the monarchy permitted those who converted to remain with its protection. Some accepted conversion, but the majority—an estimated 100,000 to 300,000 Jews—remained steadfast and left the land they and their ancestors called home for centuries. No means of coercion could control their will. Prohibited from leaving with their valuables, they left virtually penniless, fleeing only with their memories of what Spain once was in bygone eras. They always maintained the hope that conditions in Spain would improve, but

[5]Rabbi Eliyahu Ki Tov, *The Book of Our Heritage*, trans., Nathan Bulman, *Sefer Ha-Todaah* (New York: Feldheim Publishers, 1978), vol. 2, 285.

those hopes were dashed with the expulsion. The Abarbanel described the grief of the people when they heard the decree in his introduction to his commentary on the Book of Kings I, "such dread and anguish was not known since the exile of Judea from its foreign soil."

The pace of the Exodus accelerated during the traditional three weeks of mourning that precede Tisha B'Av, the day of national mourning over the destruction of the First and Second Temples and other tragedies that befell the Jewish people on that day. As the days before the final day of the expulsion approached, groups of Jews left Spain accompanied by musicians. Although music is prohibited during these three weeks, the sages of the era allowed it during that particular time to raise the hopes of a downtrodden people who withstood the pressure and did not convert.

The Abarbanel places the final day of departure from Spain on Tisha B'Av. "It turns out that the day set for the departure from Spain was the ninth of Av, but the king did not know the character of the day when he issued his edict. It was as if he had been led from above to fix this time."[6] It was also the same day that several professed Jews from Spain set sail with Christopher Columbus toward the New World. With one decree, Europe's most prosperous and affluent Jewish community, which had achieved great heights, was declared evicted and homeless, facing an uncertain future.

For most of the refugees the ordeal was far from over. Tens of thousands crossed over into Portugal where they would again face forced conversions and expulsion five years later. Others, in their search for refuge, were often robbed or murdered, or they suffered starvation. Such was the case for many of those who reached North Africa. In many cases the exiles were not permitted entry. The most fortunate were those who reached the Turkish Empire, where they were welcomed by the sultan.

---

[6]Isaac Don Abarbanel, *Commentary on Jeremiah*, 311:B, from Ki Tov, Rabbi Eliyahu, *The Book of Our Heritage*, trans. Nathan Bulman (New York: Feldheim Publisherrs, 1978), vol. 2, 285.

The ninth of Av—August 2, 1492—was a day of tragedy for Spanish Jewry. Tisha B'Av—the day of Jewish catastrophe, destruction, and misfortune —is epitomized by the expulsion from Spain.

THE CHMIELNICKI REVOLT

The world was often a place of chaos for the Jews of the fourteenth, fifteenth, and sixteenth centuries. Yet they felt they had one safe haven—Poland. Although the Jews of Poland did face persecution on occasion, it did not compare to the suffering of Jews in other lands. From the middle of the thirteenth century, the rulers of Poland had offered the Jews unprecedented freedoms in Europe. Under the Charter of Bolesav the Pious in 1264, Jews were granted protection, security, freedom of religion, and land ownership. These rights were reaffirmed and increased in the middle of the fourteenth century by King Casimir the Great, who allowed the Jews the right of self government. For the next three hundred years, this climate of tolerance in Poland attracted Jews from other parts of Europe.

Jews arrived following expulsions in other lands such as Hungary in 1360 and Germany and Bohemia in 1394. Jews also fled to Poland following persecutions such as the Black Plague massacres of Jews throughout Europe in 1348–1349. In that era, Poland lived up to its traditional Hebrew acronym *Po Lin*, meaning "rest here." Over time, an immense Jewish community grew in Poland where the Jews lived as an autonomous entity and issued their own laws under a central body known as the "Kahal." Within that environment, the Jewish community thrived as it produced a wealth of Talmudic scholars whose commentaries on the Bible and Talmud and decisions on matters of Jewish law remain invaluable. It was the "golden era" of a community whose refugees emptied the Jewish communities of Western Europe. At the time it was not only the largest Jewish population in the world, but possessed the vast majority of world Jewry itself. However, the relative calm would not last. It was shattered with a catastrophe of unspeakable proportions—the Chmielnicki Revolt.

Bogdan Chmielnicki served as a cavalryman for the Poles and Cossacks during Poland's war against Turkey. In late 1647, he was a bitter man who had suffered a personal humiliation by the Polish governor Czehryn. The governor's soldiers entered Chmielnicki's home, arrested his wife, and took many of his personal possessions. His new enemy was now the Polish hierarchy and he began to foment a rebellion against them. The thousands of Ukrainians who joined him were an assorted group of criminals, bandits, highwaymen, and dispossessed serfs. They saw rebellion as their opportunity to settle scores with their Polish Catholic overlords. Ukrainians and Orthodox Ruthenians prepared for war against the Polish enemy. To add strength to Chmielnicki's forces, an alliance was forged with their former enemies, the Tartars of Crimea—a tribe that had drifted into the Ukraine centuries earlier.

In the war between the Ukrainians and the Poles, the Jews—who were natural allies of the Polish noblemen and some of whom were employed by the Poles as tax collectors—were caught in the middle. The Ukrainian peasants possessed a strong hatred for the Jews, the close allies of the Polish nobility who the peasants also despised.

Rabbi Nathan Nata Hanover, a chronicler of the revolt, wrote of the uneasiness that existed between the peasant and the Jew prior to the revolt, "The Jew was the noble man's tax farmer, as was customary . . . of most Jews in the kingdom of the Ukraine. For they ruled in every part . . . a condition which aroused the jealousy of the peasants."[7] Some Jews did work for Polish overlords; however, most Jews of Poland during that era lived in poverty, lacking the bare essentials.

When thinking about Tisha B'Av—the day that marks the many disasters that befell the Jews—it is fitting to recall the horrors

---

[7]Rabbi Nathan Nata Hanover, *Yeven Metzulah (Abyss of Despair)* (Hahistadrut Haclalit Shel Haovdim B'Eretz Yisrael, 1964), 24.

perpetrated by the Cossacks who fought under Bogdan Chmielnicki. The horrors of that era are commonly known as Gezeirot Tach V'Tat—*Gezeirot*, the hebrew word for "decree," implying that the sufferings were heavenly ordained; *Tach V'Tat*, the Hebrew letters corresponding to the date 5408–5409 in the Jewish calendar and 1648–1649 in the Gregorian calendar. These are the years of the Chmielnicki Revolt. The massacres perpetrated by Chmielnicki and his Cossacks against the Jews went beyond the many horrors already experienced by Jews over centuries of persecution. The brutality and the extent of the deaths were unprecedented in the long history of anti-Jewish persecution in Europe.

When the combined forces of the Ukrainians and Tartars advanced toward Poland, unimaginable horrors awaited Polish Jewry. Chmielnicki routed the Polish army at Yellow River on May 19, 1648, and Hard Plank on May 26, 1648. The victories added momentum to the revolt; serfs throughout the Ukraine revolted against their Polish overlords. With Chmielnicki's successes, many Poles also joined his forces.[8] Then, as chaos reigned, the destruction began.

In each town the Cossacks approached, Poles and Jews faced the Cossack's barbarism. Many Jews fled to the large cities for protection. Of the Jews who remained, thousands were found murdered in the most barbaric ways. Hanover, in his account *Yeven Metzulah*, described the sadistic brutality of the Ukranians:

> Some had their skin torn off which they threw to the dogs. Some had their hands and legs chopped off which were thrown on the road to be crushed by wagons and horses. Some had deep wounds inflicted upon them and then they were thrown outside so that they should not die quickly, suffering in their blood and pain until their souls departed. And many were buried while they were still alive. And they slaughtered chil-

[8]Ibid., 29.

> dren in the laps of their mothers. And many children were sliced open and cut like fish. Pregnant women had their bellies ripped open and their fetuses were ripped open before them. In others, their abdomens were cut and live cats were sowed inside, and their hands were chopped off so they could not attempt to remove the cat. The infants were hung on the breasts of their mothers. Some children were pierced with spears, roasted on the fire and then brought to their mothers to be eaten.[9]

The Cossacks also built bridges out of the bodies of Jewish children.[10]

The Tartars—allies of the Cossacks—were known to have sexually abused Jewish women. However, their primary interest was in plunder and profit. Jews found under their control were for the most part captured, held for ransom, and redeemed by Jewish communities in Italy and Turkey, as well as Amsterdam and Hamburg. Thousands of Jews managed to survive as a result. In one particular situation, the Cossacks surrounded thousands of Jews on one side and the Tartars surrounded them on the other. Knowing what their fate would be if they were overrun by the Cossacks, they decided to surrender themselves to the Tartars. As they approached the Tartars, "a Cantor among them, Rabbi Hirsch from Zivitov, was chanting the memorial prayer *Kel Malei Rachamin* for the slain in a high voice, and the people moaned in despair." When their captors heard their cries, their compassion was aroused, and they bid the people not to worry. About twenty thousand Jews were ransomed.[11]

For most Jews who sought refuge within Poland's cities, the horrors had just begun. Terrified, they waited within Poland's city walls along with Polish refugees in the hope that a miracle would

---

[9]Ibid., Ch. 4.
[10]Ibid.
[11]Ibid.

cause the defeat or retreat of Chmielnicki. In each city, Jews and Poles worked against a common enemy and prepared the best possible defenses; although the Jew often had no ally.

When Chmielnicki heard that many Jews—some of whom possessed a considerable amount of gold and silver—had gathered in the city of Nemirov, he arrived with troops. Unable to breach the city's walls, he relied upon deception and the betrayal of the Poles within the city. As his troops approached Nemirov, they unfurled Polish flags to give the appearance to the Jews within the city that the troops were Polish. The Poles within the city were notified of this deception and collaborated with the Cossacks in order to save their own lives. They instructed the Jews to open the city walls, claiming the troops were Polish and had come to the city's aid.[12] It appeared to the Jews that such was indeed the case and they opened the city gates for the troops. As the Cossacks entered the city they drew their swords and proceeded to massacre the Jews within. Many attempted to escape but were cut down by the Cossacks. Many were offered the choice of baptism or death; all refused and died martyr's deaths. The rabbi of the town, Yechiel Michaell ben Eliezer, in an address to his congregation on the Sabbath before the destruction, told them that if the enemy should arrive, the people must defy them if they demand baptism; at the cost of their lives they could not abandon their faith.[13] Throughout the two years of Chmielnicki's horrors, thousands of Jews died due to their refusal to denounce their faith, as during the era of the Crusades.[14] When the slaughter in Nemirov ended, about six thousand Jews lay dead.

The Cossacks then rode several miles to the southern end of Poland and besieged the city of Tulchin. As in Nemirov, Jews and Poles held off the enemy. The well-organized Jews actually managed to inflict heavy losses upon their enemies. However, as in

---

[12]Ibid., 37.
[13]Ibid., 38.
[14]See "Shavuot: The Ultimate Sacrifice" page 59.

Nemirov, the Jews of Tulchin were betrayed.[15] In this case, the Jews were aware of the betrayal and wanted to overcome the Poles. However, the rabbi of Tulchin warned them that such an act could jeopardize all Jews in Poland. "Listen, my brethren and my people. If you lay a hand upon the nobles [Poles], the others will take revenge against our brethren elsewhere, God forbid. Therefore if our fate be decreed from Heaven, let us accept the judgement with rejoicing."[16] When called to embrace Christianity, no one responded. Fifteen hundred Jews were massacred. News quickly spread of the horrors of Nemirov and Tulchin and both Jews and Poles prepared to meet the threat. Tragically, horrors had just begun. Over the next year the massacres would continue, and all of Polish Jewry was in grave danger.

The next target would be the city of Polona. The Cossacks and Tartars rode to the northwest—the heart of Jewish Poland—and besieged the city of Polona. This time, the Greek Orthodox betrayed the city and assisted the entry of the enemy. When the Cossacks entered, they massacred ten thousand Jews. In Polona, three hundred followers of the revered Kabbalist Rabbi Shimshon of Ostropli gathered around their leader in their synagogue wrapped in *talits* (prayer shawls) and prayed. When the enemy arrived, the Jews were massacred.[17] Soon, Tisha B'Av arrived and the Jews despaired over their fate and that of their brethren.

Panic spread over all of Poland with the fall of Polona. Chmielnicki had defeated an army of forty thousand Polish soldiers and a dark cloud hovered over Poland. Jews fled in desperation, seeking shelter as one Polish city after another fell. Polish Jewry was at the mercy of barbarians whose savage attacks threatened the entire Jewish community over the next year.

By the time the war neared its first cease fire in late 1649, 744

---

[15]Such betrayal, although not uncommon during the Chmielnicki Revolt, was not the norm either.
[16]Hanover, *Yeven Metzulah*, 41.
[17]Ibid., 49.

Jewish communities had been destroyed. Possibly over three hundred thousand Jews were murdered. For years to come, a host of invaders swept over Poland, each inflicting cruelties upon the Jews. The nightmare seemed endless.

On Tisha B'Av, it is fitting to recall the Chmielnicki Revolt and its consequences. Polish Jewry, the crown of the exile where Jewish life flourished for centuries, had been destroyed. Its end came abruptly. In time Polish Jewry would be reestablished, but a disaster of such a magnitude had not occurred since Roman times. Just as the destruction of the first two Temples had set the Jewish world in chaos, so too, did the Chmielnicki Revolt. For Jewish survivors around the world, the harsh reality set in that Jewish sufferings in exile knew no limits.

TISHA B'AV IN THE WARSAW GHETTO

Before the Germans captured the city of Warsaw in the 1939 Blitzkrieg, there were 360,000 Jews in the Polish capital. It was a city enriched by centuries of Jewish life. The Warsaw Ghetto was established November 15, 1940, in a small area within the city. It would become a halfway stop to death for hundreds of thousands of Polish and German Jews.

Jews from outlying areas poured into the ghetto. By 1940 its population reached 460,000.[18] Thousands of ghetto residents died of disease and starvation, however, the population was maintained by the continual flow of refugees. Little did they know that they were being forced into what was a holding pen for the slaughterhouse—Treblinka, the concentration camp that would destroy eight hundred thousand people, the majority of whom were Jews, in only a few months time.

On July 22, the eve of Tisha B'Av 1942, the death sentence

---

[18]Charles Roland, *Courage Under Siege: Starvation, Disease and Death in the Warsaw Ghetto* (New York: Oxford University Press, 1992), 27.

for Warsaw's Jews was issued. In the early morning hours, the Judenrat was convened and the Plenipotentiary for Resettlement Affairs ordered the "resettlement in the east of all Jews residing in Warsaw regardless of age and sex." The order called for six thousand Jews per day to be rounded up and deported.

When Warsaw was under siege by the Germans in September 1939, its Jewish Council appointed Adam Czerniakow as mayor of the ghetto. As head of the Judenrat, Czerniakow attempted to assist the many starving and destitute of Warsaw and defended Warsaw's Jews, often at risk to his own life. Czerniakow always kept a tablet of cyanide by his side in the event that the Nazis asked him to obey an order he felt he had to refuse.

His despair at the plight of the children of the ghetto tormented him. On June 14, 1942, he wrote in his diary "I commanded that the children be brought to the garden from the detention room organized by the local Ordnungsdienst. They are living skeletons, street beggars. . . . I'm ashamed to admit it's been long since I cried so. . . . Cursed are those among us who eat and drink and forget these children."[19]

A week before the announcement of the deportations, rumors had already spread in the ghetto and the Jews were gripped with terror. Czerniakow asked the Nazi officials for an explanation, but received nothing but denials. On July 22, at 7:30 in the morning, Czerniakow, along with the members of the Judenrat, were told that the deportations were to begin the next day—Tisha B'Av—and the expulsions would include children. He immediately understood the gravity of such an order and that his previous policy of cooperation with the Germans was a grievous error. This was an order he refused to sign. The night following the first deportation, he took the cyanide he had kept with him. He left the following note to the Jewish council executive: "I am powerless, my heart

---

[19]Raul Hilberg, Stanislow Starow, and Josef Kermisz, eds., *The Warsaw Diary of Adam Czerniakow: Prelude to Doom* (New York: Stein and Day, 1979), 366.

trembles in sorrow and compassion. I can no longer bear all this. My act will show everyone the right thing to do."[20]

The diary *A Cup of Tears*, by Abraham Lewin, offers the following description of the events that occurred on July 23: "Disaster after disaster, misfortune after misfortune. The small ghetto has been turned out on to the streets. . . . The people were driven from 42-44 Muranowska Street during the night. . . . Rain has been falling all day. Weeping. The Jews are weeping. They are hoping for a miracle. The expulsion is continuing. Buildings are blockaded."[21]

Chaim Kaplan, in his diary on the Warsaw Ghetto, foresaw the doom that awaited the Jews of Warsaw with the issuance of the decree. He described the decree as "the total destruction of the Jewish nation." He cites several signs—all ominous—and surmises that the deportations can only be a death sentence and those who deny it "grasp at straws."[22] In a July 26 entry, Kaplan writes, "We, the inhabitants of the Warsaw ghetto are now experiencing the reality. Our good fortune is that our days are numbered—that we shall not have to live long under conditions as these."[23] According to the decree, all were to be deported except for the Judenrat and those who worked in German industries.

At Treblinka, there was a sign outside the death camp that attempted to maintain calm. It stated, "Do not worry about your future. . . . all of you are headed for the east, to work; while you work, your wives shall take care of your houses. But first you must bathe and your clothes must be cleaned of lice."[24] Only moments

---

[20]Ibid., 23.
[21]Abraham Lewin, *A Cup of Tears: A Diary of the Warsaw Ghetto* (Oxford: Basil Blackwell in Association with the Institute for Jewish Studies, 1988), 136.
[22]Abraham I. Katch, trans. and ed., *Schroll of Agony: The Warsaw Diary of Chaim Kaplan* (New York: Collier Books, 1973), 380.
[23]Ibid., 383.
[24]Hilberg, Starow, and Kermisz, eds., *The Warsaw Diary of Adam Czerniakow*, 46.

later, after merciless beatings by SS and Ukrainian guards, the Jews from the Warsaw Ghetto were herded into the crematoria.

On July 29, the second round of Warsaw's deportations began. A proclamation was posted by the Jewish police (most of whom were concerned, foremost, in saving themselves) urging Jews to volunteer for resettlement. The SS, along with Latvian and Lithuanian troops, closed off individual blocks and brutally forced the masses out for deportation. Many were shot on the spot; others were savagely beaten. When the crowd's numbers reached a few thousand, they were herded off to the "Umschlagplatz"—a deportation railway yard to be transported. Every morning and evening the roundups took place. Over the month of August, 142,525 were deported, with 135,120 Jews being sent to Treblinka. By the middle of August it was widely understood that "resettlement" was a myth. Enough evidence had already reached the ghetto by word of mouth from witnesses to the Nazi camps that resettlement actually meant death at Treblinka. By October 3, approximately three hundred thousand Jews were deported[25] including most members of the Judenrat. Many were deported on September 21—Yom Kippur, the Day of Atonement.

On Tisha B'Av 1942, the well-organized Nazi killing machine was set into high gear and its horrors knew no bounds. That day marked the forthcoming end of Warsaw Jewry.[26] Soon other ghettos would face the same fate. A chronicler of the Warsaw Ghetto, Emanuel Ringelbaum, called the eve of that Tisha B'Av in

---

[25]Yisrael Guttman, *Jews of the Warsaw Ghetto 1938–1942*, (Bloomington: Indiana University Press, 1982), 211. That figure belongs to the Jewish Underground report sent to London in November 1942, although other Jewish chroniclers speak of as many as 350,000 who were deported.

[26]Of the forty thousand Jews who remained in the Warsaw Ghetto following the deportations, several hundred armed themselves and fought against their oppressors when they came to liquidate the ghetto in April 1943.

1942 "the blackest day in Jewish history in modern times. From that time, mass deportations and executions began."[27]

Hillel Seidman, in his diary of the Warsaw Ghetto, wrote in an entry he entitled "The Night of Tears:"

> As night falls I finally reach home, my brain bursting with terrifying images. Crossing our courtyard I notice our small *shtiebl.* [Because of the danger of being caught out on the street, every block organized its own private minyan.] About twenty men sit on upturned benches—it's Tisha B'Av tonight! Two flickering candles at the temporary amud dimly light up the bent heads, with their eyes staring into the far distance, as that heartrending tune wells up: "Eichah. . . ."
>
> The tune that was perhaps first composed at the exile from Jerusalem and has since absorbed the tears of generations.
>
> Every age has its particular Eichah. But somehow this Eichah from our generation has a special ring to it, different to that from any previous calamity. Perhaps it is the very last Eichah.
>
> "How alone it sits, the great city of many inhabitants. . . ." Indeed how alone, how forlorn we are today.
>
> "All her pursuers entrapped her in dire straits. . . . I called to my friends but they betrayed me." How true, how real those ancient lamentations read; how accurate they describe our present catastrophe. That was when it all started, when we were driven from our land and lost our sovereignty 1,872 years ago. Today is but another link in a long chain.
>
> We Jews of Warsaw, sons of those exiles, sit on the ground to mourn our own personal *churban,*[28] the destruction

---

[27]Jacob Sloan, ed. and trans. *Notes from the Warsaw Ghetto: The Journal of Emmanuel Ringelbaum* (New York: Schocken Books, 1974), 126.
[28]destruction

of a major *kehillah*[29]—the largest and most vigorous in Europe—which resulted from that earlier *Churban*.[30] We weep at our fate, a nation without a land, within the grasp of our fiercest enemy and condemned to death. We grieve both for the loss of the Beis Hamikdash[31] and the extinction of our lives. True, our lives were full of suffering, yet we always harbored hopes that will now never be realized. Yes, our lives were tough but despite everything they were still rich and purposeful. Now, however, our enemies scheme to wipe us all off the face of the earth.[32]

THE HISTORY OF THE WESTERN WALL

Tisha B'Av is a day of mourning and despair, but within the sadness of the day there is also a message of hope. That message being that despite much suffering, the Jews will survive and be redeemed as promised by the prophets of old. That message of Tisha B'Av is conveyed in the history of the Western Wall.

The Byzantine emperor Constantine adopted Christianity in the early part of the fourth century. Upon the defeat of the emperor of the east, Licinius at Chrysopolis on September 18, 324 C.E., Constantine became ruler of the Holy Land.

Constantine built churches throughout the land and strongly encouraged the proselytism of Jews. It is theorized that Constantine enacted anti-Jewish laws.[33] He also reinstated legislation of the

---

[29]community

[30]the destruction of the Temple in Jerusalem

[31]holy Temple

[32]Dr. Hillel Seidman, *The Warsaw Ghetto Diaries* (New York/ Jerusalem: Targum/Feldheim, 1997), 55–56.

[33]Michael Avi Yonah, *The Jews Under Roman and Byzantine Rule: A Political History of Palestine from the Bar Kochba Revolt to the Arab Conquest* (Jerusalem: Magnes Press, The Hebrew University, 1975), 165.

Roman emperor Hadrian 117–138 C.E.. Following his suppression of the Bar Kochba Revolt (132–135 C.E.), Hadrian enacted laws that prohibited the entry of Jews into Jerusalem or the surrounding region of Judea. Over time those laws remained on the books but were not enforced by all emperors; many allowed Jewish pilgrimages on the holidays.[34] Constantine reinstated those laws, but with some changes. Jews were again permitted to reside in Judea. In addition, he also allowed the Jews to enter Jerusalem and pray at the Western Wall on one day annually—Tisha B'Av.

Being the last standing wall surrounding the Temple, the Western Wall already possessed a special significance to the Jews. Perhaps the emperor permitted the Jews access to the Western Wall on Tisha B'Av so they could revel in their sufferings and misery; maybe he had the notion that such thoughts would lead them to apostasy. But the sight of the remnant of the Temple gave the Jews hope and a sense of resolve rather than weakening them. They saw it as a sign of strength and took solace upon their annual opportunity to visit the site of their beloved Temple. The Talmudic sages of that era spoke of the special and eternal nature of the Wall. Rabbi Acha stated that the *Shechina*, special Divine Presence of God, will never depart from the Temple's Western Wall. The Midrash cites a quote from Solomon's Song of Songs, "Behold, He stands behind our wall."[35]

The Temple was destroyed, but a part remained. The Western Wall served as a reminder that the Temple could never be totally destroyed. The hope for its rebuilding remained strong in that era and over the centuries. The seemingly minor changes in the laws by Constantine allowed the Jews some solace and inspiration on their day of mourning.

---

[34]Ibid., 164.

[35]"My beloved is like a gazelle or a young hart: behold, he stands behind our wall, he looks in at the windows; he peers through the lattice." Midrash Tanchuma Exodus, 10; Song of Songs; Exodus Raba 2:2.

THE TENTH OF AV: WHILE THE TEMPLE WAS IN FLAMES

Tisha B'Av is preceded by a period of intense mourning for nine days. In commemoration of the destruction of the First and Second Temple, various activities that signify celebration or bring joy, such as listening to music and eating meat or drinking wine cease.[36] However, the mourning doesn't end with the fast day on the ninth of Av; it continues until midday on the tenth of Av. The First and Second Temples were set aflame on Tisha B'Av, but the fires continued to destroy both Temples the following morning as well. That is why many activities prohibited during the nine days are also prohibited on the tenth of Av until midday.[37] The Talmudic sage Rabbi Yochanan stated, "Had I been alive in that generation, I would have fixed [the mourning] for the tenth, because the greater part of the Temple was burnt on that day."[38]

Several events occurred on the tenth of Av that had a profound effect upon the history of the Jews. These events resulted in tragedies of untold proportions to the Jewish people.

Expulsion from France

On July 22, 1306, the tenth of Av, the Jews of France were arrested and ordered to leave the country. The Jewish community was not aware of the planned expulsion because France's king, Phillip the Fair,[39] did not want them to flee in advance with their assets. The monarch's motive for expelling the Jews was to some extent financial. Phillip's fiscal policies played havoc upon the French monetary system[40] and he saw expulsion as the way to shore up

---

[36]*Orach Chaim*, "Laws of Tisha B'Av," sec. 551; *Chayei Adam*, "Laws of Tisha B'Av," ch. 133.
[37]*Orach Chaim*, "Laws of Tisha B'Av," sec. 558, paragraph 1.
[38]Babylonian Talmud, Taanit 29A.
[39]He was given this name due to his appearance.
[40]Simon R. Schwarzfuchs, "The Expulsion of Jews from France

France's economic woes by plundering the wealth of the exiles. No doubt, frustration at centuries of failed attempts to force the Jews into apostasy was also a contributing factor. There had been some expulsions from local provinces in prior years, but this act which expelled Jews from most of France was by far the most significant expulsion to date in medieval Europe. The numbers tell the magnitude of the tragedy. Approximately one hundred thousand, including the young, old, and infirm, were forced to wander in search of new homes; many perished along the way.

Less then ten years later, Louis the X invited the Jews back to France under certain conditions; few returned. The expulsion ended an era of Jewish history that was one of the great eras of Jewish scholarship—that of the Tosaphists of France whose commentaries added great illumination to Talmudic texts. The expulsion also set a precedent for other mass expulsions to follow. Such expulsions plagued the Jews of Europe in the Middle Ages, reinforcing their sense of instability as they were often forced to migrate to different lands.

Barred from England

In the late nineteenth century, England was a haven for tens of thousands of Jews fleeing from oppression in Russia. The immigrants made their way to the east end of London and created a closed Jewish world not unlike the *shtetles* of their former lands. For years, the flow of Eastern European Jews into crowded ghettos in England's cities slowly aroused the opposition of many British lawmakers, especially those who were more conservative. Some as far back as the 1880s dubbed the immigration wave "the alien invasion."[41] There was an atmosphere of opposition to the migrations of Jews from Eastern Europe who were viewed as an outside

1306," ed. A. A. Newman and Solomon Zeitlin, *Jewish Quarterly Review* 75th Anniversary Edition (Philadelphia, 1967): 486.

[41]David Feldman, *Englishmen and Jews: Social Relations and Political Culture 1840–1914* (New Haven/London: Yale University Press, 1994), 281.

element that could not be absorbed into English society, or a "state within a state."[42] As xenophobia heightened, laws were proposed to limit the flow of "aliens" into Great Britain.

On August 11, 1905, the tenth of Av, the Aliens Act was passed. This act entitled an immigration officer the right to deny entry to an "undesirable immigrant," which was defined by the bill as one who had no means of earning a living, one who is judged to be a lunatic, or one who was convicted of a nonpolitical crime. The bill also allowed for the expulsion of those that had already immigrated and were deemed undesirable.

A dark and ominous cloud threatening Jewry would soon appear over Europe. As Nazism rose in the late 1930s, Jews in search of refuge would eventually have to look to areas outside England.[43] However, the legislation had other implications as well. The British legislation was not only the beginning of a policy that would enforce increasingly stricter measures against immigration to England, but it also impacted American immigration policy. When the Alien Act became law, Americans who were dissatisfied with the level of Eastern European immigration looked toward the bill as an example of immigration control. By 1924 with the Johnson Reed Amendment, strong American nativist anti-immigration forces succeeded in restricting the flow of Jews from Eastern Europe. The immigration restrictions remained enforced throughout the era of Nazism and the Holocaust, denying European Jewry that desperately needed sanctuary.

Massacre in the Holy Land: The Closure of Palestine to Jewish Immigrants

On the tenth of Av in the year 1929, Arab hostilities toward Zionism exploded into full-scale riots. The Arabs of Jerusalem were well aware of the significance of the Western Wall to the Jews and

---

[42] Ibid., 295.

[43] After the passage of the Aliens Act, the flow of Jewish immigrants was reduced by forty percent.

used Judaism's holy site as a means to express their opposition to the Balfour Declaration of 1917, which called for a Jewish state in Palestine. On Yom Kippur 1928, the British gave in to an Arab demand to remove the *mechitza*, the divider separating men from women when in prayer. Right in the middle of Yom Kippur services, British soldiers entered the grounds of the Western Wall and removed the *mechitza*.

This event typified the growing sympathy of the British with Arab concerns. The Arabs saw it as a sign of British weakness and complicity toward their demands. Emboldened, the mufti of Jerusalem, Haj Amin Al Husseini, engaged in inflammatory anti-Jewish rhetoric inciting the Arab masses into revolt against the Jews within the land. At the initiative of the mufti's supreme Muslim Council, Arab workers set about building operations around the Wall to disturb Jewish worshippers there.[44] As the issue was argued, the British decided that the construction might continue provided that the Jews were not disturbed during their usual times of prayer.[45] Neither side was satisfied with the decision.

On Tisha B'Av of the next year, members of the Zaev Jabotinsky Youth Movement, Betar, organized a peaceful demonstration. As the pious converged upon the Wall, a contingent of Betar members arrived to protest British policies concerning the Wall. With permission granted by Britian's acting high commissioner Sir Harry Luke and with a police escort, the group came out in support of the right of Jews to pray at the Wall and in protest of the British decision to remove the *mechitza*. An Arab counter-demonstration soon formed as Husseini raised the charge that the Jews were attacking the Muslim holy places. The mufti's charges whipped the masses into a frenzy.[46] At the Western Wall, Jews were attacked as a newly opened door located near the Wall and the

---

[44]Howard Sachar, *A History of Zionism: From the Rise of Zionism in Our Time* (New York: Alfred A Knopf, 1979), 173.
[45]Ibid.
[46]The following day, sporadic attacks against the Jews began around Jerusalem. JTA, "Arabs in Armed Attack on Wailing Wall Area: Injure

Jewish worshippers was made use of by the perpetrators, contrary to British assurances to the contrary.[47] Two were injured and many religious articles were destroyed. On the next day, the seventeenth of August—the eleventh of Av—thousands of Arabs armed with clubs, swords, and daggers converged upon the Mosque of Omar to hear the impassioned speeches by their leaders.[48] Soon the cry "slaughter the Jews" was heard. Over the next few days there were attacks at Mount Scopus and the Bucharian section of Jerusalem where young Abraham Mizrachi was mortally stabbed. An ominous tone was set at Mizrachi's funeral. As angry Jews voiced their protest against British policies, the British responded by attacking mourners. Twenty-six were wounded, one subsequently died. Again the Arabs and their leaders, emboldened by the apparent pro-Arab signals, steadily increased attacks against Jews.

Over the next ten days, rioting would take the lives of 133 Jews, with 339 wounded. When the British police, initially slow to act, finally restored order, it again became more clear that solutions to the conflict between Arab and Jew were not forthcoming.

Throughout the Arab world the conflict and the issue of Jewish settlement, initially overlooked, became a highlighted issue. Massive demonstrations were held throughout Arab countries in sympathy with the Arab cause in Palestine. In Iraq, ten thousand rallied in a mosque in memory of the Arab victims of "British Zionist aggression," and then poured out into the streets in angry demonstration. Such opposition further pressured the British to yield to Arab terms, which demanded they prohibit Jewish immigration into Palestine. The British responded over time with severe restrictions against immigration. The first of the riots, resulting in an increasing wave of anti-Zionist violence and anti-Zionist pressure, began on August 16, 1929—the tenth of Av. On the tenth of

---

Jews, Tear Prayer Books," *Jewish Daily Bulletin* 1444 (August 19, 1929): 1.

[47]Ibid.

[48]"Arab Attacks on Jews Spread over Palestine," *Jewish Tribune* 95, no. 9 (August 30, 1929): 1.

Av, the first major expulsion was enacted in Europe. The events of the day also contributed to the closure of the west to Jewish immigrants, and so, too, the sanctuary of the Land of Israel was denied to the Jews in their greatest hour of need.

A MESSAGE THAT WAS CAPTURED IN JERUSALEM ONE SHABBAT MORNING

The Haftarah (prophetic portion) read on Shabbat Nachamu, the Sabbath of Comfort which follows Tisha B'Av, expresses the message of conciliation expressed by the prophet Isaiah to a nation that would endure a prolonged exile. In the Old City of Jerusalem in 1920, a particular event on Shabbat Nachamu captured the essence of its theme.

During the First World War, the British government foresaw their victory over Turkish forces in Palestine as imminent and issued the Balfour Declaration supporting Jewish aspirations for a Jewish Homeland. Not long after the declaration was issued, opposition mounted from members of Britain's government and military administration who were against Zionism. However, the British government was under the leadership of the staunch Zionist Lloyd George, who was determined to stand by the Declaration. George appointed a Jew and Zionist, Sir Herbert Samuel, as the first British high commissioner of Palestine. Samuel's appointment signified the beginning of the British mandate over Palestine.

On July 1, 1920, Samuel disembarked a British battleship at the port of Haifa as the new commissioner or, as his biographer put it, "the first Jewish ruler in Palestine since Hyrcanus the second" (whose reign ended 40 B.C.E.)[49] Samuel seemed to be the answer to the Zionists' prayers. A Zionist leader, Arthur Ruppin, described in

---

[49]John Bowle, *Viscount Samuel: A Biography* (London: Gollancz, 1957), quoted in Conor Cruise O'Brien, *The Siege: The Saga of Israel and Zionism* (New York: Simon and Schuster, 1986), 155.

his diary the ceremony held nine days later on the Mount of Olives in honor of Samuel's appointment. "Until now, pronouncements about a Jewish National Home . . . had only been words on paper; but now they rose before us embodied in the person of a Jewish High Commissioner. . . . Many of the Jews present had tears in their eyes."[50]

Just a few weeks later, on the morning of Shabbat Nachamu, Samuel set out on foot toward the famous Churva Synagogue in the Old City of Jerusalem. Surrounded by an entourage of advisors and guards, he entered the Old City's Jaffa Gate and headed toward the Jewish Quarter. As he entered, spectators gathered on the streets, which were adorned with flowers, to glimpse the man who represented their highest hopes and dreams. As he passed by, the onlookers cheered and expressions of joy resonated. A sense of euphoria quickly came over the crowd.[51]

Samuel entered the Churva Synagogue where there was not an empty seat. He had arrived prepared to chant the Haftarah. Soon the *gabbai* (sexton) summoned him to the Torah, calling out the familiar words *Ya'amod HaNasi Ha'Elyon* (may the High Commissioner arise). As Samuel stood up, the entire congregation also rose to their feet in a show of respect and admiration. Samuel made his way to the *bimah* (platform from which the Torah is read) and proceeded to recite the blessings over the Torah and then the blessings over the Haftarah. The British high commissioner began chanting the Haftarah, echoing the words of Isaiah, which express the hopes and dreams of the nation. "Comfort, comfort My people, says God. Speak to her heart of Jerusalem and proclaim to her that her time [of exile] has been fulfilled, that her iniquity has been conciliated, for she has received for the Hand of God double for all

---

[50]Arthur Ruppin, *Memoirs, Diaries, Letters* (New York: Herzyl Press, 1971), 186.
[51]*Pillar of Fire: The Jew Returns and the Arab Awakens*, Gideon Dror, dir., Rachia Wellner, ed., The History Channel, 1995, videocassette.

her sins."[52] The entire congregation shuttered upon hearing the words that embodied their greatest hopes and dreams. It was a moment of intense emotion. An aid to Samuel described the scene as "a golden moment where the Jews in the synagogue felt as if the hour of redemption had arrived."[53]

Unfortunately, Samuel did not live up to the people's hopes and expectations. Despite his devotion to Zionism, he was caught between two sides. As Arab riots increased and pressure against the Zionists intensified in British circles, Samuel made concessions to the Arabs and their British sympathizers. Jewish immigration restrictions were imposed and Haj Amin Al Husseini—a vehement anti-Zionist and later an open supporter of Nazism—was appointed by Samuel to the position of *mufti* (religious interpreter) of Jerusalem. A British policy of appeasement was set into motion. The restoration of the Land to the Jewish people would be a slow arduous process fixed with obstacles.

However, the course of events did not change the impression of that Shabbat Nachamu morning. That morning was a special moment that would live forever in the memories of those present. It was a moment that belonged not to the messenger, but to the message—the age-old message of hope brought on Shabbat Nachamu.

---

[52]Isaiah 40:1–2.
[53]Dror and Wellner, *Pillar of Fire.*

6

Tu B'Av

THE FAIRS OF POLAND: WHERE MATCHES WERE MADE

To make a successful match is cause for great joy. Tu B'Av is generally known as the Jewish "Sadie Hawkins Day." It is a time when matchmakers are busy applying their trade. Weddings are also often held on that day. The Talmud states that both Yom Kippur and Tu B'Av were the most joyous days of the year, for on those days the young women of Jerusalem would don borrowed white garments (in order not to shame those who owned none) and dance in the vineyards chanting "Young man, lift up your eyes and see what you choose for yourself. Do not set your eyes on beauty, but set your eyes on a good family."[1]

In earlier times, there were different settings for the making of matches. In those days, matches were often made at fairs where the multitudes gathered. In the book *Yeven Metzula* by Rabbi Nathan Nata Hanover, the author describes how thousands con-

[1]Babylonian Talmud, Taanit 26B.

verged upon the fair in Poland in the years prior to the Chmielnicki massacres (1648–1649). The open fairs of the summer were held on the seaside villages of Zaslow and Yerislav and attracted great numbers of people.[2] The fair was a place for socializing, conducting business, and relaxation. It served as a brief respite from the difficulties of life.

Tu B'Av marked the end of the summer sessions in the yeshivas of Poland and thousands of students would converge upon the fair with their instructors. There, they studied with students from other yeshivas.

Naturally, the fair was also an ideal place for networking and the arrangement of marriages. Rabbi Hanover wrote, "Whoever had a son or daughter of marriageable age journeyed to the fair, and there arranged a match. There was ample opportunity for everyone to find their type and suit.[3]. . . . hundreds and sometimes thousands of such matches would be arranged at the fair."[4]

A rabbinical ruling was issued regarding matchmaking at fairs. A convention of Poland's rabbinical leadership, the Council of the Four Lands, which met at a fair in Lublin, Poland, in 1580, ruled that the payment of more than one fee to the matchmaker (for a successful match) was prohibited, even if more than one matchmaker was involved. They further stipulated that the fee would be set according to the means of the families of the bethrothed.[5]

The fairs in Poland were a substitute for the open fields in biblical times. The times, circumstances, and locations in which marriages were arranged have frequently changed over time and they continue to change. Diverse situations, however, offer the same opportunities for those in search of their *bashert* (destined one) and allow for the continuity of the Jewish people.

---

[2]Rabbi Nathan Nata Hanover, *Yeven Metzulah (Abyss of Despair)* (Hahistadrut Haclalit Shel Haovdim B'Eretz Yisrael, 1944), 63.
[3]Ibid., 63.
[4]Ibid.
[5]Shmuel A. Arthur Cygielman, *Jewish Autonomy in Poland and Lithuania until 1649* (Jerusalem: Zalman Shazar Center for the Furtherance of the Study of Jewish History, 1991), 263.

A DAY OF RESTORATION

Tu B'Av, which follows Tisha B'Av by just six days, is a contrast to the sadness of Tisha B'Av. Tu B'Av is a day of joy, and the events that occurred on Tu B'Av throughout history reflect that joy and signify the theme of restoration.

The Israelites paid heed to the negative report of ten of the twelve spies that questioned the feasibility of their mission into the Promised Land on Tisha B'Av; they wailed and bemoaned their fate forgetting the Almighty's promise to bring them into the land.[6] As punishment, all the men aged 20 and up, except those from the tribe of Levy and the spies Joshua and Caleb, were condemned to die in the wilderness and would not enter the promised land.[7] On the last Tu B'Av of the Israelite's sojourn in the wilderness, the deaths resulting from the "sin of the spies" had ended.[8] As on Yom Kippur, when Moses returned to the people with a second set of tablets and announced to the people that they were forgiven,[9] likewise that Tu B'Av was a sign of Divine forgiveness.

Yeravam ben Nevat who reigned over Israel from 928–907 B.C.E. was the first king to lead the kingdom of Israel, which had split off from Judea. Yeravam was a learned man but also one of great ambitions. When he participated in a failed revolt against King Solomon (before the national split), he fled to Egypt. Upon hearing of the king's death, he returned. King Solomon's son and heir to the throne, Rehaboam, levied high taxes from the people. The funds were needed, but high taxation, whether in ancient or modern times, will often leave a political leader with a popularity problem. It also helps the political opposition. Yeravam seized upon the issue of taxation. He approached the king, addressing the people's grievances: "Your father made our yoke hard. Now lighten

---

[6]Numbers 24.
[7]Numbers 14:23; Deuteronomy 1:35.
[8]Babylonian Talmud, Baba Batra 121:A.
[9]Rashi's Commentary on Deuteronomy 18:13 and on Exodus 33:11. Midrash Tanchuma, Parshat KiTisa, no. 31.

your father's hard work and his heavy yoke which he placed upon us, and we shall serve you."[10] Rehaboam approached his father's advisors and asked them how he should respond. They answered that he should address them in a conciliatory manner with kind and respectful words and that would win the people's loyalty, "then they will serve you for all time."[11] Rehaboam unwisely disregarded their counsel and chose to listen to his own younger advisors who recommended that he respond harshly to Yeravam's requests.[12] He told the people, "I shall add to your yoke, my father flogged you with whips and I will flog you with scorpions."[13] The ten tribes of northern Israel responded to Rehaboam's words by seceding from the House of David. The nation was now divided between Judea in the south and the Israelite kingdom of the ten tribes to the north.

As the king of the newly separated kingdom of Israel, Yeravam's true motives became clear. Well aware that the thrice annual pilgrimages by the Israelites to the capital city of Jerusalem located within the kingdom of Judea would result in his being dethroned or perhaps assassinated, he prohibited those pilgrimages. In its place he set up two altars and golden calves, one in the city of Dan and the other in Beit El, resembling the golden calves the Israelites had fashioned at Mount Sinai. Although his original intentions were for the altars to serve as alternatives to the Temple Service in Jerusalem, they were soon used for idolatrous practices as those resembling the heathen practices of the Gentiles around them.[14] Well aware that the people were still attached to Jerusalem and would continue to make the pilgrimages, Yeravam stationed guards at the roadways as he closed off those roads leading to Jerusalem.[15] In addition, he postponed the holiday of Succot by one month so the people would travel to the altars of Dan and Beit El and not be tempted to go to

[10]1 Kings 12:4.
[11]Ibid., 12:7.
[12]Ibid., 12:10–11.
[13]Ibid., 12:14.
[14]Ibid., 12:29, Radak (Rabbi David Kimchi).
[15]Talmud Bavli, Baba Batra 121B.

the Temple in Jerusalem. By such changes, Yeravam hoped to sever the people's connection to Jerusalem.

For years to come, the Israelites traveled to Dan and Beit El on pilgrimages where they immersed themselves in the ways of idolatry and the heathen. This continued with the ascension to the throne of Hosea ben Elah, the last king of the kingdom of Israel.[16] However, Hosea broke ranks with his predecessors and removed the guards posted on the roads to Jerusalem, opening Jerusalem to pilgrims from the north.[17] The day he did this was Tu B'Av.[18]

Such a move could have sparked a national revival. A reconnection of the people to their capital. It could have led to a reunion of the kingdoms. Instead it turned out to be a lost opportunity. The king gave the people the option to go to Jerusalem but he did not mandate its requirement. By then, the people were immersed in idolatrous ways and were far removed from Jerusalem spiritually. Thus, they overlooked the opportunity and, instead, continued to bow down to false gods and heathen altars. A great moment turned out to be a great disappointment.[19]

Almost one thousand years later, the Roman emperor Hadrian ruthlessly suppressed the Bar Kochba Revolt, forcing the fleeing Judeans into the fortress of Betar—a city several miles south of Jerusalem. The Jews in Betar held out until the Romans entered the city (on Tisha B'Av) and proceeded with the city's conquest while brutally putting the Judeans to the sword. Following the carnage, tens of thousands lay dead on the open fields of Judea. Afterwards, Hadrian, who sought any means to humiliate and degrade the Jews, prohibited their burial. It was not until the ascent of the next emperor, Antoninus Pius (138–161 C.E.) that burial was finally permitted. That day, too, was Tu B'Av.[20] According to the Talmud,

[16]Vanquished eighth century B.C.E.
[17]Babylonian Talmud, Taanit 30B.
[18]Ibid.
[19]Jerusalem Talmud, Taanit 4:7.
[20]Babylonian Talmud, Baba Batra 121A.

the corpses of the slain miraculously did not decay over the years.[21] On that Tu B'Av, respect was given to the remains of Judea's martyrs and the spirits of the survivors of Hadrian's destruction, the remnants of the defeated nation of Judea, were rejuvenated as they finally buried their kin.

Over one thousand years later, in the twelfth century, religious fanaticism arose in North Africa threatening the stability of neighboring countries. The Almohades (Unitarians), a Muslim religious and political movement under the leadership of Oped al Mumin that originated in the Atlas Mountains of North Africa, sought to spread Islam by force and they began to conquer vast territories throughout North Africa.[22] In the conquered territories, they initiated inquisitions and persecutions against both Jews and Christians, many of whom were given the choice of conversion or death. The more the Almohades conquered, the more havoc they caused. At the height of their empire, they controlled North Africa and the southern half of Spain. The Almohade threat prompted thousands of Jews to flee to the Christian controlled northern half of Spain and to France. Among those who fled was the family of Moses Maimonides, who left Cordoba, Spain, in 1165 and traveled to Fez, Morocco, which was not yet under Almohade control. At the height of their power, the Almohades sent tremors into the Jewish communities who were in a high state of alert in fear of being overrun. But soon their fears would be calmed. On Tu B'Av, July 16, 1212, the Almohades were defeated in battle in Las Navas, Spain, and their power was broken.

The Battle at Las Navas marked the beginning of their decline. Afterwards, independent kingdoms were established in their place and Jewish communities could again practice their Judaism in the open within a more tolerant atmosphere. On that Tu B'Av, Jewish communities were relieved of a great menace. For the next 150

---

[21]Babylonian Talmud, Baba Batra 121A.
[22]*Encyclopedia Judaica* (Jerusalem: The Macmillan Co., Keter Publishing House, 1972), 2:663.

years, Spanish Jewry experienced an era in which the freedoms granted allowed them to achieve great heights, all in part from the result of a battle fought on Tu B'Av.

In another part of the world far away from Spain, over four hundred years later, the Jewish community of Cochin, India, was in dire need of religious items. Such supplies were necessary to help maintain proper ritual observance, as well as to educate the next generation.

In 1662, the Portuguese, who had controlled the region for one hundred years, swept into Cochin from nearby Cranganore, murdering, plundering, and destroying homes and synagogues. That year, the Dutch (who were friendly toward the Jews) failed in an attempt to take the city, which only worsened the plight of their allies, Cochin's Jews. The Portuguese vented out their wrath upon them and again the Jews of Cochin faced grave dangers. But less than a year later, the Dutch took control of Cochin and were naturally welcomed by the Jewish community as heroes. Their rule ushered in an era of tranquility for the Jews.

Almost immediately, communication was established between the Jews of Holland and Cochin. The Jews of Cochin comprised two small communities. Each community lived different lives and was separated from one another. One community was referred to as the "White Jews" because of their lighter complexion, while the other community was called Malabari or "Black Jews." The White Jews had migrated from European lands, which accounted for their lighter complexion, while the Malabari were most probably from Arabian lands. The dark appearance of the Malibari was also a result of the native Indians who had converted to Judaism and joined their ranks. The Dutch rabbi, Menashe ben Israel, described the Jews of Cochin as having four synagogues—one, the Paradesi, for the white community, the other three for the black Jews.[23]

When both communities lived under Portuguese rule, supplies

---

[23]In an appeal for readmission of Jews expelled from England, submitted to Oliver Cromwell in late October–early November 1655.

of religious articles were sparse due to their relative isolation and their persecution by the Portuguese. When the Dutch took control, the Malabari appealed to the Jewish communities of the Arabian Peninsula for help, while the White Jews, who had built a strong connection to Holland's Jews, appealed to the Dutch for religious materials. Their appeals were soon answered.

The response to the White Jew's appeal was answered with a shipment from Holland consisting of a supply of Torahs, books of Jewish law, copies of the Talmud and other religious items such as *tefilin* and *mezuzahs*. The day of the shipment's arrival was Tu B'Av 1686.[24] Other shipments would follow. The White Jews of the Paradesi synagogue began to celebrate Tu B'Av and the following seven days as a minor festival. This festival celebrated a time when desperately needed books and religious items reached them.

On that Tu B'Av in 1686, a community was provided the means to build a future. Over time the Jewish community of Cochin, which numbered several hundred families, would increase. By the twentieth century, the Jews of Cochin numbered several thousand, many of whom would make *Aliyah* after the establishment of the State of Israel.

Just as many tragedies occurred on Tisha B'Av, many joyful days and events occurred on Tu B'Av. Tu B'Av is a day of restoration and a day of rebuilding. Just days after the destruction of the Temple is mourned, a celebration arrives that reinforces hope for the future.

---

[24]J. B. Segal, *A History of the Jews of Cochin* (London: Valentine Mitchell, 1993), 44.

7

Rosh Hashanah

TRUE REPENTANCE

Rosh Hashanah is a time for personal introspection. A time to assess one's deeds. On one particular Rosh Hashanah, the Jewish people assembled in Jerusalem and collectively reflected upon their misdeeds. On that Day of Judgement, the Jews stood together before their Heavenly Judge. The positive direction that the nation took on that Rosh Hashanah greatly impacted the future of the Jewish people.

In 538 B.C.E., the Jews of Babylonia, who had been exiled in the years prior to the destruction of the Temple (586 B.C.E.) and following the destruction, were living under a new empire. Persia engulfed Babylonia and King Cyrus of Persia granted the Jews the right to return to Judea, rebuild the Temple, and restore the nation in its land. He issued the following proclamation: "So says Cyrus King of Persia. All the kingdoms of earth had Hashem, God of heaven, delivered to me and He has commanded me to build Him a Temple in Jerusalem, which is in Judea. Anyone among you of His entire people, may his God be with him, let him go up to Jerusalem which is in Judea, and build the Temple of Hashem, God of Israel—He is the God!—which is in Jerusalem."[1]

In total, 42,360 Jews answered the call and went to Judea.[2] Although opponents of the establishment of a Jewish commonwealth interfered and prompted the next Perisan king, Darius, to suspend construction of the Temple, it was completed by 517 B.C.E., fulfilling the biblical prophesy that the exile would last seventy years.[3] In Judea, there was already a large community of Jews who were not exiled.

A scribe and eminent Torah scholar named Ezra, who was also head of the Anshei Knesset HaGedolah,[4] [Men of the Great Assembly] remained for some time in Babylonia until the death of his teacher Baruch ben Neriah, who was too weak to make the trip.[5] "He left for Judea with the king's approval and the king's protection accompanied by fifteen hundred Jewish returnees to Zion"[6] and arrived after a four-month journey.[7] When Ezra arrived, the Second Temple had already been rebuilt.[8]

In Judea, Ezra was informed of the decay of religious observance in the land; the Jews gave little financial support to the Temple as well. Even more distressing was the news of widespread intermarriage. Even the son of the high priest had a Gentile wife.[9] Dismayed, Ezra realized that the new Jewish State was in rapid decline. Out of a sense of urgency, he called for an assembly in Jerusalem. There Ezra rebuked the people: "You have transgressed

---

[1]Ezra 1:2–5.
[2]Ezra 2:64.
[3]Jeremiah 25:11–12.
[4]The 120-member legislative body of the Jewish people that was composed of the most eminent Torah scholars.
[5]Shir HaShirim Raba 5:5; Babylonian Talmud, Megillah 16B.
[6]Ezra 7:14 and 7:26. Ezra arrived in the seventh year of the reign of Cyrus' successor Darius.
[7]Ibid., 7:9. He left in the month of Nissan and arrived in Av.
[8]Rashi's and Metzudot Tzion's commentary on Ezra 7:1.
[9]Ezra 10:18.

and harbored alien wives, adding to Israel's iniquity. Now, confess before Hashem, God of your forefathers, and perform His will." Ezra then asked the men who had intermarried to sever their ties with their families: "separate yourselves from the peoples of the land and from alien wives."[10]

It was a harsh request, yet the people responded in acquiescence: "True, we must do as you say."[11] Ezra motivated the masses of Judea to return to the observance of the laws of the Torah. In the attempt to ensure that the changes were lasting and not merely temporary, he instituted *takkanot* (decrees) aimed at preserving Jewish families and ensuring observance of the Sabbath and other Jewish rites. However, Ezra had no police force at his disposal and could not enforce the laws. Thus, over some time, the people reverted back to their old ways. For the next twenty years Judea continued in its decline.

When Nehemia, a cupbearer of the king, heard of the dismal state of affairs in Judea, he received permission from the king to go and act as military governor of Judea. In Judea, Nehemia went about the task of building the walls around Jerusalem and ensuring that the markets were closed on the Sabbath and that the people contributed to the upkeep of the Temple. In 444 B.C.E. Nehemia and Ezra again summoned the masses to Jerusalem.

The masses of Judeans assembled at the "Water Gate" on Rosh Hashanah.[12] The purpose of the assemblage, as was the prior assembly, was to inspire the Judeans to mend their ways and commit themselves to a Jewish future. Ezra stood before the nation and prepared to read the Torah out loud. "And Ezra opened the Torah scroll before the eyes of the entire people, for he was above all the people, [on a platform] and when he opened it, all the people stood. And Ezra blessed the Lord, the great God and the [people] answered 'Amen, Amen,' with the uplifting of their hands, and they

---

[10]Ibid., 10:10–11.
[11]Ibid., 10:12.
[12]Nehemia 8:1.

bent their heads and prostrated themselves to the Lord on their faces to the ground."[13]

From the early morning hours, Ezra read the Torah to the masses.[14] There, Ezra inspired the people and instilled in them a sense of awe.[15] Those who did not understand the Torah reading heard translations given by Ezra, Nehemia, the priests, and Levites.[16] Inspired by the event, the people reflected upon their past misdeeds and lack of piety. The mood turned melancholy as the people openly wept.[17] Seeing the genuine regret of the people and their outpouring of emotion, Ezra reminded them that the day was Rosh Hashanah, a holiday. "Today is a holy day to the Lord your God; neither mourn nor weep."[18] And he told them, "Go, eat fat foods and drink sweet drinks and send portions to whoever has nothing prepared, for the day is holy to our Lord, and do not be sad, for the joy of the Lord is your strength."[19] It was Rosh Hashanah, a day to be confident in God's judgement.

The following day, the second day of Rosh Hashanah, the people returned to learn and understand more of their Jewish heritage. They gathered to hear the explanations of the sages. There they were reminded of the importance of the observance of the upcoming Succot holiday and were instructed to prepare *Succot* (booths) for the holiday.

On that Rosh Hashanah, a dramatic change had taken place. The groundwork for the second Jewish commonwealth was paved. A massive festival of repentance preceded the coming era of the second Temple. Not only did the event occur on Rosh Hashanah, but also on that day—which signifies a specific time for personal examination and spiritual renewal—the community examined itself

---

[13]Ibid., 8:5–6.
[14]Ibid., 8:3.
[15]Ibid., 8:8.
[16]Rashi's commentary on Nehemia 9:9.
[17]Nehemia 8:9.
[18]Ibid., 9:9.
[19]Ibid., 9:10.

and earnestly reflected its deeds. They didn't just regret their misdeeds, their outpouring of emotion and their readiness for change signified the beginnings of a new era. That day was the quintessential Rosh Hashanah. One that helped to shape the future of the Jewish people.

NEW BEGINNINGS

Rosh Hashanah, the New Year, signifies new beginnings in Jewish history and in the history of the world. According to tradition, Adam and Eve were created on Rosh Hashanah.[20] Rosh Hashanah also represented a new beginning for several major Jewish communities throughout history.

The first Jews to arrive in America, which set the stage for the establishment of future Jewish communities, came from lands of persecution in search of sanctuary. Many of the Jews who immigrated to America first settled in the port city of Recife, Brazil, which was under the control of the tolerant Dutch during the seventeenth century. In 1634, the Dutch states general issued a proclamation guaranteeing freedom of religion to Jews and Catholics in Brazil.[21] It was a haven amidst a "New World" that, predominately under Catholic rule, was replete with inquisitions and *auto-da-fe* (act of faith). When the Dutch captured Recife in 1624, a city now existed where Jews could openly proclaim their allegiance to Judaism without persecution. The many Jews who were living as Morranos in the region immediately ended their secrecy.

Recife became a haven for small groups of Jews from both Ashkenazi and Sephardi backgrounds who arrived there in their

---

[20]Babylonian Talmud, Sanhedrin 38B.

[21]Abraham P. Bloch, *One a Day: An Anthology of Jewish Historical Anniversaries for Every Day of the Year* (Hoboken: Ktav Publishing House, 1987), 65.

search for freedom. They left behind the horrors of the past and built a community with several synagogues, the largest among them named Tzur Israel—Rock of Israel. It was their continual search for sanctuary that would soon lead some of Recife's Jews to the shores of New York (then New Amsterdam) and the formation of the first Jewish community in North America. The Jews, in fact, were the first group in America to struggle for its freedom.

The sanctuary Jews found in Recife ended in 1654, when the Portuguese captured Recife. According to Portuguese policy, the residence of professed Jews was prohibited. They offered the Jews terms that permitted them to remain in Recife for three months. The agreement stated that "those subjects who did not desire to remain in Recife and Mauricia could remain in Brazil for three months [from January 26, 1654 on]."[22] Considering Portuguese treatment of Jews elsewhere, these were very generous terms. The community possessed no Morranos,[23] so they were permitted to leave. The few who chose baptism remained.

Many families left Dutch Brazil for Holland, others went to Surinam on the northern coast of South America, which already possessed a Jewish community that would in ten years increase immensely. However, some had other plans. A few groups of Jews planned to travel to North America. One group of twenty-three left Recife on the boat *Valck* bound for Martinique, beginning a most arduous journey. They encountered adverse winds and were driven off-course to Spanish-held Jamaica.[24] In Jamaica, this small group had to prove that they never accepted baptism; therefore, they were not subject to the inquisition and permitted to leave. They found a small vessel, the *Sainte Catherine*, and sailed to New Amsterdam.

---

[22]Arnold Wiznitzer, *The Exodus From Brazil and Arrival in New Amsterdam of the Jewish Pilgrim Fathers, 1654* (Philadelphia: American Jewish Historical Society, December, 1954), XLIV:282.

[23]Article six in terms of capitulation between the defeated Dutch and the victorious Portuguese. Quoted in Wiznitzer, *The Exodus From Brazil*, 44:82.

[24]Ibid., 44:94.

The entire journey took about four months. They arrived in New Amsterdam in late August 1654.

The group consisted of four men, six women, and thirteen children.[25] Upon arriving in New Amsterdam, they found a few other Jews already there.[26] They were also recent arrivals. On Rosh Hashanah, September 12, 1654, the adult men, along with their Bar Mitzvah-aged sons and the few others who were present, assembled for the first services held in New York.[27] Members of the congregation Tzur Yisrael of Recife were now transplanted to New Amsterdam and became a part of the beginning of the first congregation in America—Shearit Yisrael (Remnant of Israel).

In their search for freedom, twenty-three Jews in transit found what seemed to be a safe haven in New Amsterdam. They did have to contend with the local governor, Peter Stuyvesant, who attempted to deny them citizenship and ordered them to leave. However, with the help of the Dutch West India Company, the Jews of New Amsterdam prevailed and were allowed to remain on the condition that they provide for the needy among the Jewish community. Soon, more Jews arrived in America from all corners of the globe.

Rosh Hashanah was the first holiday celebrated by the Jewish community of New Amsterdam (known as New York by 1664) and it marked the establishment of American Jewry. In time, their discovery would eventually draw millions of Jews seeking the same relief from oppression that they had found.

ROSH HASHANAH IN ENGLAND: ONE YEAR LATER

As New Amsterdam's Jewish community assembled for Rosh Hashanah prayers, the Jewish community of England was in the

[25]Ibid., 44:92.
[26]Ibid., 44:92.
[27]Ibid.

process of reestablishing itself. On July 18, 1290, all the Jews were expelled from England by order of King Edward I. Three hundred and fifty (350) years later, a petition was filed for their readmittance. During the latter portion of that time, there were small groups of Morranos in England who had fled Spain and Portugal. They came to England with the hope of finding a place of refuge for themselves and others in need. That was also the hope of Menasseh ben Israel (1604–1657), a rabbinic scholar from Amsterdam who was born a Morrano in Madeira, Portugal. Menasseh ben Israel fervently sought the admittance of Jews to England for other reasons as well. He believed that it would bring the redemption of the Jews closer by completing the dispersion of the Jews to the "ends of the Earth," as is foretold in the Bible.[28] The Bible states that the imminent redemption of the Jews would occur following their complete dispersion.[29]

In 1650, ben Israel commenced a campaign with the publication of the document *Hope of Israel*, which contained his messianic views. It was intended for the English Parliament.[30] The Lord Protector of England, Oliver Cromwell, was likely to be receptive due to his tolerant nature and puritan views of the Bible. Menasseh ben Israel, aware of the possibilities, opened up conversations with the English mission, St. John, in Amsterdam. He then filed a formal petition in October 1651.[31] Cromwell headed the committee appointed to deal with the matter, and two passports were sent to ben Israel to come to England and discuss the matter with them.[32] Before he could leave, however, war broke out between Spain and England and he consented to his family's pleas not to go.

At the war's conclusion, ben Israel was not able to make the

---

[28]Deuteronomy 26:24.
[29]Deuteronomy 26:24.
[30]*The Jewish Historical Socity of England, Sessions 1924–1927* (London: Spottiswoode, Ballantyne, and Company, LTD., 1928), IX:117.
[31]Ibid., IX:117.
[32]Ibid., IX:117.

journey due to illness. His brother-in-law, Manuel Martinez Dormido, and his son, Samuel Soeiro, went in his stead. It is a matter of history that Cromwell favorably received the two, but the Council of State rejected their requests on December 5, 1654.[33] When his son returned to tell ben Israel the news, despite illness and opposition by family, the determined ben Israel departed for England on September 2, 1655. Following an eloquent appeal presented to the Lord Protector on December 4 of that year, a council of notables met to consider the question.[34] The judge decided that there was no statute to keep the Jews from entering the country. However, the opposition was strong and they demanded conversion to Christianity as a prerequisite to the Jews' admittance.[35] Menasseh ben Israel's trip did not appear successful but, in actuality, it softened the opposition.

The following March, the Morranos within London presented a new petition asking only for the right to a burial ground and the right to observe their religious rites and ceremonies. This request was granted—a non de-facto recognition of the Jews of England.

Their achievement fell short of ben Israel's expectations, but it did ensure the continuation of Jewish life in England and protect their religious rights as well. Over time more Jews would stream into England. The official readmittance of Jews was inevitable. It can be said that ben Israel's efforts were ultimately successful. He plowed the road that others paved.

Just as Rosh Hashanah 1654 was one of great significance for the Jews of New Amsterdam, so, too, was Rosh Hashanah one year later for England's Jews. In 1655, Menasseh ben Israel arrived in England just before the Jewish New Year, which began that year on October 2. According to the Jewish Historical Society of England, it is probable that he organized the first openly held Rosh

---

[33]Ibid., IX:118.
[34]*Encyclopedia Judaica* (Jerusalem: The Macmillan Co., Keter Publishing House, 1972), 6:752.
[35]Ibid., 6:753.

Hashanah services and delivered a sermon. Even if this was not so, that Rosh Hashanah was of great significance to the Jews of England because a dignitary arrived as an advocate on their behalf just prior to the holiday. If there could be one date that marks the decisive point in the gradual resettlement of Jews in England, Rosh Hashanah 1655 would suffice.[36]

THE RAMBAN SYNAGOGUE: HOPE AMIDST DESPAIR

A great rabbinic luminary of the thirteenth century, the Ramban,[37] revived Jerusalem's diminishing Jewish community. His contributions toward rejuvenating Jewish life in the Holy City are everlasting. The day of the opening of the synagogue, which marked the Jewish community's revival, was Rosh Hashanah—the day of Creation, the day of beginnings.

The Ramban lived during an era when the land of Israel was in a state of chaos following a series of conquests. Armies frequently swept over the land wreaking devastation as they fought for its control. The greatest prize—Jerusalem—suffered most. Waves of conquerors repeatedly sacked Jerusalem. From the Crusades in 1099 to Saladin in 1187 to Frederick the Second in 1229 to the Mongols in 1259 to the conquering Egyptian Mamelukes a year later in 1260, little remained of the once magnificent city.

The Mongol invasion was amongst the worst, leaving Jerusalem a city of ruins. Prior to the invasion, some Jews fled; most of those that remained were killed. A year later, the Egyptian Mamelukes, who were more tolerant, captured Jerusalem and allowed Jews to live in the city; only a trickle returned.

In 1267, the Ramban made *Aliyah.* Aware of the dismal situation in the Holy Land, he already planned Jerusalem's revival

---

[36]*The Jewish Historical Society of England*, 118.
[37]Rabbi Moshe ben Nachman (Nachmanides), 1195–1270.

before he arrived. Just before his departure from his native Spain, the Ramban delivered a sermon during the holiday of Shmini Atzeret on the Book of Ecclesiastes. He spoke about the eternal holiness of the Land of Israel and then immediately proceeded to speak of the importance of giving charity.[38] He was, perhaps, preparing his congregants to support the building of religious institutions within Jerusalem and the land of Israel.

After a long and perilous journey, the Ramban, over seventy years old, arrived in the port city of Acco. After a brief stay in this city, the Ramban left for Jerusalem and arrived on the ninth day of the month of Elul.[39] As he approached the city's gate he tore his clothes in mourning over the destruction of the Temple in accordance with Jewish law. The Ramban entered the city and saw its desolation as he recited passages from the Psalms and the Book of Lamentations. As he approached the Western Wall, he again tore his clothes while uttering the 79th Psalm, "Nations have come within Your inheritance defiled Your Holy sanctuary and they have laid Jerusalem in heaps."[40]

In a letter to his son, Nachman, regarding the situation in Jerusalem, he wrote, "Many are its forsaken places, and great are the wastes. The more sacred the place the greater devastation it has suffered. Jerusalem is the most desolate place of all." There was virtually no Jewish community left in Jerusalem. The Ramban continued, "There are two brother dyers by trade . . . There are ten men who meet and on the Sabbaths they hold service at their home." But amidst the sorrow, he saw hope adding, "But even in its destruction it is an exceedingly good land."[41]

Immediately, he began to revive Jerusalem. He chose one of

---

[38]Ramban (Nachmanides), *Writings and Discources*, trans. Rabbi Dr. Charles B. Chavel (New York: Shilo Publishing House Inc., 1978) Ramban, *Discourses on the Book of Ecclesiastes*, 212–215.
[39]The Ramban's personal account, which is found in *Kitvei HaRamban (Writings of the Ramban)* (Avrahaim Ya'ari, *Igrot Eretz Yisrael*).
[40]Psalms 79:1.
[41]Avraham Ya'ari, *Igrot Eretz Yisrael* (Tel Aviv: Gazit, 1952), 85.

the many ruined houses in Mount Zion—one which possessed marble pillars and a beautiful arch—and began constructing a synagogue. In just three weeks, the synagogue was in use, just in time for Rosh Hashanah. Torah scrolls that had been removed from the city before the Mongol invasion eight years earlier were brought to the synagogue. Word of the Ramban's presence in Jerusalem brought some new residents. On Rosh Hashanah, he delivered a sermon urging the new arrivals to remain in Jerusalem. Once again, there was a Jewish community in the Holy City.

The next task was to set up a yeshiva in Jerusalem. This would attract students from around the land and other countries as well and further enlarge the community. As expected, students came to Jerusalem to study with the revered scholar, teacher, and leader.

Over time, the Jewish community of Jerusalem steadily grew and it was once again the center of Jewish life in Israel. Around the year 1400 the synagogue was relocated north of Mount Zion. Sephardim and Ashkenazim prayed and studied together in the Ramban Synagogue until the spring of 1588 when the local Muslim judge prohibited the use of the synagogue. For the next 380 years the building was used as a workshop.[42] By then, however, the Jewish community was well established.

In one year, the Ramban built a Jewish community that would continue until the Jordanian occupation of the Old City in 1948. A year after he reestablished the Jewish community in Jerusalem, the Ramban returned to Acco to lead the congregation there until his death two years later.

Rosh Hashanah that year marked the reestablishment of Jerusalem's Jewish community. Today, the Ramban Synagogue is again in use. Its presence serves as a reminder of that early settlement which—diminutive though it was—preceded the many to follow; the synagogue stands as a cornerstone to the modern city of Jerusalem.

---

[42]The synagogue was reopened in 1967.

ROSH HASHANAH IN NAZI-OCCUPPIED DENMARK

On the eve of Rosh Hashanah 1943, an entire Jewish community was hidden by their neighbors from those who sought their annihilation. When Yom Kippur arrived members of that community were safe, at arms length from danger.

Adolph Hitler felt a kinship with the people of Denmark because of their common Nordic background. But he was very mistaken. In reality, the Danes and the Germans shared little in common. They were, in fact, worlds apart. The Danes proved themselves to be humanitarians and heroes in a world of apathy and indifference toward Hitler's victims.

On April 9, 1940, the Germans invaded and occupied Denmark. The Germans guaranteed that the independence and liberty of the Danes would be respected. In turn Prime Minister Thorvald Stauning, in a proclamation issued that day, urged the people not to resist the German occupation in order that, "quiet and order prevail."[43] Following the German occupation, life continued as usual for the people of Denmark and the Jewish community. The Nazis, aware that anti-Jewish laws and activities would be strongly opposed by the Danes, initially left the Jews unharmed. The Jews, however, still maintained a low profile. Communal activity continued but in a private manner so as not to attract attention. Amidst global chaos there was a strange calm in Denmark.

Denmark's first Jews, Sephardim from Portugal, arrived in 1622. By 1782, the Jewish community became a mixture of Portuguese and German Jews numbering 1,830.[44] At the turn of the nineteenth century about fifteen hundred Jewish immigrants arrived from Russia. By the Second World War, Danish Jewry numbered about 7,500.

---

[43]Rabbi Ib Nathan Bamberger, *The Viking Jews: A History of the Jews of Denmark* (New York: Shengold, 1983), 131.
[44]*Encyclopedia Judaica* (Jerusalem: The Macmillan Co., Keter Publishing House, 1972), 5:1538.

Perhaps the Nazis were testing the loyalty of the Danes toward their Jewish citizens. In December 1941, an attempt was made to destroy the synagogue in Krystalgrade by fire. The Danish police prevented this attempt. Again a year later, another attempt was foiled. The police, along with a newly formed unit of Jewish youth, together protected the synagogue.[45]

In a personal letter from King Christian X of Denmark to Chief Rabbi Moses Friediger following the first incident, stated, "I have heard about the attempted fire at the synagogue, and I am very happy that there was only slight damage. I beg of you to give my congratulations and best wishes for the New Year to your congregation."[46]

In the summer of 1943 as the tide of the war shifted toward the allies, acts of sabotage against the Germans increased throughout German-occupied territories. Many of the Danes began to join the resistance and engage in anti-German sabotage. After the Danish government refused to try those responsible, the Germans dissolved the government and declared martial law. The situation facing Danish Jewry began to appear ominous.

On August 29, prominent Danish citizens, including several Jews, were arrested. The situation worsened as the Germans began to forcibly obtain records of the Jewish community.[47] On September 18, a special group of Gestapo commandos arrived with orders to begin the liquidation of Danish Jewry. The planned arrests of the Jews were set for Wednesday night, October 1—the first night of Rosh Hashanah. The Jews were to be seized and deported to concentration camps by ships.

The events leading to the salvation of Danish Jewry are remarkable. On September 18, German ambassador to Denmark Werner Best, notified the German director of shipping in Denmark, George F. Duckitz, that ships would be anchored in the harbor.

---

[45]Bamberger, *The Viking Jews*, 135.
[46]Ibid., 135.
[47]Ibid., 140.

Best also notified Duckitz that these ships were to be used to transport Jews. Duckitz had no intention of cooperating with the Gestapo. One week later he flew to Sweden and pleaded with the Swedes, who agreed to accept the Jews provided the Germans agreed. Duckitz returned to Copenhagen and waited for a response. By September 28, he had received no response and secretly went to a meeting of the Danish Socialist Democrats and told them of the German plans for Danish Jewry.[48] Those in attendance immediately informed members of the Jewish community. The news spread quickly, people were warned to leave their homes immediately. Most members of the Jewish community found refuge in the homes of their Christian neighbors. On the night of October 1, when Gestapo commandos invaded the residences of the Jews, they found them empty. Over the next week, hundreds of Danes clandestinely smuggled the Jews from their places of hiding to boats that brought them to Sweden. The last group arrived on Friday morning October 9, Yom Kippur eve.

Due to the efforts of the Danes, the Gestapo's plans were thwarted. Over six thousand Jews escaped, while the 464 who remained were deported to Theresienstadt.[49] Not all heeded the warnings. Since the Jewish community had already lived under Nazi control for over three years, some did not believe the deportations would actually occur. Others were arrested because they lived in more remote areas and were not informed of the dangers. There were also those who had no place to go or who considered themselves too old to flee.[50] The Danes continued to intercede on behalf of the Jews while they were under Nazi internment. They sent them food parcels and needed supplies. In total, fifty-two of the deported Jews did not return, a figure far lower than any other Jewish community under German occupation.

The Germans figured the Danes would betray the Jews and

[48]Ibid., 142.
[49]Ibid., 143.
[50]Ibid.

reveal their hiding places. They even offered the incentive that imprisoned Danish troops would be released in return for some measure of cooperation. But even this did not elicit their cooperation.[51]

Over the first three years of German occupation, the humanity of the Danes discouraged the Germans from pursuing the Jews. When they did, the Danes made great efforts to protect them and ensure that they would not become victims of the Holocaust.

The family of a Danish Jew, Rabbi Ib Nathan Bamberger, was forewarned of the Nazis plans on September 29. They left their home as Rosh Hashanah was arriving. He records in his book *The Viking Jews* that the Danes protected their property even after they fled, "The table was set, candles placed in candlesticks, and the traditional holiday bread baked. When, after twenty months, in May 1945, we returned to Copenhagen and reentered our home, everything was exactly as we left it! The Danes had seen to it that no one entered our home during our absence. Similarly, the Danes watched the synagogues, the Jewish schools, the community center and many Jewish apartments. No looting, stealing, or other mischievous acts occurred there."[52]

World War Two is a dark era of history for those who either kept silent, betrayed the Jews, or cooperated with the Nazis. There were many individuals who made valiant efforts to save Jews, but the Danes as a nation conducted themselves heroically. Their name has been etched in history for their decency and humanity.

The Talmud states that Rosh Hashanah is the day of judgement for humanity for the coming year, while Yom Kippur is the day that judgement is sealed. As the liturgy of the High Holidays states, "On Rosh Hashanah it is written and on Yom Kippur it is sealed." Indeed, in 1943, Danish Jewry was predestined to survive.

---

[51]Ibid.
[52]Ibid., 146.

8

Yom Kippur

FOLLOWING KING DAVID'S EXAMPLE

Yom Kippur is a time to focus on improving one's relationship with the Creator through repentance. However, true repentance requires confronting one's feelings of guilt. King David's repentance following the Uriah-Batsheba incident underscores the theme of Yom Kippur.

King David arose one night and went to the roof of his house. As he gazed over Jerusalem, he noticed Batsheba in her home and he took an interest in her. The king sent messengers and brought her to his palace. There, David had relations with her.

At the time, Batsheba and her husband Uriah were technically divorced. Before Uriah, a soldier, left for battle he gave his wife a conditional divorce that would take effect retroactively in the event of his capture or disappearance. It would allow her to remarry after a certain period of time if he did not return after the battles were fought. It was a divorce based upon the condition that they would reunite upon the soldier's return. Such a promise was often made prior to battle in biblical times lest the soldier be taken captive.[1]

---

[1]Rashi, Tosafoth, Talmud Bavli, Ketubot 9b.

David sent a message to Uriah in the field ordering him to return to his home. Uriah disobeyed the king as he relayed a message to David that his place was with his fellow troops. He defiantly told the knig, "The ark and Israel and Judah dwell in booths, and my lord Joab and the servants of my lord are encamped in the open field; and shall I come to my house to eat and to drink and to live with my wife? By your life and the life of my soul, if I will do this thing."[2] Uriah's defiance of the king is likened to an act of rebellion against the kingdom, which according to Jewish law is punishable by death. Out of anger, David ordered the general in command, Joab to place Uriah in the most dangerous position of front line combat. "Place Uriah at the forefront of the fiercest battle, and go away from him, so that he will be hit and die."[3] Uriah was subsequently killed in battle.

The prophet Nathan went to rebuke David. He told the king a parable with the intention that the story would prompt the king to search his own deeds. He told of two men who lived in a city—a poor man who had just one lamb and a wealthy man who took the poor man's sole possession, one sheep, to feed a wayfarer.[4] David, who possessed whatever he wanted, represented the rich man. The wayfarer symbolizes man's evil inclination, the capacity to do wrong.[5]

David heard the tale and expressed his revulsion toward the wealthy man. "As the Lord lives, the man who has done this is liable to death."[6] Nathan then accused David of being that man, saying, "Why have you despised the word of God to do what is evil in His eyes?"[7] As David heard the prophet's reprimand, he could have rejected Nathan's accusation that no doubt threatens the prestige of the king. However, he responded with the brief words "I have

---

[2]Samuel 2, 11:11.
[3]Ibid., 2:15.
[4]Ibid., 12:5.
[5]Rashi, Babylonian Talmud, Succah 52b.
[6]Samuel 2, 12:5.
[7]Ibid., 12:9.

sinned to God." At that moment of truth, David looked into himself and came to terms with his own wrongdoing.

Nathan accused the king of acting in a manner beneath his dignity, but made no mention of adultery. Furthermore, when the prophet Samuel later told David that he would not build the Temple, the reason given was that he spilled blood in wars that the Israelite nation fought out of necessity for its very survival, no mention was made of David's actions with Batsheba and Uriah.

David's remorse for his actions ran deep. Out of regret, he composed Psalm 51, "Abundantly cleanse me of my iniquity, and from sin purify me. For I recognize my transgressions, and my sin is before me always. Against You alone did I sin and that which is evil in Your eyes did I sin."[8]

What compelled David, Israel's greatest king, to act in the manner in which he did? David acted upon zeal. David, who possessed Divine spirit, envisioned that Batsheba would be the mother of Israel's next king. He foresaw destiny and attempted to control and hasten it.

As David foresaw, his union with Batsheba eventually brought into the world Solomon, who would succeed David to the throne and build the Temple. Although David did not build the Temple, he did everything but construct its walls. He conquered the city, built it up, procured the spot for the Temple, prepared many of the supplies needed for the Temple, and composed the Psalms sung there by the Levites. The Temple itself is often refereed to as the "House of David." The favor David found with God is unquestionable. "Since David did what was just in the eyes of the Lord and he did not turn away from all that the Lord commanded him, all the days of his life except in the matter of Uriah the Hittite."[9]

In the Bible, the heroic actions of the righteous are recorded as well as their misdeeds. There is no one who has not sinned. The

---

[8]Psalm 51:4–6.
[9]1 Kings, 15:5.

Midrash relates that King David asked God not to record (in Scripture) the sin committed. God replied, "Do you want the people to say, because God loved David He forgave him?"[10] David was forgiven because he confessed and repented.

David's episode with Batsheba exemplifies the meaning and message of Yom Kippur.

INAPPROPRIATE CELEBRATIONS

The violation of the sanctity of Yom Kippur—most notably the refusal to fast—signifies the distancing of one's self from Judaism. On Yom Kippur there have been those who not only refused to fast but, out of self-hatred, have used Judaism's holiest day as a time to make a statement against their own Jewishness.

By the turn of the century the Lower East Side of New York was one of the most densely Jewish areas in the world. For the new immigrants, life drastically contrasted from that of the past. The world of the *shtetle* was a bygone era whose memory was faded by the new reality of a society that offered new possibilities. Only a small percentage of immigrants maintained the old traditions, although most of the immigrants were not willing to make a total departure from their Jewish traditions.

The "New World" for many immigrants was replete with dreams and ideals of social utopias reflecting the radicalism of the times. The Lower East Side had its fill of anarchists, socialists, and radical reformers. Often the young, poor immigrant's socialism was an expression of his desire to heal the world of the ills of poverty from which the majority of immigrants suffered. Frequently such rebels caused havoc within their own families when they displayed their flagrant disregard for Jewish tradition. Many traditional or Orthodox families suffered the shock of having a radical in their

---

[10]Midrash, Sifri, Va'etchanan 1.

own midst. Most immigrants did not anticipate they would have to pay this price by coming to America.

To the horror of the Orthodox, and the non-observant mainstream immigrant, the radicals frequently attacked the beliefs and practices of their own people. Anti-religious tracts, pamphlets, and newspaper articles featured in the Yiddish press frowned upon the "backwards" ways of Judaism within a rapidly changing world. The long history and lore of the Jews was not merely forgotten but became the subject of scorn and attacks. The only reality to the revolutionaries of the late nineteenth century were those ideologies akin to radicalism.

Then came the greatest outrage, the desecration of the holiest day of the Jewish year—Yom Kippur—by Jewish anarchists. The anarchists advocated abrupt revolution by small groups of radicals, unlike the socialists who believed in collective action over the course of time. The anarchists acted out their hostility against their own Jewishness. They organized Yom Kippur Balls that caused anxiety and indignation within the Jewish community. In 1889, Jewish "workers" were invited to spend Yom Kippur night at the Clarendon Hall on Thirteenth Street.[11] The invitation was not to use the hall as a makeshift synagogue but for a party with food and drink. Due to the huge wave of protest, the doors to the event were not opened. But the self-haters were persistent. The next year, the New York anarchists attempted to arrange another Yom Kippur Ball at the Lyceam Theatre in Brooklyn. A ticket to the Yom Kippur Ball read: "Grand Yom Kippur Ball with theatre. Arranged with the consent of all new rabbis of liberty. Kol Nidre Night and day of the year [5651], after the invention of Jewish idols. . . . The Kol Nidre will be offered by Johann Most. Music, dancing, Marsellaise, and other hymms against Satan." The planned party also provided attendants with an ample supply of ham and drink. Again, outraged Jews protested to the mayor who ordered the police to prevent the

[11]Phillip Goodman, *The Yom Kippur Anthology* (Philadelphia: Jewish Publication Society of America, 1971), 331.

meeting.[12] However, the mayor was sharply criticized by the press for the restrictive measure and, eventually, the Yom Kippur Ball was held.

The Yom Kippur Ball also began to spread to other cities and continued to be a weapon in the radical's battle to agitate and infuriate the Jewish community. One can only imagine the horror and the remorse so many immigrants felt upon hearing of such events. Their memories of the *shtetle* no doubt contrasted greatly with the realities of the New World. While attending the Kol Nidre service they must have contemplated those differences as others made a mockery of the Day of Atonement.

THE INDOMITABLE SPIRIT OF YOM KIPPUR

A rare, annual appearance to a synagogue generally implies a lack of interest, a weakening link in the chain of tradition. However, in the former Soviet Union, attending synagogue even just once a year on Yom Kippur represented the continuity of that chain.

In Soviet Russia, despite the onslaught against religion and especially Jewish observances, most Jews in the Communist Party did not show up to work on Yom Kippur. The following example demonstrating the tenacity of Kolkhoz[13] members in observing the High Holidays is found in Joshua Rothenberg's *The Jews of the Soviet Union*. He wrote:

> The "Collectivization Day" established by the government to be feted on October 14 fell in 1929, on Yom Kippur. Knowing that the Jewish Kolkhozkiks would not voluntarily participate in the festivities, the Executive Committee of the Supreme Soviet saw fit to change the date of the "Collectivization Day"

---

[12]Alter F. Landesman, "Radical and Social Movements," in *Brownsville: The Birth and Development and Passing of a Jewish Community in New York* (New York: Bloch Publishing Company, 1969), 109.
[13]collective settlement

> for the Jewish Kolkhozes, so that the "Jewish members could participate in celebrating their holiday of their own free will and not because they were forced to."[14]

It should be noted that, true to form, the most devout of the Jewish communists sought to end the Jewish observance of Yom Kippur. The Yevsekszia—the Jewish wing of the Communist Party—insisted that Collectivization Day not be postponed.[15] The Yevsekszia organized concerts and meetings on Yom Kippur night. They also organized voluntary work groups on Yom Kippur called "Yom Kippurniks."[16] Unlike their counterparts in New York who held parties, these Jewish warriors against Judaism entered synagogues, disrupted services and gave inflammatory speeches. Sometimes fights would break out that were followed by arrests and jail sentences.[17]

Over time, the Soviets increased their anti-Jewish campaign and traditional observance suffered. The Jews became further distanced from their heritage. Although attendance in synagogue on Yom Kippur dwindled, it always continued. The Soviet Jew simply could not be kept away from the synagogue on Yom Kippur. The Yiddish writer H. Rabinkov, who was active in the "atheist movement," stated, "You may conduct with us as many anti-religious meetings as you can stand, but you are wasting your words. We are, you should know, like those cavalry horses: when they hear the trumpet, on they go. The same with us: as soon as Rosh Hashanah and Yom Kippur arrive, on to the synagogue we go and nothing will hold us back."[18] In the Soviet Union, the Jewish spirit could be wounded but not broken. Yom Kippur was never forgotten.

---

[14]Joshua Rothenberg, *The Jewish Religion in the Soviet Union* (New York: Ktav Publishing House, 1971), 75.
[15]Ibid., 75.
[16]Ibid.
[17]Ibid.
[18]Ibid., 76.

So it was, decades later, in the 1960s, that perhaps tens of thousands of Jews continued to make their way to those synagogues that still existed. One eyewitness described Yom Kippur at the synagogue of Kiev—a city of two hundred thousand Jews. "When I arrived, the path leading to the synagogue was already thick with crowds of Jews. I shouldered my way inside with great difficulty. Thousands of people, possibly tens of thousands, stood jammed together near the entrance in the alley."[19] According to another eyewitness, the synagogue, "could scarcely accommodate a few hundred worshipers."[20]

Rulers came and went; the Soviet Empire fell and the Yevsekszia is no longer around. On Yom Kippur, against all odds, Jews of the Russian republics of the former Soviet Union who live there or in other lands still fast and fill the synagogues on Yom Kippur. It is poetic justice that their prayers were answered.

AN EMERGENCY DECREE

Rabbi Samsom Raphael Hirsch (1808–1888), an eminent scholar and leader of German Jewry, was appointed at the age of 22 to lead the congregation of the city of Oldenburg. It was during this time in his career that he authored two of his treatises on Judaism, which are still widely read, *The Nineteen Letters* and *Horeb*. During this time, Rabbi Hirsch also sought to maintain the sanctity of Yom Kippur, whose message was being forgotten by many in his community. He noticed that many members of his community were not keeping their oaths and relied upon Kol Nidre to absolve them. Using a measure known as *Hora'at Shaah* (emergency decree), Rabbi Hirsch[21] decreed that Kol Nidre not be recited in synagogue

[19]Ben Ami, *Between Hammer and Sickle* (Philadelphia: Jewish Publication Society of America, 1967), 75.
[20]Ibid.
[21]According to rumors and the diary of historian Heinrich Graetz.

on Yom Kippur night. Thus, those who abused the purpose of Kol Nidre would no longer be able to do so, and violations of the Torah's laws of honesty would be prevented.[22]

The solemnity of Kol Nidre can be lost in the broken words and vows that people utter and its sanctity can be diminished by those who think they can be absolved of their broken promises at Kol Nidre. Rabbi Hirsch's act reminded his community, and serves as a reminder to all, that all the prayers, chest-pounding, and verbalization of sin on Yom Kippur is merely a physical exercise if it is not accompanied by intent and resolve.

---

[22]Leo Jung, ed., *Guardians of our Heritage* (New York: Leo Jung, Bloch Publishing House, 1958), 272.

9

Succot

MIGRATIONS: WANDERING IN THE DESERT

The Duke of Mannhein once asked Rabbi Tzvi of Berlin, "What is the reason that children ask the 'Four Questions' on Passover and not on Succot? After all, on Succot you have more customs than on Passover, especially since you leave your homes and live in temporary booths." "Let me explain it to you," replied Rabbi Tzvi. "On Passover a child sees the family seated around a table with many tempting dishes, and they are freely relaxed in a way we Jews are not permitted to always enjoy. Therefore the child is surprised and asks the questions. But what does the little one see on Succot? The people of Israel leave their homes and sit outside without a roof over their heads. This is no surprise, for even a child knows this is the way for Jews in the Diaspora."[1]

The experience of the Israelites wandering in the desert is a microcosm of the history of the Jews in the Diaspora. Throughout

---

[1]Phillip Goodman, *The Succoth and Simchat Torah Anthology* (Philadelphia: Jewish Publication Society of America, 1973), 100.

history, expulsions and migrations have been a reality of life. Just as the Israelites in the Sinai wilderness wandered from place to place, so, too, did the Jews throughout history. "These are the journeys of the Israelites who had left Egypt in organized groups."[2] The Bible lists the numerous places of that long journey. The Israelites unfurled and pitched their tents forty-two times in their many travels over forty years.

The many migrations of the Jewish people have been in the search for sanctuary. Persecutions and expulsions have sent Jews on a never-ending search for protection and safety.

It was the search for safety and prosperity that brought Jews to America's shores. The first wave of Sephardim arrived in the eighteenth century as escapees from the intolerance of Inquisition rule. In the middle of the nineteenth century, the next wave of Jewish immigrants arrived from Bavarian provinces of Germany following upheavals, and revolutions that increased the tide of American Jewish immigrants. Then, the largest wave of immigrants from eastern Europe came in the years 1881–1921, escaping persecution and poverty. Over the past seventy-five years, waves of immigrants have continued to arrive from different countries. They came fleeing persecution, but their travels and migrations continued.

Although by volition and not by the force of persecution and expulsion, American Jews have been constantly on the move. The most common route of migration began from the inner city and moved slowly toward the suburbs, and then even farther out to other cities and smaller towns. In America today, while the Jewish population of New York has not increased in recent years, it has in many other major cities. American Jews are constantly on the move. For every growing Jewish community in one area, there is one in decline elsewhere. Jews still migrate as if they still resided in ancestral lands of persecution, as if the restlessness of migration is something habitual.

---

[2]Numbers 33:1.

The *succah* itself is the embodiment of this history. The *succah*, with its shabby walls and open roof, serves as a constant reminder to Jews in the Diaspora that their homes, as their *succah*, are only temporary dwellings. Wherever a Jew may be, regardless of the environment one is in, their homes, which are periodically changed, are not unlike those of their ancestors in the Sinai wilderness. The Israelites, however, were actually in constant transit for only two of their forty years in the desert. They were encamped in one place—Kadesh Barnea—for thirty-eight of their forty years. Likewise, there are times when a home for the Jews in the Diaspora may last long and seem permanent. Such was the case in Spain during the "Golden Era" or in Poland prior to the massacres of the seventeenth century. And just as the Israelites sojourned in Kadesh Barnea for a long duration, they would ultimately have to move on. Throughout Jewish history, some Jewish communities remained in their adopted lands for centuries while others only remained for a short time, but what they have in common is the eventuality of their flight. Such is the nature of Jewish existence.

DIVINE PROTECTION

> You shall dwell in Booths for seven days, every member of Israel shall dwell in Succoth. In order that your future generations shall know that I housed the Israelites in booths when I took them out of Egypt.[3]

The *succah* is constructed as a temporary dwelling exposed to the elements. Its fragile walls serve as a constant reminder that the only true security in the world comes from the Almighty. However, the security provided by the *succah* does not exclude the realities of the natural order. On Succot, one does not invite danger or illness and is not forced to live in the *succah* in certain specific situations where

[3]Leviticus 23:42–43.

there is excessive hardship.[4] Thus, people are accustomed to leniency when it comes to the requirement of sleeping in a *succah* in areas where danger lurks or where the weather is intolerable.[5] Just as one would not invite trouble or suffer in one's home, likewise in the *succah*. The exceptions are those who are very scrupulous in their observance of the Torah's commandments.[6] There are those who ignored all the dangers and at great risk made special efforts to fulfill the basic commandment of dwelling in the *succah*. The amount of time in which they could spend in their *succoth* was minimal. Nonetheless, whatever time they spent was remarkable considering the circumstances.

During the Holocaust, there were brave Jews within the concentration camps who disregarded all dangers and constructed and dwelt in *succahs*. As they sat inside the *succah*, they, too, were reminded of their ancestors who sojourned in the Sinai wilderness for forty years.

Rabbi Zvi Hirsch Miesels, a Holocaust survivor, recorded the heroism of those in Auschwitz. Some acts of heroism included those who constructed and used *succahs* within the concentration camps. The following are accounts from his book:

> I was also able to fulfill the mitzvah of Succah. In one corner of the camp some Jews worked on the repair of beds and sofas. I asked them for a few boards, which I joined together covered with *sechach*.[7] The sitting in the *succah* involved considerable danger since the SS men passed by the place at all hours of the day in order to supervise the work of the Jews. If they found anyone eating in the *succah*, they would beat him murderously. In this fashion they caught my son Zalmon eating in the *succah*, it was only through a miracle that he remained alive

---

[4] *Orach Chaim*, "Laws of Succah," section 640, paragraph no. 4.
[5] Ibid., section 639, law no. 2, Ramah.
[6] Ibid., Ramah.
[7] According to the Jastrow *Dictionary of the Talmud*, the term literally means overhanging boughs or twigs.

after the beating about the head and body which they inflicted on him. Thus, one can see the extraordinary sacrifices which the Jews, even in the dreaded camps of death, were able to make to fulfill the *mitzvoth* of the Almighty, whenever and however a mitzvah came their way.[8]

This was not the only *succah* in Auschwitz. Rabbi Jacob Aaronson writes:

> In 5704 (1943) we built a *succah* in Auschwitz. . . . At the edge of the camp, between us and the residences of the SS guards, there were long rows of large barrels. Between the rows there was room enough for a large *succah*. We set up a third wall alongside two rows of barrels [a *succah* needs three walls in order to be suitable for use]; and covered the *succah* with *sechakh*. No one was aware that this was a *succah* except those to whom the secret had been imparted. The first night of Succoth, we went there secretly, recited *kiddush* over a bit of bread which we had saved from the morning, and ate the required *ke'zayit* [olive-sized amount] hastily. This, because the spot where the barrels were stored was surrounded by an electrified fence; the camp inmates discovered there were punished by death. I was in doubt as to whether I should recite the benediction of *Lei-shev BaSuccah* because of this danger, since according to the *Rama* in the *Shulchan Aruch*, if one sits in a *succah* built in a "place of danger" he may not be fulfilling the mitzvah at all. Nonetheless, the blessing spontaneously rose to the lips as well as the *Sh-he-heyanu* benediction, joyously, because we were able to erect a *succah* in the very "jaws of the lion." Many of the prisoners ate in that *succah*. . . . One would leave and another would enter.[9]

---

[8]Irving Rosenbaum, *The Holocaust and Halakhah* (Hoboken: Ktav Publishing House, 1976), 115.
[9]Ibid., 116.

Jacob Koretz writes of the many Jews who built *succoth* in the ghetto of Pietrkov:

> In my courtyard there were two *succoth*. In one of them there sat a Jew singing *zemirot*[10] in a very loud voice. I entered and asked him if he didn't realize where we were; how he dared sing so loudly as if nothing had happened. He just shook his head and continued with his *zemirot*. When he finished he turned to me and said, "what can they do to me? They can take my body—but not my soul! Over my soul they have no dominion! Their dominion is only in this world! Here they are the mighty ones. All right. But in the world to come, their strength is no more."[11]

Regardless of the situation a person may find himself in, one can rest under the protective shade of the *succah*. Even in the Nazi death camps, numerous prisoners were able to sit in the *succah* and sense the constant protection of the Almighty.

THE ELUSIVE *ETROG*

> The Talmud states, "Our rabbis learned, 'And you shall take' (Leviticus)[12] [the Four Species] means that they are to be taken by each individual. 'For yourselves' (Leviticus)[13] implies that it must belong to you. This comes to exclude [the Four Species] which are borrowed or stolen. From here, the Sages stated that a person does not fulfill his requirement with a *lulav* on the first day of the holiday which belongs to someone else unless he gives it to him as a gift." (Succah)[14]

---

[10]Sabbath or holiday songs
[11]Rosenbaum, *The Holocaust and Halakhah*, 116.
[12]Leviticus 23:40.
[13]Ibid.
[14]Babylonian Talmud, Succah 41b.

The Talmud continues on the subject by presenting an example of five of the greatest sages of the Mishnah—Rabban Gamliel; Rabbi Joshua; Rabbi Elazar, the son of Azaria; and Rabbi Akiva—who were traveling on a ship as Succot arrived. Only Rabbi Gamliel had a *lulav*, which he purchased at the very high price of one thousand Zuz.[15] After Rabban Gamliel made the benediction over the waving of the *lulav*, he gave it as a gift to Rabbi Joshua who did the same and then gave it to Rabbi Elazar ben Azaria who did the same, until each sage fulfilled the Torah's commandment of holding the *lulav* and *etrog*. It can be inferred by the fact that only one of the sages possessed an *etrog*, which he purchased at an exorbitant cost, that the precious commodity was in very short supply at that time.[16]

When Succot approaches in today's times, most people are able to purchase an *etrog* at their local synagogue or Judaica store. But, like the above case, *etrogim* have often been difficult to obtain. Such was also the case in Vilna, Lithuania, one year in the early nineteenth century.

As the holiday of Succot approached, the Vilna Gaon (Rabbi Eliahu, son of Rabbi Shlomo Zalman, 1720–1797) began to grow uneasy, realizing that the fulfillment of the mitzvah of the Four Species was in jeopardy. For months, the community of Vilna sent messengers searching for *etrogim*, but none could be found. The news was received with shock. Could it be possible that the community would have no *etrogim* for the holiday? The community leaders decided to send one more messenger to travel from city to city to find an *etrog*, no matter what the cost. With time running out, the messenger was forced to return home empty handed. However, stopping at an inn on his trip homeward, the messenger

---

[15]Ibid.

[16]Rashi's commentary on Talmud Bavli Succah 41b and Tosafot's commentary on Baba Kama 9a state that the unusually high price Rabban Gamliel paid was attributed to his love of the Torah and its precepts.

noticed that the innkeeper himself owned a beautiful *etrog*. The messenger offered a hefty price, but the innkeeper refused to part with the *etrog*. After the messenger revealed that he was seeking an *etrog* for the Vilna Gaon, the innkeeper immediately reconsidered and exclaimed, "I will agree to give my *etrog* to the Vilna Gaon as a gift, but only on the condition that when the Vilna Gaon fulfills the mitzvah, it is in my name."[17] When the messenger returned to Vilna on the eve of Succot and presented the *etrog* to the Vilna Gaon, he explained the condition with which it was given. The rabbi complemented the messenger and exclaimed with joy, "The truth is, no one knows how great the rewards for *Mitzvos* are! But it is certainly worth forfeiting my reward in the World-to-Come in order to fulfill the mitzvah of *etrog* properly in this world."[18]

Many such stories exist. There were many times when obtaining an *etrog* was nearly impossible. In the twelfth and thirteenth centuries, it was very common for communities, because of the scarcity of *etrogim* in France and Germany, to purchase only one with the understanding that each member of the entire community would make use of it.[19] In the *shtetles* of eastern Europe, communities also often relied upon a single *etrog*. Over the course of the holiday, the communal *etrog* would pass through so many hands that by the end of the holiday it would become unrecognizable, darkened by fingerprints. In one case, a town in southern Germany in Western Bohemia, Kuttenplan, taxed the entire community in 1576 in order to obtain a single *etrog*.[20]

There were many reasons why *etrogim* was sparse. Before the era of modern transportation, the sending of an adequate supply

---

[17]Meaning that in the World-to-Come he would receive the reward for the Vilna Gaon's fulfillment of the commandment.
[18]This is a common story. The rendition here is taken from Rabbi Aharon Yisroel Kahan, *The Taryag (613) Mitzvos* (Brooklyn: Keser Torah Publications, 5747), 200 and *Sefer HaMoadim*, 380–381.
[19]Babylonian Talmud, Succah 41b, Tosafot.
[20]Goodman, *The Succoth and Simchat Torah Anthology*, 161.

of *etrogim* to far distances was extremely difficult, so supplies were limited. During wars, *etrogim* could not be transported by any means between the combatant nations. Such was the situation during the rule of Emperor Napoleon, whose conquests divided Europe between northern countries—where *etrogim* do not grow—and southern European countries. During the Second World War, few *etrogim* were available and Jewish communities throughout the world made good on a very limited supply.

Under oppressive regimes, *etrogim* were often prohibited or discouraged. In the Soviet Union in the 1920s, when obtaining *etrogim* was extremely difficult, the Yiddish newspaper *Der Emes*[21] described an arrangement made by two neighboring towns to share an *etrog* over the holiday. Every day, a non-Jewish messenger would carry the *etrog* from one town to the other. Under Nazi occupation, S. B. Unsdorfer in *The Yellow Star* describes how the entire Jewish community of Slovakia had just one *etrog*. He writes, "a trusty gentile was asked to tour the Jewish communities by car with this one set of *Arba Minim* (Four Species), congregants were informed beforehand at what day and hour they had to assemble in the synagogue in order to have a chance of making the blessing on the *Arba Minim*."[22]

There were other ways of making the *etrog* difficult to obtain. In 1744, Maria Theresa of Bohemia imposed a very heavy tax on *etrogim*. The *etrog* tax continued for fifty-five years. There were also times when unscrupulous merchants deliberately destroyed supplies in order to increase their prices.

According to Jewish law, an *etrog* can be preserved from one year to the next as long as it maintains its character and does not dry

---

[21] *Der Emes* (October 8, 1922), quoted in Joshua Rothenberg, *The Jewish Religion in the Soviet Union* (New York: Ktav Publishing House, 1971), 91.

[22] S. B. Unsdorfer, *The Yellow Star* (New York/Jerusalem: Feldheim, 1983), 22.

out.[23] The Mishnah states that a dry *etrog* cannot be used. However, the term "dry" needed elaboration especially in areas where *etrogim* were in short supply. The issue was dealt with in several works of Jewish law. The redactor of the *Shulchan Aruch* (Code of Jewish Law), Rabbi Moses Isserles (1530–1572), who lived in Poland, stated that an *etrog* from the following year cannot be used if it is completely dry.[24] However, the implication is that if the whole *etrog* is not completely dry then it is permissible. Rabbi Yisroel Meir Kagen HaCohen, better known as the Chafetz Chaim (1838–1933), who authored the Mishna Berurah,[25] comments that as long as the entire *etrog* appears to maintain some degree of moisture, it is permissible. A commentary on the Mishna Berura, also by the Chafetz Chaim, known as the *Shaar Tzion*,[26] states that he himself saw an *etrog* preserved in a metal utensil and stored in a cool place for over a year and he found that it was moist and therefore permissible according to all rabbinic views.[27] Preservation of an *etrog* was within the realm of possibility for the many Jews who struggled each year to obtain one. This was a comforting notion to many.

Fulfilling the mitzvah of "taking an *etrog*"[28] may not be a luxury anymore in most areas, but it is still a privilege. In instructing the use of the *etrog*, the Torah states, "and you shall take for yourselves."[29] Perhaps the verse can also be viewed as stating

---

[23]*Orach Chaim*, "Laws of Lulav," section 645, paragraph 1; *Be'er Hatev, Mishna Berura.*

[24]*Mishna Brurah, Orach Chaim*, "Laws of Lulav," section 640, paragraph 1, Ramah.

[25]The *Mishna Berura* is a definitive analysis and explanation of the *Shulchan Aruch, Orach Chayim*, which deals with laws of prayer and holidays. It serves as a guide to many contemporary halachic issues.

[26]*The Shaar Tzion*, also composed by the Chafetz Chaim, elucidates and quotes source footnotes on the *Mishna Berura.*

[27]*Orach Chaim*, "Laws of Lulav," section 645, paragraph 1, Shaarei Tzion.

[28]Leviticus 23:40.

[29]Ibid.

that times will come in history when the individual will not "take for yourself" in the singular but "yourselves" in the plural, stressing that each individual member of the community will fulfill his commandment with the use of the same *etrog* out of necessity.

A TIME FOR GUESTS: RETURNEES TO JERUSALEM

Since the time of the Roman invasion of Judea in 63 B.C.E., until the Six Day War of 1967, Jerusalem's Old City was under foreign rule. Those who visited Jerusalem for the Succot holiday celebrated together in communal *succoth*, which were constructed for that purpose. The tradition dates back to the beginnings of the era of the Second Temple. The biblical Book of Nechemia describes how the Judeans, who returned to Jerusalem from Babylonian-Persian captivity, constructed communal booths.[30] That Succot, the holiday was celebrated with a special enthusiasm as it had not been celebrated since the time of Joshua when the Israelites entered the Land of Israel. "And all the congregation of the returnees from the captivity made Succot and dwelt in the booths, for they had not done so since the days of Joshua, the son of Nun, until that day, and there was exceedingly great joy."[31]

Since the destruction of the Second Temple in 70 C.E., those who visited Jerusalem for Succot also had the custom of encircling the city seven times. They circled the city on the first day of Chol HaMoed (the intermittent days of the holiday) as they focused their eyes upon the remains of the destroyed Temple on the Temple Mount. This custom was based upon the line in a Psalm, "Walk about Zion and go about her; count the towers thereof. Mark well her ramparts, traverse her places."[32] Those who encircled Jerusalem

---

[30]Nechemia 8:17.
[31]Ibid.
[32]Psalm 48:13–14.

did so with the hopes and prayers that their actions would hasten the realization of the Psalmist's words—that Jerusalem would again be a city rebuilt with towers and ramparts surrounding its core, the rebuilt Temple. Over time, the pilgrimages on Succot were eventually suspended for a variety of reasons.

When Zionist youth began immigrating to the land, the custom was revitalized. In 1904, in the early days of the Second *Aliyah*, a group of farm workers from the new emerging settlements of Petach Tikveh, Rehovot, Nes Ziona, and Hadera went to Jerusalem to celebrate the holiday.

As they entered Jerusalem, they were greeted warmly by the city's elders. In the tradition of providing those who needed provisions for the Yom Tov, the chief rabbi of Jerusalem, Rabbi Shmuel Salant[33] sent them some money, which they refused having already saved up for the journey. The pioneers built a large *succah* from mats on the roof of the house where they lodged, located in the Bet Yisrael quarter. On the first evening of Succot, they went as a group to synagogue and then returned to their *succah*. When they returned, one of the leaders of the group, Aaron David Gordon, recited the holiday *Kiddush* in a loud and clear voice—loud enough to make their presence heard throughout the immediate area. Soon, residents of the Jewish quarter gathered in their *succah* and joined in the holiday by rejoicing, singing, and dancing. When the *Chol HaMoed* arrived, the young pioneers also adopted the custom of circling the walls of the Old City. Together they encircled Jerusalem. Once again Jerusalem had welcomed its guests for Succot, a custom which was prohibited by the ruling authorities of Jerusalem for centuries. The custom continued until 1947, when the Jordanians came to occupy the Old City of Jerusalem.

Each year, Jerusalem welcomes more guests who come to the city for Succot. With their presence, the spirit of the holiday

---

[33]Rabbi Shmuel Salant (1816–1909) was the chief rabbi of Jerusalem from 1878 until his death.

increasingly livens, brightening the face of the Holy City. Upon seeing the *succot* throughout the city and observing the crowds assembled in prayer at the Western Wall, one can almost imagine the spiritual greatness of the city during Temple times and ponder what lies in store for Jerusalem in the future.

RECOGNIZING THE CREATOR

Succot serves as a reminder that all achievements come with Divine help. The Bible warns the Israelites that when they enter the Promised Land, the prosperity they will enjoy should not be taken for granted. "Be careful not to say, it was my strength and personal power that brought me all this prosperity."[34] The guidance of the Almighty should never be forgotten. Such recognition applies to success on the battlefield as well.

A famous poster from the Yom Kippur War shows an Israeli soldier clenching a *lulav* and *etrog* while immersed in prayer. On his face one can see the intensity of his prayers and the weight of responsibility that was placed upon his shoulders as Israel fought for its survival. There were also earlier times in history when the Four Species were brought to soldiers on the front lines of battle.

A bundle of letters written by Simon Bar Kochba, commander of the Bar Kochba Revolt (132–135 C.E.), was discovered by a member of the archeological expedition of the Bar Kochba Caves.[35] The expedition, which was headed by the famed Israeli general and archeologist Yigal Yadin, revealed many fascinating finds. One remarkable letter reveals how Bar Kochba sought to obtain the Four Species for his soldiers for the upcoming holiday of Succot. The letter, translated from its original Aramaic states:

> Simon to Judah Bar Manasseh who lived in Qiryath Arabvaya,
> "I have sent to you two donkeys that you shall send with them

---

[34]Deuteronomy 8:18.
[35]In these letters Bar Kochba was referred to as Ben Kusba.

two men to Yehonatan and to Masabala in order that they shall pack and send to the camp, toward you, palm branches [*lulavim*] and citrons [*etrogim*]. And you, from your place, send others who will bring you myrtles [*hadassim*] and willows [*aravot*]. See that they are tithed[36] and send them to the camp. [The request is made] since the army is big. Be well."[37]

Bar Kochba, no doubt, sought weapons to wage war against the oppressive rule of the Romans, but he also sought ritual objects at great expense. The Bar Kochba Revolt was fought for Jewish survival and independence against the emperor Hadrian, who sought to eliminate Jewish observances and rites in Judea.[38] In their fight for Jewish continuity, the Judean warriors sought the graces of the Almighty—Israel's greatest ally.

Eventually, however, it seems Bar Kochba might have overlooked this important lesson. His apparent military might prompted him to beseech God's neutrality, as if to say that victory against the forces of the mighty Roman Empire can be achieved by his own efforts alone. The Talmud[39] states that Bar Kochba expressed this by quoting a certain passage from the Psalms as he prepared for battle, stating "It is not You, O Lord, who has forsaken us; do not go forth, O God with our legions."[40] Bar Kochba's overconfidence in his own prowess was soon forgotten as Judea's initial military successes were followed by defeats and destruction at the hands of their enemies. Eventually, the Romans laid siege to town after town in Judea until the city of Betar—Bar Kochba's last stronghold—was captured.

---

[36]The separation of the priestly gifts and tithes.
[37]Descriptions, along with photographs of the Bar Kochba letters, appear in Yigal Yadin, "The Great Find," *Bar Kochba* (New York: Random House, 1971).
[38]See "Lag B'Omer and Yom Ha'atzmaut: The Twilight and the Dawn," pg. [cross-ref].
[39]Babylonian Talmud, Gittin 57A.
[40]Psalms 60:12.

Yet it is not his over-confidence and the revolt's failure that should be remembered on Succot but rather his ensuring that his soldiers would have *lulavim* and *etrogim* for Succot at their disposal. Bar Kochba's example of dedication to perform the commandment on the battlefield should serve as an example. When grasping the Four Species during the holiday of Succot, one should remember that victory and success must not be taken for granted. The very message of Succot—that everything comes from the Almighty—must be taken to heart.

ON THE WAY TO THE PROMISED LAND

The Exodus from Egypt prepared the Israelites for Mount Sinai and the receiving of the Torah. Their wandering in the desert for forty years—commemorated by Succot—prepared the Israelites for their eventual entry into the Promised Land. Long before Operation Magic Carpet on September 24, 1950, brought fifty-three thousand Yemenite Jews to Israel, many Jews of Yemen were already preparing for that journey.

There has been a Jewish community in Yemen since the destruction of the First Temple in 586 B.C.E. In their isolation, they endured centuries of persecution under Muslim rule, while tenaciously clinging to their fervent and unwavering belief in the eventual redemption of Israel. In the mid-nineteenth century, small groups of Yemenite Jews began to make the long journey by land and sea to the Promised Land. Over time, several factors would increase the small trickle of immigration. Oppression under Ottoman rule and an epidemic in 1879 severely worsened the situation for Yemenite Jewry. In addition, stories and rumors appeared that industrialist and philanthropist Edmund Rothchild, regarded by the Yemenite community as the "king" of the Jews, was purchasing land for Jewish settlement.

As Zionism took shape in the west in 1881, the *Aliyah* of groups of Yemenite Jews was already being organized clandestinely.

Simultaneously with the first wave of *Aliyah* from Eastern Europe, the Jews of Yemen began to leave the country in appreciable numbers. The largest group consisted of a caravan of a few hundred families. Their enthusiasm reflected their dreams, and those of their forefathers, of returning to the Promised Land. When they decided to make the long and arduous journey to the Land of Israel, the festival of Succot arrived and together they dreamed of their future and destiny on that Succot.

The celebration of that Succot is described by an anonymous author:

> And they celebrated the festival [of Tabernacles] with great rejoicing. And throughout the whole festival, day and night, men and women spoke only of the subject of Eretz Yisrael [the land of Israel]. And all the Jews who were in the capital of Yemen, Sana'a, and all the Jews of Yemen agreed together to sell all their houses and all their goods in order to use the money to journey to their country. And almost all of them neither slumbered nor slept at night, out of their longing and desire and the burning enthusiasm of their love for Eretz Yisrael. And so strongly did this love break out in their heart, that they cast away all their money, selling all their houses and possessions at an eighth of the value, in order to find money for the expenses of the journey by land and by sea.[41]

That Succot embodied the ancient dreams and hopes of Yemenite Jewry. As their ancestors dwelt in the Sinai wilderness, the stops on their journey were their opportunity to reflect upon the upcoming entry into the Promised Land. On Succot, Yemenite Jews about to embark to the Promised Land rejoiced in the coming fulfillment of their dreams.

---

[41]Bat Yaor, *The Dhimmi* (Rutherford, New Jersey: Fairleigh University Press, 1985), 376. *The Exodus From Yemen* (Tel Aviv).

WHEN THE JOY OF SUCCOT WAS CELEBRATED ON CHANUKAH: THE FIRST CHANUKAH CELEBRATION, A SEMI-SUCCOT

In the year 165 B.C.E., the holiday of Succot was not celebrated with its usual joy. The celebrations were subdued by a strong sense of loss along with the anxiety of anticipation. The sense of loss was because the Temple of Jerusalem was under the control of the Hellenists and their Syrian overlords, the anticipation came with the hope for the restoration of the Temple.

At this time, the Maccabees had led the nation in a revolt for almost three years. In the months prior to Succot, they had won two major victories at the Judean cities of Beit Horon and Emmas, but Jerusalem remained under the control of the enemy. The victories had not yet achieved the freedom for which they longed. When Succot arrived that year, they observed the holiday without its usual joy for they were hidden in the Judean hills aloof from the enemy while the Temple of Jerusalem was defiled by the Hellenists. The memories of the holiday, bringing the holiday sacrifices, celebrating the *Simchat Beit HaShoevah* (water drawing celebration) in the Temple courtyard, and entering the Temple courtyard with *lulav* and *etrog* in hand were sweet and not in the far distant past. For three years, Antiochus Epiphanes persecuted the people, and for almost three years Judah Maccabee and his followers hid in the Judean hills from the enemy. The people of Judea observed Succot as best as they could and waited for the time when it could again be celebrated upon the hallowed grounds of the Temple.

Not long after Succot in 165 B.C.E., a very decisive battle took place. General Lysias of Syria, who had directed the campaign from afar, personally moved tens of thousands of troops to Beit Tzur, located about twenty miles south of Jerusalem. There, Judah and his army of Maccabees, which numbered ten thousand men,[42] came out and routed the enemy. Lysias returned to Syria to bring an even

---

[42]Josephus Flavius, *The Complete Works of Josephus*, trans. William

larger force. In the meantime, Jerusalem was open to the Maccabees. Judah assembled the people and told them to go to Jerusalem. "Judas assembled the people together, and told them, that after these many victories which God gave them, they ought to go up to Jerusalem."[43] The Maccabees purified themselves and then entered the hallowed grounds of the Temple and proceeded in its purification.

The Second Book of Maccabees describes how they celebrated Chanukah in place of Succot:

> Now it so happened that the cleansing of the sanctuary took place on the very day on which it had been profaned by aliens, on the twenty-fifth day of the same month, which is Kislev. And they celebrated it for eight days with gladness like a Feast of Tabernacles [Succot], remembering how, not long before, during the Feast of Tabernacles they had been wandering like wild beasts in the mountains and caves [and were unable to celebrate the holiday].[44]

The holiday was celebrated symbolically. As Succot, it lasted for eight days, the ritual objects of Succot were used, and the Hallel prayers sung at Succot were sung on Chanukah as well. "Bearing wands wreathed with leaves and fair boughs and palms, they offered hymns of praise to Him who had prospered the cleaning of His own place."[45] Why did the Hasmoneans celebrate Chanukah in the manner of Succot, but not Passover, Shavuot, or any other Jewish holiday? Perhaps it is due to the many references to Succot as the Holiday of Joy and the references that connect Succot to future Messianic times.

Whiston (Grand Rapids, Michigan: Kregel Publications, 1981), vol. 7, chapter 7, verse 5.
[43]Ibid.
[44]The Second Book of Maccabees, 10:1–2.
[45]Ibid., 10:5–7.

Judah Maccabee and his court established a new eight-day holiday to be kept. The Maccabees, in the second of two letters to the Jews of Egypt, instructing them to keep the ordained holiday of Chanukah in the coming year, likened Chanukah to Succot. "See that you keep the days of the Feast like Tabernacles in the month of Kislev. . . . Whereas we are now about to celebrate the purification of the Temple in the month of Kislev, on the fifth and twentieth day, we deem it our duty to inform you, that you may keep the Feast like Tabernacles."[46]

On Chanukah, the Maccabees brought *lulavim* into the rededicated temple, as they chanted Psalms—praises to the Almighty who granted them victory.[47] With joy and celebration, they observed those holidays, which they had longed to keep within the sacred walls of Jerusalem. They celebrated Chanukah, a holiday separate unto itself, but in their celebrations they recalled Succot, the time of joy which was sorely missed by the people of Judea. In effect, they recaptured that joy on Chanukah.

JUDGEMENT DAY

The last day of Succot—Hoshanah Rabbah—is considered a day of judgement like Yom Kippur. The name Hoshanah Rabbah means many salvations, which refers to the prayers for salvation that are recited at the end of morning services on Succot. The final seal on the verdict placed upon a person on Yom Kippur is rendered on Hoshanah Rabbah.[48]

On Hoshanah Rabbah the nations of the world are judged as well. "On the seventh day of Succot [Hoshanah Rabbah], the judgement of the nations of the world is finalized. Sentences are

---

[46]Ibid.
[47]Ibid.
[48]Jerusalem Talmud, Rosh Hashanah 4:8.

issued from the residence of the King. Judgements are aroused and executed on that day."[49]

On Hoshanah Rabbah in 1947, a judgement was meted out against the leaders of Nazi Germany for their crimes against humanity in what was the most famous of all war trials.

The trials began on October 18, 1945, when twenty-one leaders of the third Nazi regime stood before the international military tribunal for their crimes in Nuremburg, Germany, the city where Nazi laws against the Jews were decreed in 1935. The counts in the indictment were: conspiracy to commit crimes named in the other three counts, crimes against peace, war crimes—violations of the laws or customs of war—and crimes against humanity.

Twenty-one defendants were judged before the court whose proceedings lasted for almost a year. On October 1, 1946, the sentences were determined. Twelve were given the death penalty, three were given life sentences, four received various prison sentences, and three were acquitted. Many of those sentenced to death played a major role in the extermination of European Jewry. The following defendants received the death penalty:

> Hermann Goering, Hitler's right-hand man—the Reichmarshal. On July 31, 1941, he directed Himmler and Heydrich to bring about "a complete solution of the Jewish question in the German sphere of influence in Europe."[50] Goering committed suicide on the day planned for his execution.
>
> Joachim Von Ribbentrop was a diplomat who helped plan German designs against England, France, and Czecheslovakia. In September of 1942, he ordered the German diplomatic

---

[49]Zohar Vayikra Rabba 316, quoted in Avraham Yaakov Finkle, *The Essence of the Holy Days: Insights from the Jewish Sages* (Northvale, New Jersey: Jason Aronson, 1993), 135.

[50]Harry Shneiderman and Morris Fine, eds., *American Jewish Year Book 1947–1948* (Philadelphia: Jewish Publication Society of America), 49:584.

representatives accredited to various satellites to hasten Jewish deportations to the east.[51]

Ernest Kaltenbrunner was an SS chief who became chief of the RSHA[52] on January 30, 1943. Under his knowledge and command, the SS and RSHA oversaw and played a major role in the murder of millions of Jews.[53]

Alfred Rosenberg was the chief ideologist of Nazism who spread the doctrine of hatred through the German media. Appointed by Adolph Hitler as Reich minister in the eastern occupied territories, he also helped plan the extermination of Jews.

Hans Frank was made governor general of the occupied Polish territory on October 12, 1939. Frank was a willing participant in the murder of at least three million Jews.[54]

Wilhelm Frick was largely responsible for bringing the German nation under the rule of the NSDAP (National Socialist German Workers Party). Frick drafted many laws intended to keep Jews out of German life and helped to formulate and implement the Nuremberg Laws of 1935.

Julius Streicher was Germany's chief Jew baiter. Streicher incited millions of Germans with his propaganda spread largely by the newspaper, *Der Shtrumer*. In 1938, he was already calling for the extermination of the Jews.

Following the trials, there was some criticism over the exoneration of three of the twenty-one defendants, once Germany's

---

[51]Martin Gilbert, *The Holocaust: A History of the Jews of Europe During the Second World War* (New York: Holt Rinehart and Winston, 1986), 439.
[52]A German abbreviation of Reichssicherheitshauptamt (Reich security main office).
[53]Ibid., 440.
[54]Ibid., 442.

leading industrialists and backers of the Nazi regime. The three, although not directly involved in German military affairs, had nonetheless made significant contributions to the rise of Nazism and were thus viewed as criminals. There were other criticisms of the trials as well.

The Jewish periodical *The Jewish Examiner* echoed the views of many at the time that there could be no justice to match the severity of Nazi crimes. In an editorial entitiled "The Verdict," *The Jewish Examiner* stated, "The verdict rendered by the International War Crimes Tribunal at Nuremburg can scarcely be called justice. The spectacle of Goering, Shtricher, Ribbontrop and the other sadistic criminals dangling at the end of a rope can not atone for the millions who were tortured at Bergenbelsen, Dachau, Buchenwald, and the other infernos operated by Nazi Germany."[55]

Indeed, there could never be true justice in the courtroom. However, the verdicts rendered did serve a purpose. Nuremberg was the most highlighted of war crimes trials and was an example followed by many others. On December 1, 1946, the United Nations War Crimes Commission announced that Great Britain, the United States, France, Greece, Norway, Czechoslovakia, and Poland had tried 24,365 people for war crimes. Of these 1,432 were sentenced to death, 16,413 to prison, and 6,520 acquitted. In addition, thousands were executed by the Soviets in Russian occupied territory and in trials under German denazifacation laws.[56]

Despite all the trials, there were thousands who directly and indirectly played a role in the murder of millions of Jews and non-Jews who would never face justice. But the trials sent the message to those involved in heinous acts that in the future they, too, could be held accountable for their actions by the nations of the world.

Before the eyes of the world, the sentences of the Nuremburg defendants were carried out. One by one, ten of humanity's most ruthless villains that ever lived were brought to the gallows. That

[55]*The Jewish Examiner* (October 4, 1946, 36:14) 4.
[56]Shniederman and Fine, *American Jewish Year Book*, 590.

day was October 16, 1947, the same day as Hoshanah Rabbah—when the nations of the world are judged.

THE JOY OF SIMCHAT TORAH IN THE SOVIET UNION

The holiday of Simchat Torah celebrates the completion of the annual weekly reading of the Torah. Not of biblical origin, the celebrations of Simchat Torah, which take place on the holiday of Shmini Atzeret, most probably began in the ninth century in Babylonia where the cycle of completing the reading of the Torah annually became the accepted practice.

In the former Soviet Union, many young people who seldom attended synagogue participated in Simchat Torah celebrations in an attempt to experience the kind of Jewish life that was denied them under Soviet rule.

This interest in Simchat Torah began in the early days of Communist rule. In one such instance, after the conclusion of services on Simchat Torah in one small Soviet town, the worshippers went out into the street and began dancing. Many young people joined the group, among them were members of the Komosol (Communist Party). The Simchat Torah festivities enraged the local party officials, who investigated the incident and found the local rabbi responsible. He was charged with counter-revolutionary propaganda. Thanks to the intervention of one judge, he was saved from a long-term incarceration.[57]

Although the rabbi was blamed, what surely angered, and even startled, the party officials so was the persistent involvement of the young and especially the young Communists. Many questions puzzled the Soviet officials in the decades to follow. What were they doing there? And why celebrate Simchat Torah? What was it about Simchat Torah that captured their attention?

---

[57]Joshua Rothenberg, *The Jewish Religion in the Soviet Union* (New York: Ktav Publishing House, 1971), 83.

Beginning in the early 1960s, a slight easing of Soviet restrictions against Jews allowed large Simchat Torah celebrations to be held. Over the following years in major Soviet cities such as Moscow, Leningrad, Minsk, and Tblisi, Jewish youth came out in the tens of thousands to synagogues to celebrate Simchat Torah. Their appearance was not motivated by traditional religious observance of which they knew little, rather they came to participate in the merriment and joy of the holiday. They sang and danced and rejoiced as a celebration of their Jewish identity.

By 1962, the Simchat Torah celebration had already become a significant event with thousands in attendance, most of whom were youths.[58] The next year, the celebrations brought an estimated fifteen thousand Jews to the Moscow Synagogue and ten thousand to Leningrad.[59] The Jewish Telegraphic Agency, quoting from *Le Monde*, noted the remarkable exuberance and spirit of the Simchat Torah 1963 celebrations: "the majority of young people sang and danced in front of the synagogue. The crowd, which in spite of official anti-Jewish measures, tried to openly demonstrate its attachment to Judaism, was far larger and more enthusiastic than in previous years."[60]

A member of an Israeli family that showed up at the Moscow Synagogue reported, "When we got there, it was already hemmed by thousands of people who filled the street from end to end. Everyone made way for us, as our children were the only ones who carried flags, and you could hear Jews whispering to one another, 'Amolige Kinder—children of the past.'"[61]

The Hebrew writer and wife of an Israeli diplomat Yemima Chernovitz-Avidar witnessed the Simchat Torah celebrations in Moscow and reported, "Like waves in a stormy sea, the people burst out dancing into the street. And the outside crowd, which

---

[58]Jewish Telegraphic Agency, no. 203 (October 22, 1962): 1.
[59]Ibid., no 198 (October 18, 1963): 1.
[60]Ibid. (October 17, 1963): 197:3.
[61]Ben Ami, *Between Hammer and Sickle* (Philadelphia: Jewish Publication Society of America, 1967), 92.

could not make a way for itself into the synagogue, greeted those coming out with the traditional song, 'Lomir ale yneinem di Yidn mekabel ponim zain.' . . . The dancers formed circles inside circles and the blowing of the horns of the cars trying to get through were of no avail. The street was closed and the crowd was in command."[62]

Elie Wiesel, who witnessed the Simchat Torah celebration in Moscow, dubbed the event in *The Jews of Silence* "The Festival of Youth" and paraphrased a Talmudic phrase, "He who has not witnessed the rejoicing of the law in Moscow has never in his life witnessed joy."[63] In describing the events of the night, Wiesel wrote, "How many were there? Ten thousand? Twenty thousand? More. About thrity thousand. The crush was worse than it had been inside the synagogue. They filled the whole street, spilled over into the courtyards, dancing and singing, dancing and singing. They seemed to hover in mid-air, Chagall-like, floating above the mass of shadows and colors below, above time, climbing a Jacob's ladder that reached to the heavens, if not higher."[64] To the outside observer as well as the Soviet authorities, the immensity of the celebrations remained an enigma.

For centuries, Simchat Torah has been observed with merriment and joy. Young Soviet Jews who rarely celebrated any other Jewish holiday celebrated Simchat Torah, venturing out from their hovels of religious estrangement and turning it into a history-making extravaganza. They were in attendance out of a need to express themselves as Jews. On Simchat Torah, which celebrates Israel's possession of the Torah, young Soviet Jews, sensing a need to express themselves as Jews, ventured to the existing, but dwindling, synagogues throughout the Soviet Union.

---

[62]Reported in *Davar* on October 10, 1965, quoted in Rothenberg, *The Jewish Religion in the Soviet Union*, 80.
[63]Ibid., 45. The Mishna Succah 5:1 states, "Whoever has not seen the Simchat Beit HaShoeva has not witnessed real joy in his life."
[64]Elie Wiesel, *The Jews of Silence* (New York: Holy, Reinhart, and Winston, 1966), 60.

10

Chanukah

CHANUKAH IN THE DAYS OF HELLENISM AND COMMUNISM

The events that surround the story of Chanukah occurred long ago and seem very distant, but they have recurred time and again. The Lubavitcher Rebbe Menachem Mendel Schneerson once said, "Chanukah teaches us that the sanctity and purity of Jewish life must be preserved at all costs."[1] This battle to preserve the sanctity of Jewish life did not just occur during the time of the Maccabees but has reocurred many times throughout history. The saga of Chanukah also took place in the twentieth century over a seventy-year span following the Communist Revolution in the Soviet Union. The similarities between the Chanukah of the Maccabees and the saga of Soviet Jewry are striking.

In ancient Judea, Antiochus Epiphanes, king of the Seleucid Empire, ascended the throne in 175 B.C.E. Epiphanes desired

[1] Y. M. Kagan, *A Thought for the Week: Adapted from the Works of Rabbi Menachem M. Schneerson, Lubavitcher Rabbi Shlita* (Michigan: Merkos L'Inyonei Chinuch Inc., 1968), 50:19.

uniformity of lifestyle within his kingdom and ruled that all peoples should adopt the ideals, customs, and forms of idolatry of his people. It was not an unreasonable request for the nations of the world who worshipped many deities, but for the Jews such a demand could never be obeyed. Thus, for several years, the Judeans maintained their traditions in isolation in Antiochus Epiphanes' kingdom; yet they were initially tolerated.

Over two thousand years later, following the October Revolution of 1917, the new Soviet regime also sought to unite all elements within their domain under the banner of Communism. Josef Stalin described Soviet policy regarding assimilation of nationalities as "the flourishing of cultures, nationalist in form and socialist in content, in the conditions of a proletariat dictatorship in one country, for the purpose of their fusion into one common socialist culture, common in both form and content, with one common tongue."[2] The notion of fusion of nationalities—or assimilation—drew support from many within the Jewish community. For those Jews, Communism appeared to signal the dawning of a new era of acceptance and an end to centuries of persecution under Czarist regimes. In due time, it became clear that the change of government in Soviet Russia presented new threats and dangers to Jewish survival.

Just a year following the revolution, a process to destroy the spiritual life of Soviet Jewry was set in motion, a process that would intensify over the years. In the years prior to the revolution, the handwriting was already on the wall. The father of modern communism, Karl Marx—a Jew himself—laid down the framework for the Soviet perceptions of Jews. In Marx's view, Jewish emancipation meant the abolishment of Judaism, or as he termed it the "emancipation of society from Judaism." Following the revolution,

---

[2]Josef Stalin, *Marxism and the National and Colonial Question*, 26, quoted in Lionel Kochin, "Soviet Theory on the Jews," in *The Jews in Soviet Russia Since 1917*, 3rd ed. (Oxford/New York/London: Oxford University, 1978), 59.

the Soviets sought to destroy the spiritual life of Soviet Jewry. Their objective was forced assimilation.

In ancient Judea, Jews had been in contact with adherents of Hellenism—the culture and religion of ancient Greece—since the invasion by Alexander the Great in 325 B.C.E. Over time, there were some Jews who took some interest in Hellenism, which embodied the worship of many deities, Greek culture and arts, and stressed physical and material pleasures. By the time of Antiochus' rule, a minority of Jews within Judea fully embraced Hellenism and its ideals.

During the early years in the rule of Antiochus Epiphanes, the Jewish Hellenists demonstrated their eagerness to adopt the predominant world culture. The Book of Maccabees states, "When Antiochus issued his decree that all must follow his laws, they [Jewish Hellenists] consented. They profaned the Sabbath and sacrificed to heathen altars."[3]

The Jewish Hellenists, or *Mityavnim*, no longer wanted to be regarded as outsiders within the Hellenistic world. They perceived the Torah and its laws as barriers that set them apart from the world in which they fervently sought acceptance. These Jews, who were amongst the upper class, sought to popularize Hellenism in Judea. "In those days there went out of Israel wicked men who persuaded many saying let us go out and make a covenant with the heathen that are around us; for since we had departed from them, we've had much sorrow."[4]

Menaleus, the Jewish high priest and a Hellenist who attained his position by offering a substantial bribe to Antiochus, was a zealot in his war against the Judaism of his fathers. Menaleus requested from Antiochus the right to build a Greek stadium in Jerusalem. He told the emperor that "they [Jewish Hellenists] were desirous to leave the laws of their country, and the Jewish way of

---

[3]The Second Book of Maccabees, 1:40.
[4]Ibid., 1:33.

living according to them and to follow the King's laws and the Grecian way of living."[5]

Such views no doubt influenced the king; he surely perceived the possibility that the Jews could indeed be swayed and thus pressured. When he eventually initiated the persecutions against the Jews, he acted under the influence of the Jewish Hellenists. "Then certain of the people who were so forward went to the king who gave them license to do the ordinances of the heathen."[6]

While Judea had its *Mityavnim*, Soviet Russia had its Jewish Communists. In Soviet Russia, as in Judea, there was little change in policy toward the Jews who had lived in autonomous communities for centuries, although the revolution itself had already produced some change. A 1917 report stated, "one of the chief aspects of the revolution is that the removal of the external pressure had brought, and is bringing about, a relaxation of the bonds which have . . . kept together all classes and Jews for centuries."[7] The feeling among Jewish revolutionaries was that the revolution itself would change the Jewish community. The initial Soviet policy toward Jews officially condemned all forms of anti-Semitism. Soviet premier Vladimir Lenin often denounced the pervasiveness of anti-Semitism in Russia as dangerous to the "revolution." In Lenin's view, the Jews would eventually assimilate if left alone. As the *Mityavnim* of ancient Judea, the Jewish Communists also sought the elimination of Jewish observances as a means to gain complete acceptance within Communist society. On October 20, 1918, the Jewish Commissariat, a wing of the Communist Party, passed a resolution that called for suspending the operation of Jewish institutions within Jewish quarters. The leaders argued that

---

[5]Josephus Flavius, "Antiquities of the Jews," in *The Complete Works of Josephus Flavius*, trans. William Whitson (Grand Rapids, Michigan: Kregel Publications, 1981), book 7, chapter 5, verse 1.

[6]The Book of Maccabees, 1:34.

[7]Zvi Yechiel Gittleman, "The Jewish Sections of the Communist Party and the Modernization of Soviet Jewry" (Ph.D. diss., Columbia University, 1968), 349.

Jewish institutions no longer had a place in Jewish life and were detrimental to the interests of the Jewish masses. This move attacked the base of Jewish spiritual life. As the *Mityavnim* had influenced Antiochus, the Soviet government took the cue from the Jewish Communists and officially outlawed Jewish institutions by decree nine months later. About a year later, the Jewish Communists passed another resolution outlawing all Jewish organizations. At the time, a wing of the Jewish Communist Party known as the *Yevsekszia* (Jewish section) began to function. The Yevsekszia was an entity, backed by the Soviet government, fanatically devoted to enforcing government legislation against Jewish observances as well as Zionism and the study of the Hebrew language. The first step in their campaign against Judaism was the formal abolishment of the "Kehilla" or Jewish community. From 1922–1923, over one thousand *cheders*[8] were closed. In Vitebsk alone, thirty-nine *cheders* with 1,358 students were shut down.[9] Over time, the Yevsekszia continuously issued more laws against Jewish practices as they conducted massive propaganda campaigns aimed at Jews in the Jewish press, at lectures, and at meetings. Members of the Yevsekszia who knew the workings of the Jewish community would spy on the rabbis, teachers, and laymen who continued to disseminate Jewish teachings to the Jewish masses. For years to come, the Jews feared both the government and their Jewish neighbors. Almost anyone could be a spy. Over time, observances such as circumcision and kosher slaughter were outlawed and eventually most Jewish practices became illegal. The Jews of Soviet Russia, a community immersed in a rich heritage that had withstood centuries of Russian anti-Semitism and oppression, now faced unprecedented dangers. Those who risked all and defied those edicts carried the torch of survival. As the Yevsekszia spied and informed on their fellow Jews, the *Mityavnim* in their era no doubt aided Antiochus in his campaign to root out Jewish observance.

---

[8]Literally meaning "room," refers to schools that taught Torah to Jewish boys.

[9]"The Jewish Section of the Communist Party."

The many who defied the decrees issued in both eras stood out as heroes. As the suppression of Judaism became the policy of both governments, Jews in both societies who were loyal to their traditions hid from the watchful eye of the government and continued their observances underground at great risk. In ancient Judea, thousands fled to the cover of the Judean hills to maintain Jewish observances away from the government. In hiding, their Jewish heritage was studied and the Torah's commandments were observed. Those who were found were executed. On one occasion, on the Sabbath, one thousand pious Jews found in a cave were slaughtered. Their deaths and those of others at that time gave rise to the new human phenomenon of martyrdom. In Soviet Russia, thousands also defied the decrees of their oppressors and faced imprisonment, exile, and often execution. There were many individuals who acted alone and privately maintained Jewish observance; others acted in small groups. They were the remnants of the famed yeshivas of Eastern Europe and Hassidic sects such as Chabad-Lubavitch, whose many deeds to perpetuate Judaism in Soviet Russia are legendary. These groups acted clandestinely and maintained underground networks. Being found attending a minyan in a private home or a yeshiva operating in a basement had its dangers and the many that were caught suffered the consequences. In the darkest times under Soviet rule, thousands of Jews maintained observant Jewish lives and many more also made great sacrifices to keep some level of observance. Undeterred by years of threats of imprisonment, exile, and execution, the Jews of the Soviet Union continued their struggle for spiritual survival.

In ancient Judea, Jews resisted Antiochus' decrees for three years until the rise of the Maccabees. The victory of Judah Maccabee and the liberation of the Temple in Jerusalem signified a victory for religious freedom and for Jewish survival. In the former Soviet Union, the determination of thousands of Jews paid off. In recent years, thousands of Soviet Jews in Israel, the West, and the Russian Republics have used their newfound freedoms to further their understanding, appreciation, and observance of Judaism. This is the sign of their victory, their Chanukah dedication. Both groups fought their battles for Jewish survival in different places and times but under similar circumstances. Both have their Chanukahs.

ANCIENT DREAMS AND THE RENEWAL OF HOPE

On Chanukah, in addition to pondering the Maccabee victories and the rededication of the Temple in Jerusalem, one can also reflect upon the events that transpired on Chanukah in 1917. At that time, a wave of enthusiasm and optimism spread over Jewish communities worldwide.

During the First World War, two powers fought over control of Palestine—the ruling Turks of the Axis and the British along with their allies. The outcome of the contest brought the ancient Jewish dream of the reestablishment of Jewish Statehood in the Jewish Homeland a little closer.

For almost four hundred years, the Turks maintained a tight and harsh rule over Palestine and its Jewish community. In the late nineteenth century, the Zionist movement began to take shape as Zionists began to settle the land. Yet their endeavors were thwarted under the stranglehold of the Turks. Land purchases by Zionists were generally prohibited and known Zionists were often subject to expulsion or imprisonment. During the war, however, a glimmer of hope appeared.

The British and their allies waged a campaign to wrest Palestine from the Turks. British General Edmund Allenby cunningly led his outnumbered troops to victory at the strategic Negev city of Be'er Sheba. As the success of the campaign seemed certain the British government, favorable to the aims of Zionism, issued the Balfour Declaration on November 2, 1917. The declaration sent by British foreign minister Lord Arthur Balfour to Jewish philanthropist Edmund De Rothchild called for the "establishment in Palestine of a national home for the Jewish people." England issued the declaration partly out of the desire to elicit the support of Russian Jewry behind the allied war effort and also out of the belief of many of its leaders that Zionism was the biblically-ordained destiny. All that seemed to stand in the way of the goal's realization was Britain's successful completion of the campaign. On November 6, Gaza fell to the British who then drove toward Jerusalem. With each British victory, more excitement and anticipation swept over Jewry. Aided by allied armies, the British fought their way through each town, flushing out the enemy until they reached Jerusalem.

On December 9, as Chanukah was approaching, the already defeated Turkish forces surrendered. In the battles for Jerusalem, twenty thousand Turkish soldiers and three thousand six hundred British and allied troops were killed. Two days later British troops marched into Jerusalem. Allenby humbly entered its walls through the Jaffa Gate by foot as the city's thirty-fourth conqueror.

Excited crowds of Jews stood along Jerusalem's ancient streets to welcome the city's liberators. One woman told a newspaper correspondent that the Jews "have been starving, but now we are liberated and free."[10]

The Jewish periodical *The Jewish Chronicle* described the allied conquest as an "Epochal event" and stated with mystic overtone, "It is as if Providence had placed its blessing upon an enterprise distinguished as had been the Palestine campaign by the historic [Balfour] declaration to the Jewish people."[11]

Rabbi J. H. Hertz, chief rabbi of the British Empire, forwarded a telegram to General Allenby that read, "British Jewry thrilled by glorious news from Palestine, sends heartfelt congratulations on historic entry into Holy City."[12]

With Jerusalem under British control, the British continued

---

[10]"Jerusalem Redeemed," *The Jewish Chronicle* 2542 (December 21, 1917): 5.
[11]"The Rising of Jerusalem," *The Jewish Chronicle* 2541 (December 14, 1917): 14.
[12]Ibid.

their campaign and soon ousted Turkish forces from all of Palestine. Three Jewish units participated in the completion of this conquest.[13]

Soon, the initial euphoria ended and the excitement calmed. The climate changed. Arab leaders in Palestine petitioned the British foreign office, strongly opposing increased Jewish immigration into the land. British military authorities also began to express disagreement with the aims of Zionism. Suddenly, under pressure, British commitments to the establishment of a Jewish Homeland seemed in jeopardy.

Barely a few months after the Balfour Declaration was issued, British military authorities banned its publication in Palestine. By 1919, the British military administration not only pushed for a revocation of the Balfour Declaration but also enforced stringent measures upon the Zionists. They restricted Jewish immigration into Palestine and land transfers to Jews. In addition, Hebrew was not recognized as an official language. The British even banned the public performance of the national anthem, *HaTikvah.*

Yet the hopes of the Zionists were again raised when the British civil mandate replaced a military administration in 1920. This change signified a return by the British government to its commitment to the principles of the Balfour Declaration. A Jew sympathetic to Zionism, Herbert Samuel, was appointed high commissioner and the gates were open to Jewish immigration. In the spring of 1921, ten thousand Jewish immigrants arrived in Palestine. The development of the land and its institutions accelerated as well.

These developments angered the opponents of Zionism, who reacted violently. Arab riots soon broke out throughout the land. Samuel responded by granting concessions to the rioters, succumbing to the pressures of violence and terror. Restrictions were again imposed against the Zionists. However, the task of building the

---

[13]As the Turks were in flight, the Jewish legion was the first to cross the Jordan River.

Jewish State continued despite the difficulties. Following the Arab revolt against the British in 1936, the Pehle Commission was set up, which suggested the partition of the land. The Arabs in their vehement opposition intensified the revolt putting the pressure on the British. Prime Minister Neville Chamberlin in an act of appeasement to the Arabs issued the infamous Passfield White Paper of 1939. The White Paper severely restricted Jewish immigration and called for the eventual establishment of one state with an Arab majority—a devastating blow to the Zionists, and which spelled disaster for the Jews of Europe.

The Jewish struggle for a homeland was far from over. Just as the Maccabees fought many wars and battles after liberating the Temple, the events of 1917 were significant. With the climatic events of 1917, the Jews of Israel did not yet achieve their freedom. The British mandate denied them the necessary rights that come with independence, but it did represent progress in that long journey.

Under British rule, the Jews were able to build an infrastructure, but that alone did not suffice. There would be many struggles and sacrifices made to oust the British and then defend the newborn state against its enemy's attacks. What the shift of powers during Chanukah 1917 accomplished was to bring the Jews one step closer to the eventual establishment of the State of Israel. Who knows what history will be made this Chanukah or in the Chanukahs of the future.

A CHANUKAH VICTORY

Changes in post-Holocaust Spain in the 1960s led to a shift in an age-long policy of religious bigotry. On Chanukah 1968, those changes and the first public dedication of a synagogue in centuries were celebrated hand in hand.

Over four hundred fifty years after Jews were ordered to leave Spain in 1492, official permission was granted to the Jews to reestablish a Jewish community. The liberalism of Europe in the prior century resulted in the abolishment of the centuries old Inquisition, but Jews were still officially prohibited from living in Spain. The consecration of the first synagogue, Midrash Abarbanel, took place on February 3, 1917.[14] The synagogue was on the second floor of a structure located in the city of Puerto Del Sol and its congregation consisted primarily of wartime refugees from eighteen different countries. The room housing the synagogue itself was able to hold about one hundred people.[15] Midrash Abarbanel hosted the first services that were conducted openly in Spain since the expulsion. However, the Jews were still not officially recognized, they were merely tolerated and permitted to practice Jewish rites privately.

In the 1960s, the Catholic Church adopted a variety of new positions on Catholic-Jewish relations, putting an end to some of the anti-Jewish policies of the Middle Ages. Taking the church's cue, the Spanish government, under the leadership of General Francisco Franco, began to enact legislation that seemed to show tolerance toward non-Catholics. On December 14, 1966, a referendum took place where the following statement was made: "The state shall assume the responsibility for protecting religious freedom."[16] On June 28, 1967 after much debate, law no. 44 was passed granting religious freedom to all non-Catholics.

The law "guaranteed also the public profession and practice of religion and a variety of individual rights flowing from this, e.g., equal facilities for marriage and burial for non-Catholics as for Catholics; the right to choose the faith of one's children. It also enabled all non-Catholic concessions to apply for legal recognition

---

[14]Midrash Abarbanel was named after the famed scholar and leader of Spanish Jewry in the fifteenth century, Isaac Don Abarbanel.

[15]Caesar Aronsfeld, *The Ghosts of 1492: Jewish Aspects of the Struggle for Religious Freedom in Spain 1848–1976* (New York: Columbia University Press, 1979), 30.

[16]Haim Avni, *Spain, the Jews, and Franco* (Philadelphia: Jewish Publication Society of America, 1982), 201.

by constituting religious associations," to be governed by their own statues and to "obtain juridical personality in all respects once inscribed in a special Government register provided for by the law."[17]

On December 14, 1968, the government issued a statement in which the Hebrew Congregation of Madrid was expressly recognized and "full rights of citizenship" were conferred upon the Jewish religion. In addition, the 1492 edict of expulsion was officially revoked.[18] Two days later, on December 16, the second day of Chanukah, "Congregation Beth Yaakov in Madrid was consecrated in the presence of a large congregation which included, representatives from all over Spain, Morocco, the United States, Britain, Portugal and Argentina."[19] Various Jewish and Christian organizations were also well represented.[20] At the consecration, minister of justice Antonio Oriol issued an order revoking the expulsion edict of the Catholic kings.[21] However, Spain's Jews were still subject to state inspection and supervision. It was not until 1977 when a new, more pro-democratic regime was set up after Franco's death in 1975 that the Jews were granted complete freedom of religion.

Ultimately, the final chapter of the trials and tribulations of Spanish Jewry did not end until the late twentieth century. On Chanukah 1968, the revival of a synagogue in Madrid served as testimony, proving that the might of tyrants and inquisitors does not outlast that of those who cling to their ideals. Such was Chanukah in the time of Judah Maccabee and in Madrid 1968.

---

[17]Aronsfeld, *The Ghosts of 1492*, 58.
[18]Ibid., 59. However, these rights were with limitations. No mention was made of the day to day rights of non-Catholics, who were still subject to state inspections. Their freedom was not sufficiently guaranteed.
[19]Ibid.
[20]Ibid.
[21]Avni, *Spain, the Jews, and Franco*, 202.

TWO CHANUKAH DEDICATIONS

The Maccabees battled for three years in order to liberate and rededicate the Temple in Jerusalem; the Jews of Newport, Rhode Island, waited for over one hundred years before they could construct a synagogue and celebrate a *Chanukat HaBayit* (dedication ceremony) for their new synagogue. Unlike most synagogues, the Touro Synagogue, which was first named the Hebrew Congregation of Newport and later became known as Congregation Yeshuat Yisrael of Newport, Rhode Island, experienced two dedications.

In 1758, the Jewish community of Newport purchased a parcel of land to build a synagogue in what was then part of the outskirts of the town. Almost one hundred years earlier, fifteen families, who were formerly Morranos, arrived and enjoyed the tolerance that Rhode Island displayed toward them. For those first one hundred years, the Jews met for worship in a private home.

When the Jewish community of Newport decided to take on the project of building a sanctuary, they appealed to their brethren of Congregation Shearit Yisrael in New York for needed financial assistance. The response was prompt and generous: "Conformable to your desire a *nedaba* [offering] was made in our synagogue the seventh day of Pesach [Passover] when a contribution of £149:6 was offered toward building at Newport a place of worship to the Almighty God."[22] Other appeals to Jewish communities in Jamaica, Curacao, Surinam, and London also met with helpful responses.[23]

On August 1, 1759, the ground was broken with six cornerstones. Soon the community would have a spiritual leader. Rabbi Isaac de Abraham Touro, educated in the famous academies of Europe, settled in Newport and became the synagogue's *chazzan* (cantor).[24]

As the community again ran short of funds during construc-

---

[22]Lee M. Freidman, *Pilgrims in a New Land* (Westport, Connecticut: Greenwood Press, 1979), 123.
[23]Ibid., 124.
[24]Ibid., 125.

tion, the assistance of Congregation Shearit Yisrael was again sought and received. After four years, the synagogue was completed and the day for the dedication finally arrived. The ceremony occurred on December 2, 1763, which was also the first day of Chanukah. The long awaited ceremony was a joyful event. The Torah scrolls were paraded into the synagogue and placed into the ark accompanied by the appropriate prayers. For the next thirteen years, the Touro Synagogue thrived. However, the life of the synagogue was cut short.

At the beginning of the American Revolution in 1776, the British captured Newport. The city's Jews, who were ardent supporters of the patriot cause, fled. During the British occupation, the synagogue's doors were closed. After the revolution, some Jews returned to Newport, but the Jewish community had dwindled as many members migrated to New York and other cities. By the end of the century, the synagogue stood empty, no longer functioning. It seemed that the use of the synagogue had come to an end and from then on would merely occupy the annals of colonial Jewish history.

By 1822 there were no longer any Jews in Newport.[25] However, the two sons of Rabbi Touro—Abraham and Judah—both successful businessmen and philanthropists, never forgot the synagogue. Upon their deaths in 1822 and 1854, they both left substantial gifts for its maintenance and preservation. The state of Rhode Island also enacted a statute administering funds to support the synagogue, which fell under the guardianship of Shearit Yisrael of New York. Thus, the synagogue building—though no longer used for services—remained, hosting thousands of visitors who came to glimpse this icon of colonial Jewish life.

The famed poet Henry Longfellow visited Newport in 1858 and composed a poem dedicated to the once existing Jewish community entitled "The Jewish Cemetery in Newport."

---

[25]Morris A. Gutstein, *To Bigotry No Sanction: A Jewish Shrine in America 1658–1958* (New York: Bloch Publishing Company, 1958), 93.

> Closed are the portals of the synagogue, No psalms of David now the silence break, No rabbi reads the ancient Decalogue In the grand dialect of the prophets spake. Gone are the living but the dead remain, And not neglected; for a hand unseen, Scattering its bounty, like a summer rain, Still keeps their graves and their remembrance green.

But Jewish life would return to Newport when new Jewish immigrants from Eastern Europe came to America. Just as Newport's original Jewish settlers of Spanish-Portuguese descent had fled persecution in search of a new haven, those who arrived at Newport as part of the massive wave of Eastern European Jews in the late nineteenth century also found sanctuary in Newport. Soon, the synagogue was again in use by a growing community.

On May 23, 1883—two hundred twenty-five years after the first Jews settled in Newport—a reconsecration took place.[26] The service for the event included the usual prayers for the occasion and was concluded with a memorial prayer for Isaac, Abraham, and Judah Touro. Ten years later, the Touro Synagogue was officially renamed Congregation Yeshuat Israel. As more Jews arrived, the congregation continued to grow. Today Congregation Yeshuat Israel—a national landmark since 1946—is the center of a thriving Jewish community.

In their search for freedom, the Jews of Newport found a hospitable environment. However, shortly after they managed to establish a synagogue, the community was forced to disband. Yet, the generosity of some its members—along with Rhode Island's acknowledgment of the community's contributions to the Revolutionary War—preserved the synagogue. In time, the Touro Synagogue would again be filled with worshippers. The synagogue had indeed experienced two Chanukahs—two dedications.

---

[26] Ibid., 108.

11

Tu BiShvat

PLANTING FROM THE REMAINS

Most everyone knows that the holiday of Tu BiShvat is associated with the planting of trees in Israel. Throughout the centuries, trees have been planted in Israel on Tu BiShvat as a celebration of the special qualities of the land, as well as its connection to the Jewish people. Prior to the scorching of the land by Roman legions following the Judean revolts over eighteen hundred years ago, Israel was adorned with lush forests and bountiful produce.

In the latter half of the nineteenth century when the Turks ruled the land, the first waves of Zionist immigrants began to arrive. Their objective was to develop the land and restore it to its former splendor. When Tu BiShvat arrived, they would gather together and mark the day with tree planting ceremonies. Soon, clusters of young saplings were transformed into forests. Each forest that was planted brought the dream of a Jewish State a little closer—a dream that seemed distant while the land was under the harsh rule of the anti-Zionist Turks. Just as every forest was precious, so, too, was each tree. The story of one particular tree symbolized the plight of

Zionism in its earliest days and proved that adversity might be an obstacle but not a deterrence. No impediments would prevent the development of the land of Israel.

While visiting Israel in 1898, Theodore Herzl sought an audience with German Kaiser Wilhelm II, who was also in the Holy Land. After visiting the coastal settlements of Mikve Yisrael and Rishon LeTzion, Herzl traveled toward Jerusalem. As he passed through the Judean hills, he noticed its splendor as well as its barrenness due to neglect over the centuries. However, he noticed an island of green amidst the desolation. It was a small Jewish settlement, the only one in the area. The settlement, named Motza, possessed a population of two hundred people and was located several miles west of Jerusalem. Its abundance of olive, date, and apricot trees, along with clusters of grapevines, gave it its fertile appearance.

Herzl and his entourage proceeded toward the village where he was warmly received. As he rested in the shade, he gazed upon the land of Judea. The sun began to set and a variety of lights of brilliant colors reflected upon its hills. Captivated by the sight, he told members of his entourage that he wished to plant a tree at that location. Herzl ascended the hill and planted a young cypress tree. The tree grew rapidly. Six years later, it stood tall and statuesque signifying to the settlers the Jewish people's return to Zion.

Seven years later, on the twentieth day of the Hebrew month of Tammuz 1905, Herzl died at age 45. The stunned members of the Yishuv mourned his death and continued to commemorate their leader in the years to come. On the day of his *yahrzeit* (the anniversary of his death), Zionist youth continued to ascend that hill and plant trees around Herzl's.

When World War I broke out several years later, the British and the Turks were locked in a bitter struggle over control of the Holy Land. As the tide of battle was turning in favor of the British, the Turks, suffering a wave of defeats, vented out their anger upon the Zionists. Many were imprisoned or exiled; others had their wealth and businesses confiscated. Despite the hardships, the settlers continued to develop the land. When the twentieth of Tammuz arrived in 1917, Zionist youth in accordance with the annual custom once again returned to Herzl's tree, but they found that it had not survived. The Turks had hewn it down. Scattered around the remains of the tree, the young Zionists found cones from the cypress tree, which they placed in their pockets. They returned to Jerusalem under cover that night to avoid the watchful eyes of the Turks. Those cones, which contained numerous seeds, were carefully guarded.

In 1917, the Turks were defeated and forced out of the land. The four hundred-year rule of the Turks was over. Those who collected and guarded the seeds proceeded to plant them throughout the land. Soon, from Herzl's destroyed tree, many young trees sprung forth across the land of Israel—from Galilee to the Judean hills.[1]

The settlement of Motza was likewise cut down. A wave of Arab riots against the Jews erupted throughout the Holy Land in 1929, and Motza suffered at the hands of Arabs from neighboring villages. The beleaguered settlement was soon abandoned. However, four years later a new settlement, Moshav Motza Ilith (Upper Motza) was established near that location, situated slightly higher on the same hill.[2] In clear view of the Moshav rested the remains of Herzl's cypress tree.

A tree was cut down, but its seeds remained in order to be planted in the future. On Tu BiShvat, a nation plants seeds to recover what was lost in the past. The Romans might have left the land bare, but there was always hope for its revival and the renewal of its legendary forestry. Every Tu BiShvat those seeds, which are remnants of the destruction of forests in the past, are planted to build future forests in the land of Israel.

---

[1]The story of Herzl's cypress tree is common. In his own account of his trip to Eretz Yisroel, Herzl wrote about planting the cypress tree at Motza ("Jerusalem Visit," in *Sefer HaYamin Shel Herzl*, (Nov. 1898). The facts here are based on the rendition found in Eliezer Shmuelit, "Herzl's Cypress," in *Sefer HaMoadim* 5, 446.

[2]Today, Motza Ilith is located within the expanded boundaries of Jerusalem.

12

Purim

ESTHER'S TRUE IDENTITY

> And Esther did not reveal her nationality nor her lineage, for Mordechai commanded her not to tell.[1]

The Morranos (secret Jews of Spain and Portugal) hid their Jewish faith and true identity for hundreds of years from their tormentors—the enforcers of the Inquisition. If they were discovered maintaining Jewish traditions, they would have faced the horrors of the Inquisition. The Morranos often identified their plight with that of the biblical personality Queen Esther who concealed her Jewish identity from all around her in the king's palace in the Persian capital of Shushan. It is no wonder that the fast day of *Taanit Esther* (the Fast of Esther)[2] had special meaning to the Morranos.[3]

---

[1]The Book of Esther, 2:10.
[2]This fast falls on the day before Purim to commemorate the fast the Jews of Persia commenced when they learned of Haman's decree.
[3]Cecil Roth, *A History of the Morranos* (New York: Schocken Books, 1974), 235.

For five hundred years, those Portuguese Jews who continued Jewish practices did so in terror. They struggled to maintain their Jewish lives in secrecy and elude the terrifying hand of the Inquisition. They were well aware that if discovered, their greatest nightmares would be realized. Such was the existence of the Morranos.

After King Manoel of Portugal married off his son to the daughter of Ferdinand and Isabella of Spain, he was pressured by Spain's monarch to do as they had done in 1492 and expel the Jews. Manoel ordered the expulsion, but with some reluctance for he was well aware of the vital roles which Jews played in Portugal's economy. His method of expelling the Jews differed from that of Ferdinand and Isabella. He sought to officially expel the Jews and yet have them remain in his country at the same time. He ordered the Jews to convert if they wished to remain in Portugal; and those who chose to leave were allowed to stay an additional year in the country. Most Jews chose to leave. Among those who left were Rabbi Yitzchak Karo, the uncle of Rabbi Yosef Karo who authored the *Shulchan Aruch* (*Code of Jewish Law*); Rabbi Levi ben Habib, who subsequently served as rabbi in Jerusalem; and Rabbi Abraham Zacuto, the famous astronomer. Yet the king, who did not want to lose the Jews and also considered it his religious duty "to save their souls," sought to keep them in Portugal by any means. In doing so, he would prove how ruthless he was.

On the first day of Passover, March 19, 1497, King Manoel ordered that all children between 4 and 14 years of age be taken from their parents and undergo baptism; he was thus able to forcibly baptize thousands of Jewish children. It was a scene of horror: thousands of children were torn from their parent's arms as both parents and children wept and cried out in anguish. In order that their children would not be baptized, many parents suffocated their children in their final embrace or threw them to drown in the rivers.[4]

Following the forced baptisms, many parents who initially

---

[4]Cecil Roth, *Jewish Book of Days: A Day to Day Almanac of Events*

were ready to depart, underwent baptism and remained with their children. King Manoel also ordered the Jews to gather in Lisbon prior to their departure. The twenty thousand who gathered there were forcibly herded into a pen and denied food and water for three days. After the vast majority still refused to be baptized, he ordered them into a nearby church where they were forcibly baptized and declared equal citizens of the realm.[5] When many of the families of those who were forcibly baptized began to emigrate, the king responded on April 21, 1499, by prohibiting the right of these "New Christians," as they were then referred to, to emigrate. Thus, the Portuguese king found a way to officially expel the Jews and yet also keep them in his country.

Thousands of Jews remained virtually locked into Catholicism by official conversion yet were devoted to the maintenance and continuity of their Jewish traditions.[6] Unlike the Spanish Expulsion of 1492 when all professed Jews were ordered out, thousands were forced to remain in Portugal, thereby creating a post-expulsion Morrano community larger then the one in Spain. Portuguese Jews continued to live as Jews in a land where Jews were officially forbidden. For the first twenty years, the king adhered to Pope Alexander IV's request that he should show leniency toward the Jews. However, during that time, a riot broke out in April 1506 and two thousand secret Jews were killed. This prompted the king to allow Jewish emigration, but in 1521 the king again prohibited the right of secret Jews to leave. The respite was over.

The Portuguese Inquisition officially began in 1536, when Pope Paul III issued a bill on May 23 announcing an Inquisition in Portugal. The first execution—the auto-da-fe (act of faith)—was held in 1540 and several secret Jews were burned. Although officials of the church sought out the Morranos, the Morranos

---

From the Settlement of Jews in Europe to the Balfour Declaration (New York: Herman Press, 1966), 68.

[5] *Encyclopedia Judaica* (Jerusalem: The Macmillan Co., Keter Publishing House, 1972), 13:922.

[6] Roth, *A History of the Morranos*, 231.

maintained a well organized underground network. Many managed to elude the authorities, but many did not. Over the next two centuries, over twenty thousand New Christians became the victims of the auto-da-fe. A single anonymous accusation brought to the authorities could put a suspected Morrano in grave danger. Before their inquisitors, those who denied their "guilt" were often tortured until they confessed. The guilty were imprisoned for years, banished, publicly whipped, and sometimes executed by being burned alive upon pyres.

The fires of the auto-da-fe could not destroy the will of the Morranos. Despite all, many persevered and continued the transmission of Jewish tradition for centuries. One example of such dedication is captured in an account of an inquisitor who witnessed a burning of twenty Morranos and was astonished by their bravery. "Children attended the burnings of their parents and wives of those of their husbands and no one heard them cry or weep. They said farewell as if they were parting to meet the next day."[7]

The Morranos evaded the long arm of the Inquisition by appearing to be practicing Catholics. One could visit a community of Morranos and not be aware of their presence. Such was the situation for hundreds of years.[8]

Over time, the dual lives of the Morranos took their toll on their level of Jewish observance. The historian and author Cecil Roth refers to a "Morrano religion." The Morranos maintained some basic beliefs and practices, but lost many traditions as well.[9] Some practices continued. The Sabbath and some festivals were still observed to a degree. In addition, the Morranos maintained Jewish fundamental beliefs and continued to marry only into other Morrano families. They also maintained a few prayers that were chanted in Portuguese and had some of their own liturgy.[10]

---

[7]Ibid., 240.
[8]Ibid., 235.
[9]Ibid.
[10]Cordozo de Bethencourt, "The Jews in Portugal from 1773 to

By the middle of the eighteenth century, opposition to the Inquisitions of Portugal and Spain by the other European nations mounted. The Protestant areas of northern Europe and France,[11] which experienced the beginnings of an age of enlightenment, harshly condemned the Inquisitions. Jews around the world also voiced their condemnations. Following years of such opposition, members of Portugal's hierarchy began to voice their protests against church policies as well. Change in Portugal was inevitable. Under the rule of Sebastian Joseph de Carvalhoe Mello, Marquis of Pombal, Portugal began its exit from the medieval world. On May 2, 1768, he ordered the destruction of all registers containing the names of the New Christian families.[12] Slowly, the forces of persecution began to weaken and wane. The last auto-da-fe took place in 1791.

On March 21, 1821, the Inquisition was formally abolished. By that time, it was assumed that only a few, if any, Jews remained in Portugal. But in fact thousands remained. In 1867, J. Kayserling, the eminent historian who made a lifelong study of the subject, closed his classical monograph on the Jews of Portugal with a reference to the complete oblivion of Judaism among the descendants of the New Christians. The Morranos of Portugal had no doubt declined. Aside from the difficulty of maintaining Jewish observances over the duration of centuries, those with the financial means fled Portugal. Many also assimilated, especially after the Inquisitions ended. It was generally assumed that the phenomenon of crypto-Judasim was eliminated with the end of the Inquisition and the Morrano isolation. However, there were still Morranos maintaining secret lives throughout Portugal. They were conditioned to maintain their secrecy as if it was a part of their tradition. Although the political climate of the times had changed, their habits did not.

In post-inquisition Portugal, the Jewish community of Lisbon

1902," eds. I. Abrahams and C. G. Montifiore, *Jewish Quarterly Review* 15 (1903): 261.

[11]Protestants also suffered in the Inquisition.

[12]Roth, *History of the Morranos*, 351.

numbered several hundred families. The community possessed a synagogue, Jewish school, *mikveh* (ritual bath), and even a kosher restaurant. But Lisbon's Jewish community possessed few former Morranos. Most members of the community were from neighboring countries or foreigners engaged in business.[13] A report at that time on the Jews of Portugal stated that there no longer existed a community of Morranos.[14] There were only claims of a few who lived in smaller, more remote areas distant from the inquisitor's eyes.[15]

In 1917, Samuel Schwartz, a Polish Jewish mining engineer living in Portugal, was the first to discover a community of Morranos while on a business trip in a remote town near the Spanish border named Belmonte. The encounter was purely by chance. Neither was aware of the existence of the other. Schwartz was unaware of the continued existence of Morranos in Portugal and the Morranos of Belmonte had no knowledge of any Jews other then those within their own area. For all they knew, they were the last surviving Jews in the world. It is thus understandable that they were initially suspicious of his claim to be a Jew. When they asked Schwartz to recite a prayer in order to ascertain the truth of his claim, he recited the *Shema*.[16] The Jews of Belmonte were not familiar with Hebrew, and its leaders, who were elderly women, did not recognize the prayer. What they did recognize was the name of God contained in the prayer. That was sufficient to win their trust. On that day, Schwartz discovered an unknown world, as did the Jews of Belmonte.

Around that time, a Portuguese citizen attempted to revive the Jewish community of Portugal. Barros Bastro served with distinction in the Portuguese army and reached the rank of captain. Following World War I, Bastro—born of a Jewish father but a non-Jewish mother—officially converted to Judaism and opened a

[13]de Bethencourt, "The Jews in Portugal," 271.
[14]Ibid., 273.
[15]Ibid., 274.
[16]Dan Roth, *Acts of Faith: A Journey to the Fringes of Jewish Identity* (New York: St. Martin's Press, 1982), 31.

synagogue in the port city of Porto. Bastro also organized groups of Morranos, published a Jewish newspaper, *HaLapid*, and in 1929 even opened up a yeshiva, the Rosh Pinah Jewish Theological Seminary. But with the sudden revival, old prejudices resurfaced. Catholics began to boycott the businesses of Jews active in their Jewish communities and a synagogue in Pinhel was attacked during an Easter procession.[17] The Portuguese press attacked Bastro himself. To make matters even worse, the Nazi propaganda of that era began to seep into Portugal. The backlash, along with internal conflict within the Jewish community of Porto, critically damaged the Morrano revival. Out of fear, some left Portugal; many went back to or maintained their private Morrano existence while others simply vanished, assimilating into the outside world. Little remained of Bastro's revival efforts.

In Belmonte, however, hundreds of Morranos continued to maintain Jewish lives in secrecy. They married amongst themselves and celebrated the Sabbath, Passover, and Yom Kippur. They also observed the fast day of *Taanit Esther*. However, the Morranos of Belmonte observed the fast on Purim day itself, partly out of confusion and partly as identification with Queen Esther, who concealed her Jewish identity from those around her in the king's palace in ancient Persia.

In recent decades, the Morrano community in Belmonte has ended its traditional secrecy and no longer hides its identity. Today on a narrow street in Belmonte, the recently constructed local synagogue, Bet Eliyahu, serves the one hundred fifty Jews of Morrano decent. In 1992, a rabbi from Israel arrived and taught the community Jewish laws and Hebrew and arranged for their official conversions.

Inside the synagogue, a plaque recalls the history of Belmonte. In Hebrew, it states:

> Here in this place the chain was not broken . . . Here in the village of Belmonte. In this house and the neighboring houses

---

[17]Ibid., 37.

> lay the heart of the Jewish area. A full and rich Jewish life was lived in days past. Then as a result of government decrees, the Jews of this community were pressed as the Jews throughout Spain and Portugal to change their religion and to observe their Judaism in the home.
>
> Here the candle was never extinguished. Here in the houses of this village, they kept the Jewish mitzvot in secret from 1492–1992. They transferred the tradition from generation to generation secretly. Observing Shabbat in their hearts and outwardly keeping Sunday in front of surrounding neighbors. They were forced to live double lives. They were careful not to mix Jewish and Christian customs, out of fear that they could fall into the hands of the Inquisition. They blessed the *challah* and the wine by secretly adding words to the prayers and they preserved Judaism in their inner souls.
>
> Here the Jewish soul was not lost. Here the Jewish soul remains forever. From the past, the future is born. From the ashes of yesteryear to the light of this *Beit Knesset* and this Jewish center.

As Purim arrives, the Jews of Belmonte will give reverence to the holiday as they always have, but now they can do so in the open without fear. Just as Esther concealed her identity for a special purpose, the Jews of Belmonte concealed their identity for hundreds of years as a means of self-preservation. Today, they no longer conceal their identity and they no longer live in fear.

Perhaps there are yet other Belmontes out there whose existences are still unknown. As Ephraim Ben-Israel, a Brazilian-born town planner, was quoted as saying of the other Portuguese towns in a *Jerusalem Report* article, "Nobody knows how many Jews there are in these places."[18] Who knows how many Esthers in Portugal have yet to reveal their true identities?

---

[18]Hanan Sher, "Portuguese Epilogue," *Jerusalem Report* (July 20, 1998): 31.

HAMAN'S EVIL DECREE

On April 1, 1920—the thirteenth day of the Hebrew month of Nissan—a political organization on the far right in Germany known as the D.A.P., the German Workers Party, was renamed the N.S.D.A.P., the National Socialist German Workers Party or the Nazi Party. On that day, Nazism officially came into being. The thirteenth of Nissan was also the day that Haman, the main villain of Purim, published a decree calling for the extermination of all Jews.[19]

The D.A.P. emerged in 1919 as a miniscule group of seven. Hitler joined the group and soon became its leader. Hitler transformed the D.A.P. into a larger organization, bringing in members and raising funds. Along with the group's founder, Anton Drexler, he also drew up a twenty-five point platform. One point called for the "end of predominance of Jewry in government and public life." A month later, the D.A.P. was renamed the N.S.D.A.P., better known by its abbreviated version—the Nazi Party.

The growth of Nazism was explosive. A few hundred members in 1920 expanded to over six million in less than a decade. Ironically, six months earlier, in 1919, the democratic Wiemar Republic was formed after receiving over 75 percent of the popular vote. As democracy finally arrived in Germany, the roots of Nazism had sprung. Wiemar would soon become past history and Hitler would drastically transform Germany's social and political landscape.

In ancient Persia, the Persian king Achashverosh reigned during a politically liberal era when the Persian Empire consisted of one hundred twenty-seven nationalities. Achashverosh appeared to be a tolerant ruler who showed respect toward all peoples under his rule. In Persia, the Jews prospered; so much so that most Jews chose to remain in Persia when Emperor Cyrus permitted them to return to Israel to rebuild the Temple just decades after their

---

[19]Esther 3:12.

exile.[20] The Jews' memories of Jerusalem faded in the comforts of their new surroundings.

At the beginning of the Purim saga, Achashverosh threw an elaborate seven day banquet for the entire population of the capital Shushan and also invited many subjects throughout the empire. A large representation of Jews attended. They enjoyed the festivities while they dined on kosher cuisine prepared for them. During the festivities, they watched from their specially assigned seating area without repulsion, as utensils from the destroyed Temple of Jerusalem were brought out for display.[21] Little did they know that the party would soon end and Haman, an advisor to the king, would emerge on the scene.

Hitler and Haman both rose to power intent upon annihilating the Jews.

When Mordechai would not bow before Haman as all the other servants of the king, he became enraged[22] and he used this as a pretext to pursue what he intended to do from the beginning of his ascent to political power—destroy the Jews. The Megillah's identification of Haman reveals his true intentions. It refers to him as Haman ben haMamedata HaAgagi, Haman the Aggagite—the descendant of King Agag, the king of Amalek who was the sole survivor of Israel's war fought against his nation due to the Almighty's command to destroy Amalek. Agag lived long enough to father a son and perpetuate the nation before being killed by the prophet Samuel. The purpose of Amalek's existence was to menace the Jews and challenge their existence. The Amalekites, who had the audacity to attack the Israelites as they headed toward Mount Sinai, despised the ideals, beliefs, and values of the Jews to the point of obsession. For the Amalekites, there was no room in the world

[20]Achashverosh halted construction of the Temple following a false accusation leveled against the Judeans by their neighbors. Ibn Ezra's commentary on the Book of Ezra 4:6; Rashi's commentary on Ezra 4:7.
[21]Midrash, Esther Raba on the Achashverosh Banquet, chapter 1.
[22]Eshter 3:5.

for coexistence between Amalek and the Jews, whose status as God's chosen people filled them with rage. Haman, as all Amalekites who preceded him, was fixated upon the destruction of Jewry. He approached Achashverosh with his plan. "There is a certain nation scattered abroad and dispersed among the nations in all provinces of your kingdom. Their laws are different from those of other peoples. They do not even observe the king's laws; therefore it is not befitting the king to tolerate them."[23]

In Nazi Germany, Hitler's intention to annihilate the Jews was also a product of his obsession from his earliest days as a Nazi. As the Amalekite Haman, Hitler saw two different worlds—Germany and Jewry—in which one would have to eliminate the other.

In *Mein Kampf*, Hitler declared, "there is no making pacts with Jews; there can only be the hard either-or." The implications of "either-or" are evident. As part of this perception of the Jews, he wrote in *Mein Kampf*, "Two worlds cannot face one another—the men of God and the men of Satan! The Jew is the anti-man, the creature of another god. He must have come from another root of the human race. I set the Aryan and the Jew over and against each other."[24] In a speech in a Munich beer cellar on February 27, 1925, Hitler told an audience in reference to the Jew, "Either the enemy will walk over our corpses or we will walk over his."[25]

The Nazi ideology defined the Jew by his race and ancestry. Bizarre theories of race were the basis of Nazism. Even possessing just one Jewish grandparent could be a death sentence. The last transport to Auschwitz on August 7, 1944, carried Jews who were married to non-Jews and their children. There was no escape from Hitler's obsession with the destruction of Jewry. Anyone with

[23]Ibid., 3:8.
[24]Gerald Reitlinger, *The Final Solution: The Attempt to Exterminate the Jews of Europe 1939–1945* (South Brunswick, New Jersey: T. Yoseloff, 1968), 27.
[25]Robert S. Wistrich, *Hitler's Apocalypse: Jews and the Nazi Legacy* (New York: St. Martin's Press, 1985), 29.

Jewish ancestry, no matter how far removed, faced a Nazi death sentence.

Prior to the emergence of Haman, there was no reason to suggest that the Jews were in any form of danger in Persia. The Jews, who were brought into the land as exiles of Judea by the Babylonians prior to and following the destruction of the First Temple, did initially face persecution. However the situation over the years had stabilized. Under Persian rule the vast majority of Jews did not believe that they were in any form of danger prior to the emergence of Haman.

In contrast, Hitler came forth in a Germany where the seeds for Nazism had sprung in advance. The warning signals of a dangerous undercurrent of anti-Semitism had existed in Germany for decades. Before the Nazis, there was the Christian Socialists Workers Party, the League of Anti-Semites, the German Social Anti-Semitic Party, the Anti-Semitic People's Party, and so on. Some of these parties even took seats in parliamentary elections toward the end of the nineteenth century. On April 25, 1881, as pogroms broke out throughout Russia, 250,000 Germans signed a petition to the government requesting the barring of foreign Jews. That petition also called for the dismissal of Jews from all public positions. On the eve of the 1893 elections, a major political party, the German Conservative Party, held a conference at Berlin's Tivoli Hall. Their party program adopted anti-Semitic planks. One stated, "We fight the multifarious and obtrusive Jewish influence that decomposes our people's lives."[26]

European Jewry was virtually destroyed due to Hitler's evil plan. Haman, however, was not as successful. In Persia, eleven months after dispatches hurried Haman's approved plans throughout the widths of the empire, he was defeated and his sons were hanged on the same gallows meant for Mordechai.

---

[26]Lucy S. Davidowitcz, *The War Against the Jews: 1933–1945* (New York: Holt, Rinehart, and Winston, 1975), 42.

Purim is a time to celebrate the defeat of Haman and the survival of Jewry; it is a time of "feast and joy."[27] We remember Purim's victors, but even in joy cannot help but remember the victims of the Hamans who followed. From the events in ancient Persia to the rise of Nazism, and even in our own times, Jewry has had to contend with the destructive forces of Haman. In due time, the Hamans and the evil they bear will be eliminated. The Mordechais will flourish unhindered and persecution and human suffering will end. Then the traumatic events of Purim will truly become past history.

PURIM IN STALIN'S PRESIDIUM: HOW STALIN'S RAGE SAVED THE JEWS

The following story was leaked to the press at a time when the Soviets, frequently accused of anti-Semitism, sought to improve their image. At the time, an account appeared in the *London Times* in April 1956 and in *France Soir* and *The New York Times* on June 8, 1957. These accounts depicted the events surrounding the Soviet premier Josef Stalin's last moments before his death.[28] There is no certainty if these accounts are true, but there is no evidence to the contrary. The events make up a Purim play like no other.

Around the last week in February 1953, a meeting took place between leaders of the Soviet regime. There, Stalin revealed his plans for Soviet Jewry. No Mordechai or Esther was present, but Haman was there. At the meeting, Stalin's pent-up fury reached a crescendo and exploded into an uncontrolled rage. That rage resulted in his death and perhaps in salvation for millions of others.

Not even ten years after Hitler's destruction of Europe's Jews,

---

[27]Esther 9:22.

[28]While there are contrasted details between the different accounts, a major difference is the timing of Stalin's stroke, which allegedly caused his death.

Josef Stalin was bent upon the same course. Decades of purges, executions, imprisonments, and exiles of tens of thousands of Soviet Jews had escalated during the Cold War into a full-scale attack upon Soviet Jewry. By early 1953, the media launched daily attacks against the Jews under the pretext of the infamous "Doctors Plot," which accused Jewish doctors of planning to poison government officials. As a result of the accusations of the "Doctors Plot," numerous doctors and other Soviet Jews were executed and incarcerated. Hounded by both the media and the police, the Jews of the Soviet Union lived in terror. As in Nazi Germany, they were used as scapegoats for all the Soviet Union's woes. The driving force behind the terror was Stalin.

Stalin's onslaught against the Jews was not something random; there was a calculated purpose to his madness. He had further plans against Soviet Jewry. At the time, rumors had already become widespread that he was planning to deport thousands of Jews to Biro Bidzhan (an alleged Jewish autonomous region) and Siberia. A broadcast on "Voice of America" stated, "Biro Bidzhan the 'Jewish autonomous republic' has been transformed into a concentration camp. A surreptitious tendency is observed to deport to Biro Bidzhan all Jews arrested. It is difficult to establish the number of camps in Biro Bidzhan. Suffice it to say that in one of the camps along the Biro River there are five to six departments; each department is reckoned to have 200–300 slaves."[29] Those rumors were soon the subject of a meeting Stalin had with his presidium.

Stalin told the two dozen leaders present of his plans against the Jews. As a pretext, he rehashed the usual accusations of "Zionist Imperialist Plot" and the "Doctors Plot" and spoke of the need for collective deportation of the Jews to Central Asia and Biro Bidzhan. A hushed silence followed the speech. Lazar Kaganovich, one of

---

[29] *Voice of America*, quoted in Gregory Aronson, Jacob Frumkin, Alexis Goldenweiser, Joseph Levitan, and Thomas Yoseloff, eds. *Russian Jewry 1917–1967* (New York/South Brunswick/London: T. Yoseloff, 1969), 199.

Stalin's loyal enforcers was the first to speak. He asked hesitantly whether all Jews were to be deported. Stalin replied, "a certain section." Again there was silence. Another presidium member, Vyacheslav Molotov, whose Jewish wife Paulina was exiled to the Kazakhastan wilderness a few years earlier, broke the silence and dared to object stating that the expulsion of Jews would have a negative impact on world opinion. Another longtime Politburo member, Anastas Ivanovich Mikoyan, nodded his head in agreement. The unusual display of dissent was not over. Kliment Yefremovich Voroshilov was next to speak up. Just days earlier, four government agents arrived at his home to arrest his Jewish wife. More loyal to his wife then his party, Voroshilov with gun in hand chased them away. In a dramatic gesture of defiance, Voroshilov threw his party card on the table and resolutely stated that he no longer wanted to be a part of the Communist Party. Enraged, Stalin responded shouting that only he determined who remained within the party.

As Stalin's rage reached a crescendo, he collapsed on the floor suffering a massive stroke. As he lay stricken, no specialist arrived to help him. They were all executed and imprisoned during the "Doctor's Plot." Fifteen to twenty minutes later ordinary doctors arrived. Stalin was brought to his private apartment where he lay gravely ill. Soviet party leaders surrounded him, many eagerly anticipating the imminent end of his reign. In his final gesture, he pointed his finger toward those present at his bedside, including his daughter, suggesting their guilt or complicity in a conspiracy to kill him. Then he died.[30]

Following Stalin's death, there was concern that his successors would be as evil or even worse. No one knew what to expect from the Soviets. Perhaps the Jews would be blamed for their leader's death. An editorial from a contemporary Jewish periodical con-

---

[30]For more information on the detailed sequence of events, see Louis Rappoport, "Purimshpiel," *Stalin's War Against the Jews: The Doctors Plot and the Soviet Solution* (New York: Free Press, 1990), ch. 13.

cluded its summation on Stalin's death with the following: "The fate of Jews in the Red Empire hangs in the balance."[31]

Stalin's death, which was announced on March 5, was actually cause for great relief. The purges almost immediately calmed as did the media attacks against Jews and Israel. Soon, the surviving doctors who were arrested were released. Soviet Jewry's struggles were far from over but they were relieved of their greatest antagonist.

Stalin died as he was planning Jewry's destruction in the Soviet Union. The exact day of his death remains a mystery. Perhaps he died on Purim day (March 1) itself. But one thing could be said, in the safety of their private confines Soviet Jews celebrated Purim, marking the salvation of Jewry in ancient times and in their own as well.

JEWS IN HIGH PLACES

The first Jew to achieve high office in the Diaspora was the biblical figure Joseph. After his jealous brothers sold him to a caravan of Ishmaelites, Joseph was brought to Egypt as a slave and then was later imprisoned on false charges. Joseph was released from prison after twelve years, following his interpretation of Pharaoh's dream which foretold of a coming famine. Joseph proposed a plan that would avert the coming disaster. In recognition for his achievements, he was elevated to the second highest position as viceroy in Egypt, earning the admiration of all Egyptians. He used his position to assist his brethren when they eventually arrived from Canaan.[32]

Almost one thousand years later, after the exile of the Jews from Judea prior to and following the destruction of the first Temple, Esther—a Jewess—was chosen by King Achashverosh of Persia to share his throne. Her uncle Mordechai, the Jewish scholar

---

[31]"The American Hebrew," 162, no. 45 (March 13, 1953): 4.
[32]Genesis 46–47.

and leader, knew intuitively that she would become queen and that she had been chosen for a special purpose.

When Achashverosh approved of Haman's plan for the annihilation of the Jews, Mordechai sought Esther's intervention.[33] Initially, Esther was reluctant to become involved out of fear that her intervention would result in nothing but her own death.[34] Mordechai, however, reminded her that it was her duty and responsibility to intervene on behalf of her people. He warned her, "If you remain silent at this time, relief and rescue will arise for the Jews from elsewhere and you and your father's household will perish; and who knows whether for such times as this you have attained the kingdom?"[35] Esther, therefore, assumed responsibility and acted on behalf of her brethren.

Since the era of Emancipation, public office has been more available to the Jews and many have attained high positions. In Western emancipated nations, the Jews generally possessed unprecedented freedoms. However, they also faced new and very dangerous forms of anti-Semitic propaganda that accused Jews of conspiracy and global domination. Many Jewish elected officials maintained a distance from the problems faced by their fellow Jews. They did not want to appear "too Jewish" and face charges of dual loyalty in a hostile environment where anti-Jewish sentiments thrived. They conveniently turned a blind eye to the plight of their brethren in need. Even in the most liberal societies, such Jewish politicians were distant from their own Jewish heritage and indifferent to the needs of their fellow Jews.

However, some elected Jewish officials, as Esther, did respond to the calls of Jews in need. Most notable were those politicians from the more tolerant nations of Britain, France and, especially, the United States. In these countries, helping one's fellow Jew was less likely to arouse animosity and did not necessarily raise the usual charges of disloyalty.

---

[33]Esther 4:8.
[34]Ibid., 4:11.
[35]Ibid., 4:14.

The Jews in high office who acted on behalf of their fellow Jews had diverse backgrounds, lived at different times, and had various motivations for their actions. Some entered high office with the intention of helping Jews in need, while others were compelled to act by the enormity of the problems that were facing Jews. Realizing the responsibilities placed upon their shoulders, they answered the call and fulfilled their destinies.

The following narratives are examples of Jews in high places who labored on behalf of their fellow Jews.

Joseph Samuel Bloch

Joseph Samuel Bloch (1850–1923) stood out as an activist who fought an unceasing battle against the rising tide of anti-Semitism in Austria. It was for that purpose alone that he sought political office. Bloch was a rabbi, trained in the yeshivas of Galicia, who had also earned a Ph.D. Although he was reared in the insular world of the yeshivas, he was involved in the affairs of the world around him even before he entered public office. In his political career, Bloch raised his voice against anti-Semitism and would not remain complacent. In addition, he was also an advocate of Jewish identity and fought against the rabid assimilation that threatened Austrian Jewry.

Bloch's political activism began years before his appointment to parliament in 1882. Eleven years earlier, in 1871, a priest by the name of August Rohling had published a widely distributed anti-Semitic book called *The Talmudic Jew*, which sought to prove that the Talmud is anti-Christian. Joseph Samuel Bloch, who was a pulpit rabbi serving a small congregation on the edge of Vienna at the time, responded to the attack. He publicly refuted Rohling's accusations and offered him a large sum of money if he could translate one page of the Talmud.[36] Rohling was silent in the face of Bloch's fearless response.

---

[36]Bloch did not actually possess this money, but was sure of Rohling's ignorance of that fact.

This was the first of Bloch's many public actions over the course of many years of activism. When the anti-Semites attacked, he responded. It was his visibility as a fighter for his community that caused him to be appointed, and then elected, a member of parliament.

In 1881, a blood libel case arose. An Austrian teenage girl was missing and the Jews were accused of ritual murder. Rohling, true to form, testified for the prosecution. He stated, "the shedding of a Christian virgin's blood is for the Jews an extraordinarily holy event."[37] Bloch responded by publicly denouncing Rohling as a liar. He realized this accusation would prompt Rohling to file a libel suit against him, but he also knew that this would allow him the opportunity to further defend the Jews. As a recently elected member of parliament, Bloch waved his parliamentary immunity to fend against the libel suit. Unwilling to face the well-prepared Bloch, Rohling did not appear in court—a clear admission of guilt. Thus, Bloch had scored a major victory.

Although Bloch was popular with many within the Jewish community, many Jews involved in Austria's politics and who were distant from Jewish concerns shunned him. Those Jews avoided voting on Jewish related issues and ignored the threat of anti-Semitism. Jewish members of the Vienna City Council, for instance, took a joint pledge to ignore the worst ravings of anti-Semitism. "When the president of Parliament once suggested the rescheduling of a session which fell on Yom Kippur, it was the Jewish members who objected to the idea."[38]

Bloch was their antithesis. While in office, he founded a defense organization and a newspaper devoted to defending Jews. He had gained a reputation as a defender of the Jews and soon became the recipient of numerous pleas for assistance by the Jewish community. As he put it, "My electorate district was the most densely populated one of Galicia with a majority of Jewish inhab-

---

[37]George E. Berkley, *Vienna and Its Jews: The Tragedy of Success* (Cambridge, Massachusetts: Abt Books, 1988), 79.
[38]Ibid., 83.

itants. Every one of the electorates believed himself to have a right to my time and that I was to settle all their affairs."[39]

In the Richsrath Parliament, Bloch dealt with the continuous onslaught from the anti-Semites. When a vote against ritual slaughter was proposed on the grounds of cruelty, Bloch vigorously defended it and proposed that the anti-Semites clamp down on hunting if they really wanted to protect wildlife.[40] When protests arose over the fact that the bodies of Jewish paupers were not turned over to medical schools for research, Bloch argued that every Jew, no matter how poor, receives a decent burial. "Why don't you Christians set up burial societies of your own?" he queried.[41] When Jews were accused of being too wealthy, Bloch produced evidence of Jews living in abject poverty. When a claim arose in the parliament that the Kol Nidre prayer absolves Jews from any oath, Bloch responded while irate parliament members personally threatened him with violence. His greatest victory occurred in 1893, when an apostate Jew was paid to write a bogus account of a ritual murder that allegedly took place in Russia. Bloch had the matter investigated and the hoax was exposed.

Bloch's efforts earned him respect worldwide. In 1885, Sir Moses Montefiore addressed the following letter to Bloch:

> I pray to the Almighty that He take you and yours into his keeping and that he may give you the strength to continue your noble endeavors in the interest of our holy religion, for the benefit of suffering mankind, and for the victory of Truth and Justice. May He who guides the hearts of men inspire you with sacred zeal that you do not rest until all those who suffer innocently should be freed of their oppressors and Israel shall live in peace in all parts of the earth.[42]

---

[39]Joseph Samuel Bloch, *My Reminisces* (Vienna/Berlin: R. Lowitt, 1923), 17.
[40]Berkley, *Vienna and Its Jews*, 91.
[41]Ibid.
[42]Bloch, *My Reminisces*, 208.

Bloch summed up his role in government as he reflected upon his relationship with Austrian Premier Edward Taffe. "Count Taffe was of the opinion, and said so ever so often, that as long as anti-Semitic persecutors would be delegated to parliament by an infatuated people, it would be advisable that a man should have a seat and voice capable of opposing the persecutors with the necessary energy and intimate knowledge—and that not only from reasons of justice, but even in the interest of State Government." When the prime minister thought of this role, understandably, Joseph Bloch came to mind.

Bloch's career in the parliament was ended after three consecutive sessions when his many opponents managed to drive him out of office. In the parliament, Bloch fought courageously in defense of Jewish honor and won many battles. However, he was unable to win the war against the bigotry and hatred embedded within the Austrian people.

Justice Louis Brandeis

Justice Louis Brandeis was raised in a completely secular environment and seemed an unlikely candidate to become a Jewish leader. Earlier in his life, he showed little interest in Jewish matters. He did not belong to a synagogue and his closest friends were non-Jews.[43] However, just a few years before his nomination to the U.S. Supreme Court in 1916, Brandeis had begun to become involved in Jewish affairs.

He recounted that his interest in Judaism was stirred by two experiences.[44] As a mediator of a garment workers strike in New York, Brandeis came into contact with Eastern European Jews arguing on each side of the dispute and he was impressed with their willingness to listen to the other's view. Brandeis felt a kinship to these Jews. His other experience was a meeting with Jacob De

---

[43]Howard M. Sachar, *A History of Jews in America* (New York: Vintage Books—A Division of Random House, 1992), 250.
[44]Ibid., 3.

Haas, editor of the *Boston Jewish Advocate.* An ardent Zionist, De Haas presented the case for Jewish Statehood and made an impression on Brandeis. As a result, in January 1912 Brandeis attended a Zionist dinner in honor of Zionist agronomist Aaron Aaronson. Aaronson's discussion on the progress of the development of the Land of Israel deeply moved Brandeis and he became a Zionist himself.

As a United States Supreme Court justice, Brandeis made significant contributions to the Zionist cause. As a friend of President Wilson, he discussed the Zionist plan with him and won the president's sympathetic understanding.[45] In April 1917, Chaim Weitzman wrote to Brandeis requesting that he obtain a statement of American support for a Jewish Palestine under British protectorate. Weitzman wrote that, "Such a statement would greatly strengthen our hands."[46] When plans for the Balfour Declaration—which expressed support for Jewish Statehood in Palestine—were drawn up, President Wilson did not initially support the plan. His aides opposed supporting the Balfour Declaration on the basis that the Unitd States was not at war with Turkey.[47] But Brandeis responded to Weitzman's desperate appeal and successfully lobbied the White House, which soon expressed support for the declaration.

Brandeis' immense contributions to the Zionist cause continued. As post-war decisions were being made in Potsdam concerning how to divide the new Middle East no longer under Turkish control, opposing voices to the Balfour Declaration were heard in Washington and Britain. Again, Brandeis lobbied the president and won his support. As a result, a Palestine mandate emerged that granted very limited, but improved, boundaries to the Zionists.

In 1936, Brandeis faced a great challenge and found that

---

[45]Ibid., 254.
[46]Ibid., 255.
[47]At the time, the British and the Turks were fighting over control of the land of Israel.

American influence had its limitations. Arab riots in Palestine had again pressured the British to reevaluate their commitments to the Balfour Declaration. The resulting Peel Report of 1937 suggested the partition of Palestine into Jewish and Arab states. Yet, the boundary for the Jewish State was far too small to accommodate the masses of Jews from Europe who wished to immigrate. At the time, the British, as they had done before, had further restricted Jewish immigration into the land. Brandeis met with President Roosevelt for over an hour and received the president's support for increased Jewish immigration into Palestine. However, American influence could not persuade the British, who soon ceded to Arab demands and issued the White Paper on May 19, 1939, which virtually closed Jewish immigration into Palestine.

As a Zionist, Brandeis' visions of the movement often clashed with those of Weitzman. Brandeis thought the Zionist movement should have been modeled after American principles of economics. He believed this would help Zionist settlements thrive in Palestine. Brandeis encountered opposition within the Zionist Movement that prompted him to withdraw from any official position in the movement, but his support never wavered. In 1941, Justice Louis Brandeis died, leaving behind a legacy of accomplishments. He aided in building the Zionist Movement in America and he also helped to partially assuage the fears of American Jews toward publicly addressing issues of Jewish concern. Perhaps most importantly, he had successfully assisted in forming U.S. policy regarding Zionism. He won over many friends in high places to the Zionist cause and established the beginnings of the friendly relationship between the United States and the Zionist Movement.

Secretary Henry Morgenthau Jr.

Henry Morgenthau Jr. came to occupy one of the most important positions in the nation as secretary of the treasury, and he used that position in his desperate efforts to save European Jewry from annihilation. Morgenthau fought a battle, with few allies, against the apathy and indifference of those around him.

Morgenthau was an unlikely candidate for someone who would defy the establishment in a stand on behalf of his Jewish brethren. He was born and raised within an assimilationist environment. His family, prominent and wealthy German Jews, were part of the upper class German Jewish elite. He lived in a world where WASP values and Christmas trees stood alongside Chanukah menorahs; a world where being Jewish was something to be concealed. He fraternized little with other Jews and did not even attend synagogue on Yom Kippur. When his young son, Henry III, asked his mother what his religion was, she answered, "If ever anyone asks you that question, just tell them you're an American."[48]

Henry Morgenthau Jr. was loyal to Franklin Delano Roosevelt since the beginning of his political career and had proven himself a capable administrator. As Roosevelt's career advanced, so too did Morgenthau's. When elected president, Roosevelt appointed him as secretary of the treasury. His father, who was a successful politician himself, groomed Morgenthau for office. He groomed him to serve not as an American Jew, but as a "100 percent American" with no particular affiliation with his own people.[49] As the atrocities in Nazi Europe became known, few Jews within Roosevelt's administration spoke up on their behalf. In a time when Jews sought acceptance in American society, few were willing to go beyond token efforts to challenge U.S. policy, which was making little effort to rescue Jews.

In early 1943, three senior non-Jewish members of Morgenthau's staff learned that the United States State Department was diverting money from private Jewish organizations earmarked for the rescue of Jews. They also learned that the state department was suppressing vital information on this matter. Morgenthau was made fully aware of this matter by his staff. His Jewish secretary,

---

[48]Henry Morgenthau III, *Mostly Morgenthaus: A Family History* (New York: Ticknor and Fields, 1991), 14.
[49]Ibid., 321.

Henrietta Klotz, implored him to take some action. Morgenthau listened to her pleas. Under his leadership, his committee investigated the matter. The treasury soon discovered that Breckenridge Long, who headed twenty-three of the state department's forty-three divisions, deliberately sabotaged efforts to save thousands of French and Romanian Jews. After confronting Long and his cohorts, he realized they had no intention of reversing their positions and that the matter must be brought to the president. In early 1944, the treasury made known the plight of European Jewry, producing an eighteen-page report entitled "The Acquiescence of the Government to the Murder of the Jews," which detailed the state department's sabotage of attempts to rescue Jews. Morgenthau personally brought the report over to the president. As a result, on January 22, 1944, the War Refugee Board (WRB) was established. The WRB consisted of officials from the war, treasury, and state departments. Together with John Pehle, leader of the WRB, Morgenthau conducted daring efforts to save Jews. Despite the continued opposition to the efforts of the WRB by those in the state department and others, the rescue efforts continued.

Efforts of the WRB involved elaborate and often daring schemes. The board's operative in Sweden enlisted Raoul Wallenberg's assistance in providing Swedish diplomatic protection for thousands. Ira Hirschman, the board's representative in Turkey, helped to secure the passage of seven thousand Jews from the Balkans through Turkey.

Perhaps the boldest of Morgenthau's projects involved a plan that had received the president's approval to resettle refugees in the United States, provided they return to Europe at the conclusion of the war. Close to one thousand Jewish refugees from former Vichy-controlled interment camps in Morocco and Algeria were brought to the United States in July 1944.[50] They were interned in Oswego, New York. The "Oswego Plan" could have been the beginning of a long process to save hundreds of thousands.

---

[50]Sachar, *A History of Jews in America*, 549.

However, after the one thousand Jewish refugees were settled in Oswego, opposition to such rescue efforts quickly rose. Within days, restrictionists in the senate began to protest the move, arguing that the refugees would not return to Europe and that tens of thousands would follow their path. Many patriotic groups also arose to declare their opposition to the plan. In Oswego itself, the refugees faced a tide of anti-Semitism by the locals. The local newspapers soon became a forum for those who sought a Judenrein Oswego. This strong opposition persuaded the president to discontinue rescue efforts for the refugees. Thus, another golden opportunity to save thousands was lost.

Morgenthau was forced to contend with many similar tragedies. While he did manage to save lives, his greatest obstacle was the strong tide of public opinion against such efforts. Anti-Semitism, endemic in America, had far greater impact on American policy than the efforts of a few lone individuals.

Yet despite the obstacles, the efforts of Morgenthau's treasury department continued. It is estimated that Morgenthau had a hand in rescuing over two hundred thousand Jews.

A man who initially showed little interest in Jewish problems became deeply moved when confronted with the tragedies in Europe, and he responded with action. Following the war, Morgenthau remained committed to aiding the Jewish community. He left the government following Roosevelt's death and devoted himself to many Jewish causes, utilizing his experience in administration at the treasury. He chaired the United Jewish Appeal and raised enormous sums that greatly helped the newly born State of Israel. Soon after, he founded State of Israel Bonds, which also met with enormous success.

Henry Morgenthau Jr. died on February 6, 1967. On the day of his funeral, workers from all the major Jewish organizations in New York were given the morning off in order to attend. He was not just someone who had a remarkable career as a member of the president's cabinet who also happened to be a Jew. He was a Jew who used his position to help his people in their dire time of need.

Every life he saved gave additional importance to his role as secretary of the treasury.

Joseph Samuel Bloch, Justice Louis Dembitz Brandeis, and Henry Morgenthau Jr. came from diverse backgrounds and were motivated to act by different factors. However, they each had a sense of responsibility to use their positions in government to aid and assist their people, just as Esther had done over two millennium earlier in Persia.

PURIM KATAN

Purim celebrates the salvation of Jewry during the reign of King Achashverosh of Persia. The mere survival of Jewry throughout history is in itself a miracle. There are several individual communities that also have their own unique stories of salvation. When faced with disaster, either from a tyrant or a natural disaster such as an earthquake or a plague, these communities miraculously escaped. To celebrate their salvation, those communities ordained that a special Purim be celebrated. In total there might be as many as one hundred such special Purims celebrated.[51] Often families saved from certain danger also instituted their own personal "special Purims." The message of all the Purims is the same as that of the original Purim; their deliverance was not by chance but guided by the Almighty. The following are some brief descriptions of the many special Purims.

A poet and scholar, Samuel ben Hosha'na reports that in 1323 a Muslim crowd attacked a Jewish funeral procession in old Cairo. Such attacks did occur from time to time. The Islamic Dhimmi laws

---

[51]Adopted from accounts presented by author, quoted in Mark R. Cohen, *Under Crescent and Cross: The Jews in the Middle Ages* (Princeton, New Jersey: Princeton University Press, 1993), 184–185.

prohibited the public display of Judaism or Christianity, even at funerals, and a funeral could provoke anger. Twenty-three Jews were arrested and the Jewish community locked themselves in their homes in fear as they fasted and wept. On the third day, a group of Jews appealed to the Caliph-Al Hakim to spare the imprisoned Jews. The Caliph looked into the matter and found wrongdoing on the part of the Muslims who instigated the disturbances and had the twenty-three released. Out of joy, an annual feast was instituted each year to commemorate the deliverance. Hosha'na, who himself was incarcerated, composed liturgy to be recited during the feast. Samuel ben Hosha'na, who also composed a *Megilah*, or scroll, to commemorate the event, writes, "Remember this and place it before your eyes. Tell it to your children, and their children, and their children to another generation."[52]

In the early seventeenth century, the city of Tiberius, which borders on the Lake of Kinereth in Israel's north, was reestablished by Sheikh dair el Amar who invited Isaac Abulafia to bring Jews to join the settlement. Soon the city had a sizable Jewish community. Governor Suleiman Pasha of Damascus laid siege to the city in 1743. For the duration of the siege, eighty-three days, the Jews of Tiberius helped stand in its defense. On August 27, the Pasha raised the siege, but his plans to attack Tiberius were not over. While preparing his next attack, however, he suddenly died and the Jews of Tiberius were saved from certain disaster. The Jews of Tiberius, declared both the day of the lifting of the siege—the seventh day of Elul—and the day of the Pasha's death—the fourth day of Kislev—local Purims.

Purim of Bandits

In European Turkey, near Andriapole, lies the city of Gumeldjina. In 1786, the city was attacked by bandits intent upon pillaging the town. Had they been permitted to ransack the city, its Jewish

[52]Phillip Goodman, *The Purim Anthology* (Philadelphia: Jewish Publication Society of America, 1949), 16.

community would have been in grave danger. Afterwards, the Jews were accused of allowing the bandits to enter the city. Again, they were in danger. With great difficulty, however, they managed to prove their innocence. In memory of their escaping both predicaments, a special Purim was instituted on the twenty-second day of Cheshvan for the Jews of Gumeldjina.[53]

The Purim of Sharif

The city of Tripoli, which contained a large Jewish community, was threatened with extermination when the ruler of Tunis besieged the city. The leader had threatened to kill all the inhabitants of the city. With just one last fortress to conquer, a sudden epidemic spread among his soldiers and he was forced to withdraw with the remains of his army. The Jews of Tripoli instituted that day, the twenty-fourth day of Tevet, as a Purim.

Purim Sebastiano

The King Dom Sebastiano of Portugal invaded Morocco in 1578. Two Morranos informed the Jewish community that if the invasion succeeded, all the Jews of Morocco would be forcibly converted. At the battle of Alcazarquebir, the Portuguese were defeated and Dom Sebastiano was killed in battle. That day was set aside by the Jews of Morocco as a Purim.

---

[53]Ibid., 29.

Selected Bibliography

Adler, H. G. (1969). *The Jews in Germany: from the Enlightenment to National Socialism.* Notre Dame, London, University of Notre Dame Press.

Agus, Jacob B. (1963). *The Meaning of Jewish History.* London, New York: Abelard-Schuman.

Ami, Ben (1967). *Between Hammer and Sickle.* Philadelphia: Jewish Publication Society of America.

Aronson, Gregory, Jacob Frumkin, Alexis Goldenweiser, Joseph Levitan, and Thomas Yoseloff, eds., (1969). *Russian Jewry 1916–1967.* New York/South Brunswick/London, T. Yoseloff.

Avni, Haim (1982). *Spain, the Jews and Franco.* Philadelphia, Jewish Publication Society of America.

Bamberger, Rabbi Ib Nathan (1983). *The Viking Jews: A History of the Jews of Denmark.* New York: Shengold.

Belkin, Samuel (1956). *Essays in Traditional Jewish Thought.* New York: Philosophical Library.

Berkley, George E. (1988). *Vienna and its Jews: The Tragedy of Success.* Cambridge, Massachusetts: Abt Books.

Bloch, Abraham P. (1983). *Day by Day in Jewish History: A Chronology and Calendar of Historic Events.* New York: Ktav Publishing House.

——— (1987). *One a Day: An Anthology of Jewish Historical Anniversaries for Every Day of the Year.* Hoboken: Ktav Publishing House.

Bloch, Joseph Samuel (1923). *My Reminisces.* Vienna, Berlin: R. Lowitt.

Chazan, Robert (1996). *In the Year 1096: The First Crusades and the Jews.* Philadelphia: Jewish Publication Society of America.

Cohen, Hayyim (1973). *The Jews of the Middle East.* New York/Toronto: A Halsted Press Book, John Wiley and Sons, Jerusalem: Israel Universities Press.

Cohen, Mark R. (1993). *Under Crescent and Cross: The Jews in the Middle Ages.* Princeton, New Jersey: Princeton University Press.

Collins, Larry and Dominique Lapierre (1972). *O Jerusalem.* New York: Pocket Books, A Division of Simon and Schuster.

Colson, F. H., trans., (1940) *Philo with an English Translation.* Cambridge: Harvard University Press.

Cygielman, Shmuel A. Arthur (1991). *Jewish Autonomy in Poland and Lithuania until 1649.* Jerusalem: Zalman Shazar Center for the Furtherance of the Study of Jewish History.

Davidowitcz, Lucy S. (1975). *The War Against The Jews: 1933–1945.* New York: Holt, Rinehart, and Winston.

de Bethencourt, Cordozo (1903). "The Jews in Portugal from 1773 to 1902," eds. I. Abrahams and C. G. Montifiore. *Jewish Quarterly Review* 15.

Encyclopedia Judaica 2. Jerusalem: The Macmillan Co., Keter Publishing House, 1972.

Feldman, David (1994). *Englishmen and Jews: Social Relations and Political Culture 1840–1914.* New Haven/London: Yale University Press).

Feldman, Louis H. (1960). "The Orthodoxy of the Jews in Hellenistic Egypt." *Jewish Social Studies* 22.

Finkle, Avraham Yaakov (1993). *The Essence of the Holy Days: Insights from the Jewish Sages.* Northvale, New Jersey: Jason Aronson.

Flavius, Josephus. *The Complete Works of Josephus.* Translated by

William Whiston (1981). Grand Rapids, Michigan: Kregel Publications.

Freidman, Lee M. (1979). *Pilgrims in a New Land.* Westport, Connecticut: Greenwood Press.

Gay, Ruth (1992). *The Jews of Germany.* New Haven: Yale University Press.

Gilbert, Martin (1976). *Atlas of Jewish History.* Dorset Press.

——— *The Holocaust: A History of the Jews of Europe During the Second World War.* Dorset Press.

Ginzberg, Louis (1940). *Legends of the Jews.* Translated by Henrietta Szold. Philadelphia: Jewish Publication Society of America.

Gittleman, Zvi Yechiel (1968). "The Jewish Sections of the Communist Party and the Modernization of Soviet Jewry." Ph.D. diss., Columbia University.

Goodman, Phillip (1949). *The Purim Anthology.* Philadelphia: Jewish Publication Society of America.

——— (1973). *The Succoth and Simchat Torah Anthology.* Philadelphia: Jewish Publication Society of America.

——— (1971). *The Yom Kippur Anthology.* Philadelphia: Jewish Publication Society of America.

Grayzel, Solomon (1968). *A History of the Jews from Babylonian Exile to the Present.* Philadelphia: Jewish Publication Society of America.

Gutstein, Morris A. (1958). *To Bigotry No Sanction: A Jewish Shrine in America 1658–1958.* New York: Bloch Publishing Company.

Guttman, Yisrael (1982). *Jews of the Warsaw Ghetto 1938–1942.* Bloomington: Indiana University Press.

HaCohen, Rabbi Yosef (1895). *Emek HaBacha.* Crackow: Typis, Joseph Fisher.

Hanover, Rabbi Nathan Nata (1964). *Yeven Metzulah (Abyss of Despair).* Hahistadrut Haclalit Shel Haovdim B'Eretz Yisrael.

Hilberg, Raul, Stanislow Starow, and Josef Kermisz, eds. (1979). *The Warsaw Diary of Adam Czerniakow: Prelude to Doom.* New York: Stein and Day.

Jung, Leo, ed. (1958). *Guardians of our Heritage.* New York: Leo Jung, Bloch Publishing House.

Kagan, Y. M. (1968) *A Thought for the Week: Adapted from the Works of Rabbi Menachem M. Schneerson, Lubavitcher Rabbi Shlita* 50. Michigan: Merkos L'Inyonei Chinuch Inc.

Kahan, Rabbi Aharon Yisroel (5747). *The Taryag (613) Mitzvos.* Brooklyn: Keser Torah Publications.

Katch, Abraham I., trans. and ed. (1973). *Schroll of Agony: The Warsaw Diary of Chaim Kaplan.* New York: Collier Books.

Ki Tov, Rabbi Eliyahu (1978). *The Book of Our Heritage.* Translated by Nathan Bulman. New York: Feldheim Publishers.

Kobler, Franz (1975). *Napoleon and the Jews.* New York: Schocken Books.

Kochin, Lionel (1978). *The Jews in Soviet Russia Since 1917*, 3rd ed. Oxford/New York/London: Oxford University.

Korey, William (1973). *The Soviet Cage: Anti-Semitism in Russia.* New York: Viking Press.

Korn, Bertram (1995). *American Jewry and the Civil War.* Marietta, Georgia: Bernis Publishing.

Lamm, Norman (1989). *Torah for Torah's Sake: In the Words of Rabbi Hayyim of Volozhin and His Contemporaries.* Hoboken, New Jersey: Yeshiva University Press-Ktav Publishing House.

Landesman, Alter F. (1969). *Brownsville: The Birth and Development and Passing of a Jewish Community in New York.* New York: Bloch Publishing Company.

Laqeuer, Walter (1974). *Wiemar: A Cultural History, 1918–1933.* New York: Putnam.

Levin, Nora (1988). *The Jews in the Soviet Union Since 1917: Paradox of Jewish Survival.* New York: University Press.

Lewin, Abraham (1968). *A Cup of Tears: A Diary of the Warsaw Ghetto.* Oxford: Basil Blackwell in Association with the Institute for Jewish Studies.

Margolis, Max L. and Alexander Marx (1947). *A History of the Jewish People.* Philadelphia: Jewish Publication Society of America.

Morgenthau III, Henry (1991). *Mostly Morgenthaus: A Family History.* New York: Ticknor and Fields.

O'Brien, Conor Cruise (1986). *The Siege: The Saga of Israel and Zionism.* New York: Simon and Schuster.

Pierson, Ruth (1970). "German Jewish identity in the Weimar Republic." Ph.D. diss., Yale University.

Pillar of Fire: The Jew Returns and the Arab Awakens. Directed by/edited by Gideon Dror, Rachia Wellner. The History Channel, 1995. Videocassette.

Ramban (Nachmanides). *Writings and Discourses.* Translated by Rabbi Dr. Charles B. Chavel (1978). New York: Chavel, Shilo Publishing House Inc.

Rappoport, Louis (1980). *The Lost Jews.* New York: Stein and Day.

——— (1990). *Stalin's War Against the Jews: The Doctor's Plot and the Soviet Solution.* New York: Free Press.

Roland, Charles (1992). *Courage Under Siege: Starvation, Disease and Death in the Warsaw Ghetto.* New York: Oxford University Press.

Rosenbaum, Irving (1976). *The Holocaust and Halakhah.* Hoboken: Ktav Publishing House.

Roth, Cecil (1974). *A History of the Morranos.* New York: Schocken Books.

——— (1996). *Jewish Book of Days: A Day to Day Almanac of Events from the Settlement of Jews in Europe to the Balfour Declaration.* New York: Herman Press.

Roth, Dan (1982). *Acts of Faith: A Journey to the Fringes of Jewish Identity.* New York: St. Martin's Press.

Rothenberg, Joshua (1971). *The Jewish Religion in the Soviet Union.* New York: Ktav Publishing House.

Ruppin, Arthur (1971). *Memoirs, Diaries, Letters.* New York: Herzl Press.

Sachar, Howard M. (1992). *A History of Jews in America.* New York: Vintage Books, A Division of Random House.

——— (1979). *A History of Zionism: From the Rise of Zionism in Our Time.* New York: Alfred A. Knopf.

Salamander, Rachel (1991). *The Jews of Germany, Yesterday 1860–1938.* New York: Rizzoli.

Schachnowitz, Selig (1977). *Avraham ben Avraham.* Jerusalem/New York: Feldheim.

Segal, J. B. (1993). *A History of the Jews of Cochin.* London: Valentine Mitchell.

Seidman, Dr. Hillel (1997). *The Warsaw Ghetto Diaries.* New York/Jerusalem: Targum/Feldheim.

Shneiderman, Harry and Morris Fine, eds. *American Jewish Year Book 1947–1948* Vol. 49. Philadelphia: Jewish Publication Society of America.

Sloan, Jacob, ed. and trans. (1974). *Notes from the Warsaw Ghetto: The Journal of Emmanuel Ringelbaum.* New York: Schocken Books.

Stern, Menachem, ed. (1974). *Greek and Latin Authors on Jews and Judaism.* Jerusalem: Academy of Sciences and Humanities.

The Final Solution: The Attempt to Exterminate the Jews of Europe, 1939–1945 (1968). South Brunswick: T. Yoseloff.

The Jewish Historical Society of England, Sessions 1924–1927, IX (1928). London: Spottiswoode, Ballantyne, and Company. LTD.

The Second Book of Maccabees. (1965). Jerusalem Bible Publishing Company.

Unsdorfer, S. B. (1983). *The Yellow Star.* New York/Jerusalem: Feldheim Publishers.

Yonah, Michael Avi (1975). *The Jews Under Roman and Byzantine Rule: A Political History of Palestine from the Bar Kochba Revolt to the Arab Conquest.* Jerusalem: Magnes Press, The Hebrew University.

Wiesel, Elie (1966). *The Jews of Silence.* New York: Holy, Reinhart, and Winston.

Wistrich, Robert S. (1985). *Hitler's Apocalypse: Jews and the Nazi Legacy.* New York: St. Martin's Press.

Wiznitzer, Arnold (1954). "The Exodus From Brazil and Arrival in New Amsterdam of the Jewish Pilgrim Fathers, 1654." Vol. 44. December, 1954. Philadelphia: American Jewish Historical Society.

Yadin, Yigal (1971). *Bar Kochba.* New York: Random House.

Yaor, Bat (1985). *The Dhimmi.* Rutherford, New Jersey: Fairleigh University Press.

Index

About the Author

Larry Domnitch is an educator and freelance writer who has taught Judaic studies on the high school and college levels in New York. He has taught at the Hebrew Academy of Nassau County, Magen David Yeshiva of Brooklyn, and the New Americans Division of Toura College. He holds a master's degree in Jewish History from Yeshiva University Bernard Revel Graduate School. As a freelance writer, Mr. Domnitch has frequently been published in numerous Jewish newspapers and periodicals throughout the country. Mr. Domnitch has also been active over the years in a variety of Jewish causes, including the former Soviet Jewry Movement and assisting the Jewish elderly in the South Bronx. He recently made *Aliyah* to Israel and resides in the city of Efrat with his wife and daughter.